Basic Chinese Character Course

基础汉字教程

主编　沙宗元
参编　王　静　蒋　宁
　　　钟　声　徐　丰

中国科学技术大学出版社

内 容 简 介

　　本书是为海外及来华汉语初学者编写的基础汉字教材,得到了"教育部国际中文教育重点项目"及"安徽省孔子学院师资培训基地项目"的资助。本书以国际中文教育最常用的 300 个基础汉字为纲,串联基础汉字知识,简析每个字的字理知识,以基础汉字联系相关词语,并设计多样化、趣味性的练习,实现字理明晰、字词贯通、同步训练的汉字教学目的,以期提高汉语学习者学习汉字的兴趣,提升汉字教学的效率,促进国际中文教学水平和质量的提高。本书可供海外孔子学院等机构教学使用,也可供国内高校留学生汉语教学以及来华汉语初学者自学使用。

图书在版编目(CIP)数据

基础汉字教程/沙宗元主编. —合肥:中国科学技术大学出版社,2022.9
ISBN 978-7-312-05502-7

Ⅰ.基… Ⅱ.沙… Ⅲ.汉语—对外汉语教学—教材 Ⅳ.H195.4

中国版本图书馆 CIP 数据核字(2022)第 123341 号

基础汉字教程
JICHU HANZI JIAOCHENG

出版	中国科学技术大学出版社
	安徽省合肥市金寨路 96 号,230026
	http://press.ustc.edu.cn
	https://zgkxjsdxcbs.tmall.com
印刷	安徽省瑞隆印务有限公司
发行	中国科学技术大学出版社
开本	710 mm×1000 mm　1/16
印张	19.5
字数	401 千
版次	2022 年 9 月第 1 版
印次	2022 年 9 月第 1 次印刷
定价	60.00 元

前　　言
Preface

在国际中文教学中,汉字被普遍认为是教学中的难点与重点。对于外国学习者来说,汉字学习之难主要在于两点:第一,汉字的形体结构较为复杂,存在笔画、部件、整字等多个结构层级,各层级之间又相互纠缠在一起,这一点迥异于多数学习者的母语文字系统,给他们学习、了解汉字造成不小的困扰;第二,汉字本身缺乏明确标音的符号系统,无法"见字知音",学习者掌握字音困难重重。除了以上两点,教学者对于如何在教学中恰当运用"字理"分析手段、如何采用更加科学的教学方法等方面下功夫不够,也是导致汉字难学的重要原因。

近年来,国内外出版了一些新的面向国际汉语教学的汉字教材。从总体趋势来看,编写者们越来越意识到独立成体系的汉字教材的重要性,从而试图摆脱长期以来汉字教学主要依附于语言要素和篇章教学的现实窘境。为加强国际中文教学中的汉字教学,提升孔子学院等机构汉语学习者学习汉字的兴趣,提升汉语教与学的效率,我们编写了这本《基础汉字教程》。

本书是为汉语初学者编写的基础汉字教材。教材以《国际中文教育中文水平等级标准》(2021年)一级汉字(300个)为目标汉字,并以这些汉字为线索联系约1000个词语,重点对300个汉字的"字理"与"字义"(包括字形的来源、结构的理据、读音和意义等)进行分析解说,介绍相关的汉字基础知识,帮助学习者掌握最常用的300个汉字的形、音、义,形成系统化的汉字知识,为进一步的汉字、汉语学习打下良好基础。

本书重视汉字理据分析,突出海外汉语和汉字教学的实用性及针对性。第一,注意"学"与"考"目标一致。本书300个重点汉字均来自《国际中文教育中文水平等级标准》(2021年)一级汉字,这些字是中文学习要求掌握的基础汉字;第二,教材在编写过程中,十分注意揭示汉字的"道理""规律""趣味",努力把汉字"有意思"的一面展现出来,激发学习者对于汉字学习的兴趣。国际中文教学实践证明,"理据发掘"及"趣味引导"有助于进一步激发学习者的兴趣,促进汉字学习,有事半功倍之效。反之,单调乏味的机械性识记则效率低下,往往事倍功半。

本书主要按照字的意义类属、构形特点将300个汉字进行分类,分别归入15课。每课由"汉字知识""汉字形音义""词语练习""综合练习""课外任务"5个部分组成。具体内容如下:

1. "汉字知识"部分主要介绍汉字的基础知识,如汉字简介,汉字的笔画与笔顺,汉字的结构类型、偏旁与部件,汉字的字符等。

2. "汉字形音义"部分重点对每课20个目标汉字的源流、字形演变、字音及字义的变化线索进行简要解说。分析解说以科学、简明、实用为原则,目的是让学习者知晓汉字字形、读音、字义的"道理"和"缘由",以"道理"为抓手,促进汉字的"意义识记"。

3. "词语练习"部分针对每课目标汉字所构成的相关词语,进行词语认读、字词联系、词句联系等方面的练习。

4. "综合练习"部分围绕目标汉字的形、音、义及相关词语进行更加多样化的练习,力求形式多样,突出对于重点汉字知识和内容的训练和活用。

5. "课外任务"部分设计了一些具有趣味性、实用性的汉字和词语小任务,通过完成任务,将汉字学习活动融入学生的实际生活中,激发学生的汉字学习兴趣,有效提高汉字应用能力。

本书是集体劳动和智慧的结晶。沙宗元负责全书的整体策划、结构设计,除课后练习之外的文稿撰写及全书统稿;王静和蒋宁负责全书课后练习的编写;钟声和徐丰负责部分英文文稿的翻译及修改。在编写过程中,一些老师和同学们在资料整理、文字翻译等方面提供了很大的支持和帮助,他们是李义成、夏琳玲、周舒扬、冯晓彤、郑文习、邹越、薛清威、郑慧敏、吕形、胡莹等,在此一并致谢!

编　者

2022年1月

前　言

Chinese characters have been recognized as the main sticking point in international Chinese language teaching. For foreigners, they have to deal with the following two difficulties: Firstly, the formation of Chinese characters consists of complicated structural levels such as strokes, components, independent words and so on. The above characteristic is totally different from their native writing systems; thus, it puzzles the learners in the acquisition of Chinese characters. Secondly, the lack of definite pronunciational symbolic system makes it more difficult for learners to master the characters since they cannot read the character when they see it. In addition, another important factor that affects the teaching effect is that in the analysis of Chinese characters, teachers have not made full use of the underlying rationality of Chinese characters to develop more effective teaching methodology.

Recently some new Chinese textbooks for international Chinese language teaching have been published in China and abroad. The authors of these textbooks have already realized the importance of independent and systematic Chinese textbooks, which can help present Chinese language teaching breakthrough the realistic predicament of mainly focusing on language elements and text analysis. This textbook is edited in the aim of strengthening international Chinese language teaching, enhancing the learning interest of learners from Confucius Institute and other institutes, and improving the teaching and learning efficiency.

This book is a textbook of basic Chinese characters designed for beginners. It focuses on the 300 Chinese characters listed in *Chinese Level Standard of International Chinese Education* (2021) as the 1st level commonly-used Chinese Characters. Based on these characters, around 1000 associated words have also been covered in the book. We expect to lay a solid foundation for future systematic learning by analyzing the rationality of these 300 Chinese characters including the origin, reasoning, pronunciation and meaning of these characters. This book gives priority to practicability and pertinency in overseas Chinese language teaching. First of all, it combines learning with testing as these 300 Chinese characters are listed in *Chinese Level Standard of International Chinese Education* (2021) as the 1st level commonly-used Chinese characters. Secondly, this book aims to motivate the interest of learners by uncovering the rationality, regularity and interest of Chinese characters. In the practice of international Chinese language teaching, exploration of rationality and interest guidance have been proved effective in motivating learners' interest and improving learning effect in contrast to mechanical memorization.

The 300 Chinese characters have been classified into 15 lessons according their meaning categories and structural characteristics. Each lesson consists of five parts: "Knowledge of Chinese Characters" "The Form, Pronunciation and Meaning of Chinese Characters" "Phrase Practice" "Comprehensive Practice" and "After-class Task".

1. "Knowledge of Chinese Characters" introduces basic knowledge of characters, such as history of Chinese characters, strokes and orders, structures, components, etc.

2. "The Form, Pronunciation and Meaning of Chinese Characters" briefs on the development of the characters' form, pronunciation and meaning. Through reasonable, concise and practical expression, this part presents the underlying rationality of Chinese characters and helps learners to realize meaningful memorization.

3. "Phrase Practice" is designed for practicing associated phrases composed by the target Chinese characters.

4. "Comprehensive Practice" has designed diversified practice on the form, pronunciation and meaning of target characters.

5. "After-class Task" has designed some interesting and practical tasks for learners to fulfill. It aims to associate Chinese learning with learners' daily life, thus improves learners' comprehensive application ability.

This textbook is the crystalization of collective labor and wisdom. Sha Zongyuan is responsible for the overall planning and structural design of the whole textbook, the compiling of manuscripts except after-class exercises, and the final unified manuscripts of the whole textbook. Wang Jing and Jiang Ning are responsible for the compiling of after-class exercises of the whole textbook, and Zhong Sheng and Xu Feng are responsible for the translation and revision of some English manuscripts. During compiling this textbook, some teachers and students have provided valuable support and help in material sorting and text translation. They are Li Yicheng, Xia linling, Zhou Shuyang, Feng Xiaotong, Zheng Wenxi, Zou Yue, Xue Qingwei, Zheng Huimin, Lv Tong, Hu Ying, etc. Thank them all very much!

Author
Jan., 2022

目 录
Contents

前言
Preface ……………………………………………………………………（ⅰ）

第一课　基本笔画与笔顺
Lesson One　Basic Strokes and Stroke Orders ………………………（ 1 ）

第二课　象形字
Lesson Two　Pictographic Characters ………………………………（ 24 ）

第三课　独体字与合体字
Lesson Three　Single Characters and Compound Characters …………（ 46 ）

第四课　指事字
Lesson Four　Indicative Characters ……………………………………（ 66 ）

第五课　会意字
Lesson Five　Associative Characters …………………………………（ 85 ）

第六课　形声字
Lesson Six　Pictophonetic Characters …………………………………（105）

第七课　汉字的意符
Lesson Seven　Ideographic Symbols of Chinese Characters …………（124）

第八课　汉字的音符
Lesson Eight　Phonetic Symbols of Chinese Characters ………………（144）

第九课　汉字中的记号
Lesson Nine　Signs in Chinese Characters ……………………（164）

第十课　字的本义和引申义
Lesson Ten　Original Meaing and Extended Meaning of
　　　　　　Chinese Characters ……………………（186）

第十一课　偏旁的变体
Lesson Eleven　Variant of Character Components ……………（208）

第十二课　常用的意符
Lesson Twelve　Commonly-used Ideographic Symbols ………（228）

第十三课　常用的音符
Lesson Thirteen　Commonly-used Phonetic Symbols …………（247）

第十四课　假借字
Lesson Fourteen　Phonetic Loan Characters ……………………（265）

第十五课　字和词的网络关系
Lesson Fifteen　Network of Characters and Words ……………（283）

第一课 基本笔画与笔顺
Lesson One Basic Strokes and Stroke Orders

一、汉字知识 Knowledge of Chinese Characters

(一) 了解汉字 About Chinese Characters

汉字是记录汉语的书写符号。汉字有数千年的发展历史。从古至今,汉字的发展经历了5个阶段:甲骨文(商代)、金文(商代、西周、春秋战国时期)、小篆(秦代)、隶书(秦代、汉代)、楷书(汉代以后)。

Chinese characters are written symbols used by Chinese language. During thousands of years of development, from ancient times to today, Chinese characters have experienced 5 phases: Oracle Bone Script(Jiaguwen) in Shang Dynasty; Bronze Script (Jinwen) in Shang Dynasty, Western Zhou Dynasty, the Chunqiu Period and the Warring States Period; Seal Script(Xiaozhuan) in Qin Dynasty; Clerical Script(Lishu) in Qin Dynasty and Han Dynasty; Regular Script(Kaishu) after Han Dynasty.

从古至今,汉字累积的总数很多,但是很多汉字并不经常用到,中国人日常所使用的汉字大约有3500个。与世界上其他的文字系统相比,汉字有一些自己的特点,主要是:汉字字形中蕴含着较为丰富的字音、字义以及文化方面的信息;汉字形体结构看上去较为复杂,但也有相当的规律性;在大量汉字中,常用字高度集中。

From ancient times to today, Chinese characters have accumulated a large number of characters, but many Chinese characters are not often used, only

3500 characters are commonly used in the daily life of Chinese people. Compared with the other writing systems in the world, Chinese characters have some characteristics of their own: the form of Chinese characters implicate rich information about pronunciation, meaning and culture; the complicated formation of Chinese characters has its own regularity; among the large quantity of Chinese characters, commonly-used characters are highly concentrated.

对外国学习者来说,掌握1000个左右的常用汉字以及由这些汉字构成的词语,就可以达到比较高的汉语水平。按照国际中文教育新的字词标准,达到最高等级的汉语水平,需要掌握约3000个汉字、11000多个词语。此外,汉字之中包含着丰富的中国文化内容,掌握汉字还可以更好地理解中国文化。

For foreigners, if they can master about 1000 commonly-used Chinese characters and the words formed by these characters, they can attain a high level of Chinese proficiency. According to the new standard of characters and words, the highest-level Chinese learner should master about 3000 Chinese characters and 11000 words. In addition, Chinese characters implicate rich Chinese culture which enables the learners to get a better understanding of Chinese culture.

(二) 汉字的笔画和笔顺 Strokes and Stroke Orders of Chinese Characters

笔画是现代汉字最基本的结构单位,每个汉字都是由若干个笔画构成的。古代汉字多数是由弯曲的线条构成的,而不是笔画。现代汉字的笔画系统是在楷书汉字定型以后逐渐形成的。

Strokes are basic structural units of modern Chinese characters as each character is formed by stroke(s). The ancient Chinese characters are formed by curly lines rather than strokes. The stroke system of modern Chinese characters has gradually developed to its present state after Regular Script(Kaishu) finalized the shape of Chinese characters.

汉字的笔画按照重要性和复杂程度可以分为基本笔画和复合笔画。基本笔画包括6种:一(横)、丨(竖)、丿(撇)、丶(点)、㇏(捺)、㇀(提);复合笔画共有20多种。

In terms of the importance and complexity, strokes can be divided into basic strokes and component strokes. There are 6 basic strokes, including 一(横 héng),丨(竖 shù),丿(撇 piě),乀(捺 nà),丶(点 diǎn) and ノ(提 tí). There are more than 20 kinds of compound strokes.

(三) 基本笔画 Basic Strokes

汉字的基本笔画有6种。这6种基本笔画都是构成汉字的最基本、最简单的笔画,其特点是一笔写完且不改变运笔方向。这6种笔画的详细介绍见表1.1~表1.6。

The 6 basic strokes are the simplest and most common strokes in the formation of Chinese characters. These strokes can be finished in one stroke without changing direction. Detailed descriptions of these 6 strokes see Table 1.1~Table 1.6.

表 1.1 一 héng

名称 Name	说明 Directions	运笔方向 Writing direction	字例 Example	书写练习 Practice
héng	横是汉字中使用最多的笔画,占全部汉字笔画数量的30%左右。根据横在汉字中的位置,它既可以写得短一些,也可以写得长一些。 横(héng) is the most commonly-used stroke in Chinese characters, accounting for about 30 percent of all the strokes in Chinese characters. Due to the different positions of the stroke in characters, it can either be short or long.	----▶	一 二 三	

表 1.2 丨 shù

名称 Name	说明 Directions	运笔方向 Writing direction	字例 Example	书写练习 Practice
shù	竖是汉字中使用第二多的笔画,约占全部汉字笔画数量的19%。根据竖在汉字中的位置,它既可以写得短一些,也可以写得长一些。	↓	十 中 土	

名称 Name	说明 Directions	运笔方向 Writing direction	字例 Example	书写练习 Practice
shù	竖(shù) is the second most commonly-used stroke in Chinese characters, accounting for about 19 percent of all the strokes in Chinese characters. Due to the different positions of the stroke in characters, it can either be short or long.			

表 1.3 丿 piě

名称 Name	说明 Directions	运笔方向 Writing direction	字例 Example	书写练习 Practice
piě	撇是汉字中使用第三多的笔画,约占全部汉字笔画数量的16%。撇一般位于汉字左侧的位置。根据撇在汉字中的位置,撇的长度、倾斜度都有所不同。 撇(piě) is the third most commonly-used stroke in Chinese characters, accounting for about 16 percent of all the strokes in Chinese characters. It usually appears on the left side of characters. Its length and inclination differ in different positions.		八 少 千	

表 1.4 ㇏ nà

名称 Name	说明 Directions	运笔方向 Writing direction	字例 Example	书写练习 Practice
nà	捺是汉字中较为常用的笔画之一,约占全部汉字笔画数量的10%。捺一般位于汉字的右侧位置。根据捺在汉字中的位置,捺的长度、倾斜度都有所不同。		八 人 个	

续表(Continued)

名称 Name	说明 Directions	运笔方向 Writing direction	字例 Example	书写练习 Practice
nà	捺(nà) is a commonly-used stroke in Chinese characters, accounting for about 10 percent of all the stokes in Chinese characters. It usually appears on the right side of characters. Its length and inclination differ in different positions.			

表 1.5 丶 diǎn

名称 Name	说明 Directions	运笔方向 Writing direction	字例 Example	书写练习 Practice
diǎn	点是汉字中较常用的笔画之一。点一般位于汉字(部件)中偏上的位置。根据点在汉字中的位置,点的长度、倾斜度可能有所不同。 点(diǎn) is also a commonly-used stroke in Chinese characters. It usually appears in the middle or upper part of characters. Its length and inclination differ in different positions.	↙	六 字 点	

表 1.6 ⁄ tí

名称 Name	说明 Directions	运笔方向 Writing direction	字例 Example	书写练习 Practice
tí	提是汉字中较常用的笔画之一。提多为横变化而来,一般位于汉字的左下方。 提(tí) is also a commonly-used stroke in Chinese characters. It is usually a variation	↗	块 冷 玩	

名称 Name	说明 Directions	运笔方向 Writing direction	字例 Example	书写练习 Practice
tí	of héng. It usually appears in the lower or left part of characters.			

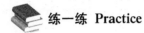
练一练 Practice

1. 说出下列笔画的名称,并用拼音写出来。同学们互相检查,看看说得、写得对不对。

Point out the name of the following strokes and spell out its pinyin. You can check with your classmates to see whether you have got the right pronunciation and writing.

　　、　　　｜　　　╱　　　丿　　　一　　　╲

　（diǎn）　（shù）　（tí）　（piě）　（héng）　（nà）

2. 老师或同学们随机说出 6 种基本笔画的名称,别的同学用手指在空中书写相应的笔画。

The teacher or classmates speak out the names of the 6 basic strokes. The other classmates write out the correspondent stroke with fingers.

3. 下面的汉字有几个笔画？分别是什么笔画？

How many strokes are there in the following Chinese characters? What are they?

例:大[3;横(héng)、撇(piě)、捺(nà)]

Example:大[three;横(héng)、撇(piě)、捺(nà)]

　六　牛　左　上　王　天

（四）基本笔顺 Basic Stroke Orders

大部分汉字由多个笔画组成。书写这些多笔画的汉字时，通常应遵循一定的书写顺序，这就是笔顺。汉字笔顺的规则（见表1.7）是在汉字发展过程中逐渐形成的，因其从人们的长期书写实践中总结而来，所以其背后有一定的科学性和理据性。按照笔顺规则来书写汉字，可以写得快、写得好看。

Most Chinese characters are formed by several strokes. We have to follow basic stroke orders when we are writing these characters. Stroke order rules (see Table 1.7) are gradually formed along with the development of Chinese characters. Since they are summed up from the writing practice, they are scientific and reasonable, which make the writing more quick as well as more beautiful.

表1.7 基本笔顺规则 Basic Stroke Order Rules

	笔顺规则 Stroke order rules	字例 Examples	仿写 Imitate to write
1	先上后下 up first then down	三：一 二 三	
2	先左后右 left first then right	人：丿 人	
3	先横后竖 héng first then shù	十：一 十	
4	先撇后捺 piě first then nà	大：一 ナ 大	

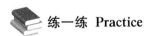 练一练 Practice

下面的汉字第一笔该写什么？
Which stroke should be the first one in each character?
四 五 六 八 九 多 少 几 两 十 千
第一笔写横（characters starting with héng）：_____
第一笔写竖（characters starting with shù）：_____
第一笔写撇（characters starting with piě）：_____
第一笔写点（characters starting with diǎn）：_____

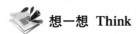 **想一想 Think**

> 汉字的第一笔不太可能写什么笔画？为什么？
> Which stroke is uncommon as the first one in Chinese characters? Why?

二、汉字形音义 The Form, Pronunciation and Meaning of Chinese Characters

 目标汉字 Learning Objective

> 一 二 三 四 五 六 七 八 九 十 两 百 元 多 少 几
> 天 个 人 系

（一）一 yī

词语：一个（one）　一天（one day）

析字：从甲骨文开始一直写作"一"，以此表示数字"一"。

Analysis of the character：It had been written as "一" to refer to number "one" since the Oracle Bone Script(Jiaguwen).

田字格书写 Writing in Tin Word Format：

书写提示：写在田字格的中间，注意笔画平直。

Writing tips: It should be written in the middle with straight stroke.

(二) 二 èr

词语：二十(twenty) 二百(two hundred)

析字：从甲骨文开始一直写作"二"，用两个平直的笔画表示数字"二"，楷书写作"二"。

Analysis of the character: It had been written as "二" to refer to number "two" since Oracle Bone Script(Jiaguwen). It had been written as "二" in Regular Script(Kaishu) with two straight strokes.

田字格书写 Writing in Tin Word Format:

书写提示："二"上面的横要短一些，下面的横稍长。

Writing tips: The upper 横(héng) is shorter than the lower one.

(三) 三 sān

词语：三天(three days) 三千(three thousand)

析字：从甲骨文开始一直写作"三"，用来表示数字"三"。楷书写作"三"，中间一横稍短。

Analysis of the character: It had been written as "三" to refer to number "three" since Oracle Bone Script(Jiaguwen). It had been written as "三" in Regular Script(Kaishu) with a shorter 横(héng) in the middle.

田字格书写 Writing in Tin Word Format：

书写提示：中间的横短一些，下面的横长一些。

Writing tips：The middle 横（héng）is shorter and the lower one should be longer.

（四）四 sì

词语：十四（fourteen）　四百（four hundred）

析字：甲骨文、金文写作"≣"，用来表示数字"四"。春秋战国时期以后写作"四"，楷书写作"四"。

Analysis of the character：It had been written as "≣" to refer to number "four" in Oracle Bone Script（Jiaguwen）and Bronze Script（Jinwen）. It had been written as "四" after the Chunqiu Period and the Warring States Period. It had been written as "四" in Regular Script（Kaishu）.

田字格书写 Writing in Tin Word Format：

书写提示：上面的笔画略宽，下面的略窄。

Writing tips：The upper part is wider than the lower part.

（五）五 wǔ

词语：星期五（Friday）　五天（five days）

析字：甲骨文写作"X"，小篆写作"X"，用这个记号来代表数字"五"。楷书写作"五"。

Analysis of the character: It had been written as "𠄡" "𠄠" and "五" in Oracle Bone Script(Jiaguwen), Seal Script(Xiaozhuan) and Regular Script (Kaishu) respectively to refer to number "five".

田字格书写 Writing in Tin Word Format：

一 丁 五 五

书写提示：下面的横比上面的横略长。

Writing tips：The upper 横(héng) is shorter than the lower 横(héng).

(六) 六 liù

词语：十六(sixteen) 五十六(fifty-six)

析字：甲骨文、金文都写作"介",表示数字"六"。之后，小篆写作"𦉢"，楷书写作"六"。

Analysis of the character: It had been written as "介" to refer to number "six" in Oracle Bone Script(Jiaguwen) and Bronze Script(Jinwen). Then it had been written as "𦉢" and "六" in Seal Script(Xiaozhuan) and Regular Script (Kaishu) respectively.

田字格书写 Writing in Tin Word Format：

丶 一 六 六

书写提示：最后的点比上面的点长一些。

Writing tips：The last 点(diǎn) is longer than the upper 点(diǎn).

(七) 七 qī

词语：七天(seven days)　七月(July)

析字：甲骨文、金文都写作"十",与"十"的写法很相似。用这个抽象符号来表示数字"七"。后来为了与"十"相区别,秦汉以后写成了"七"。

Analysis of the character：It had been written as "十" to refer to number "seven" in Oracle Bone Script(Jiaguwen) and Bronze Script(Jinwen). As it was very similar to "十"(ten), it had been written as "七" after Qin Dynasty and Han Dynasty to avoid confusion.

田字格书写　Writing in Tin Word Format：

一七

七	七	七	七	七	七	七	七	七	七	七	七	七

书写提示：第一笔是横,书写时应略微向上倾斜。

Writing tips：The first stroke is 横(héng) and it should be inclined upward slightly.

(八) 八 bā

词语：十八(eighteen)　八千(eight thousand)

析字：甲骨文、金文、小篆都写作")(",用来表示数字"八",后来楷书写作"八"。

Analysis of the character：It had been written as ")(" to refer to number "eight" in Oracle Bone Script(Jiaguwen), Bronze Script(Jinwen) and Seal Script(Xiaozhuan). Then it had been written as "八" in Regular Script(Kaishu).

田字格书写 Writing in Tin Word Format：

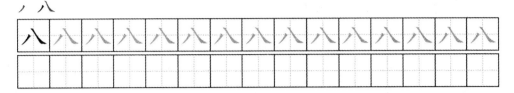

书写提示：第二笔捺的起笔，应略微比撇高一些；且两个笔画不可相连。

Writing tips：The starting point of the second stroke 捺(nà) should be a little higher and isolated from 撇(piě).

(九) 九 jiǔ

词语：九十九(ninety-nine)　九个人(nine persons)

析字：甲骨文写作"⌇"，金文写作"九"，楷书写作"九"，用来表示数字"九"。

Analysis of the character：It had been written as "⌇" "九" and "九" in Oracle Bone Script(Jiaguwen), Bronze Script(Jinwen) and Regular Script (Kaishu) respectively to refer to number "nine".

田字格书写 Writing in Tin Word Format：

书写提示：第一笔是撇，不能写成竖。

Writing tips：The first stroke is 撇(piě), not 竖(shù).

(十) 十 shí

词语：十天(ten days)　九十(ninety)

析字：甲骨文写作"丨"，后来金文写作"✝"，小篆写作"十"，楷书写作"十"。

Analysis of the character：It had been written as "丨" "✝" "十" and "十" in Oracle Bone Script(Jiaguwen), Bronze Script(Jinwen), Seal Script(Xiaozhuan) and Regular Script(Kaishu) respectively.

田字格书写 Writing in Tin Word Format：

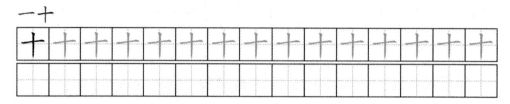

书写提示：第二笔竖从横的中间点穿过。

Writing tips：The second stroke 竖(shù) should be in the middle of the first stroke 横(héng)．

 汉字锦囊 Idea Box of Chinese Characters

有趣的数字

Fun Tips about Number Characters

汉字中表示基础数字的10个汉字在3000多年前的甲骨文中都可以见到，而且很常用。这些表示基础数字的汉字笔画都很简单，容易书写，它们可以分成两个部分：

The 10 Chinese characters for the basic numbers had been found in Oracle Bone Script(Jiaguwen) of 3000-year history as commonly-used characters. These characters have simple strokes and are easy for writing. They can be divided into two groups：

1. 字形与数字的意思联系密切。如"一""二""三""十"。

The form of some characters are closely related to the meaning, such as "一""二""三""十"．

2. 字形只是抽象的记号，与数字的意思没有关系。如"四""五""六""七""八""九"。

The form of some characters are abstract and irrelevant to the meaning, such as "四""五""六""七""八""九".

这些表示基础数字的汉字很有用，不仅可以表示汉语中的全部数字，还可以表示跟数字、序号有关的常用词语。

These characters are very useful as they can express not only all the numbers in Chinese language, but also all the commonly-used phrases related to numbers or orders.

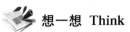 想一想 Think

汉语中的月份怎么说？星期的每一天怎么说？

What are the names of each month in Chinese language? How about the names of every day in a week?

（十一）两 liǎng

词语：两个（two） 两天（two days）

析字：金文写作"𠕓"，隶书写作"兩"，楷书写作"兩"，后来简化为"两"。古代字形为"𠕓"，表示从中间分开，因此有"分为两部分"的意思，演变出数量"二"的意思。

Analysis of the character: It had been written as "𠕓" and "兩" in Bronze Script(Jinwen) and Clerical Script(Lishu) respectively. It had been written as "兩" in Regular Script(Kaishu) and then simplified as "两". The ancient form "𠕓" symbolized separation from the middle, so it has the meaning of "being divided into two parts", which evolved the meaning "two".

田字格书写 Writing in Tin Word Format：

一丆厅丙丙两两

两 两 两 两 两 两 两 两 两 两 两 两

书写提示：两个点不能写成捺。

Writing tips: The two strokes 点（diǎn）in the middle should not be written as 捺(nà).

(十二) 百 bǎi

词语:一百(one hundred)　两百(two hundred)

析字:甲骨文写作"☒",小篆写作"☒",楷书写作"百"。古代字形本来像人的面部,因此有"白色"之义,后来人们借用这个字来表示作为数量单位的"百"。

Analysis of the character：It had been written as "☒" "☒" and "百" in Oracle Bone Script(Jiaguwei)，Seal Script(Xiaozhuan) and Regular Script(Kaishu) respectively. The ancient form was similar to the face of a person，so it was used to refer to the "white color". Then it was borrowed to refer to the number "one hundred".

田字格书写　Writing in Tin Word Format：

一ㄏㄒ万百百

书写提示:第一笔横要略长一些,中间的横要略短。

Writing tips：The first stroke 横(héng) should be longer than the middle ones.

(十三) 元 yuán

词语:元旦(the New Year's Day)　十元钱(ten yuan)

析字:古代汉字写作"☒",像站立的人形并突出其头部,本义是"人头"。小篆写作"☒",楷书写作"元"。后来由"头部"的意思引申出"开始""根本"等意思,如一年的开始——元旦。

Analysis of the character：It had been written as "☒" in ancient Chinese character，it looked like a standing person figure with its highlighted head. The original meaning of this character was "head". It also had been written as "☒" in Seal Script(Xiaozhuan)，and "元" in Regular Script（Kaishu）. Later, its meaning extended from the "head" to "beginning" "foundation", like the beginning of a new year is "元旦".

田字格书写 Writing in Tin Word Format：

一 二 テ 元

元	元	元	元	元	元	元	元	元	元	元	元	元	元

书写提示：上面的短横不能写成点。

Writing tips：The stroke on the top is a short 横(héng)，not 点(diǎn).

（十四）多 duō

词语：多少(how many)　很多(many)

析字：甲骨文写作"多"，小篆写作"多"，楷书写作"多"。表示"数量大""很多"的意思。

Analysis of the character：It had been written as "多" "多" and "多" in Oracle Bone Script(Jiaguwen), Seal Script(Xiaozhuan) and Regular Script (Kaishu) respectively to refer to "large quantities" "many".

田字格书写 Writing in Tin Word Format：

丿 ク 夕 夕 多 多

多	多	多	多	多	多	多	多	多	多	多	多	多	多

书写提示："夕"不能左右并排写成"夗"。

Writing tips：The two parts of the character should not be written as "夗".

（十五）少 shǎo

词语：很少(few)　少有(seldom)

析字：甲骨文写作"⺌"，小篆写作"ᴗ"，楷书写作"少"。古代字形用细碎的小点儿来表示"数量不多"的意思。

Analysis of the character：It had been written as "⺌" "ᴗ" and "少" in Oracle Bone Script(Jiaguwen), Seal Script(Xiaozhuan) and Regular Script (Kaishu) respectively. Its ancient forms used a few spots to refer to "few or not many".

田字格书写 Writing in Tin Word Format：

丨 丷 小 少

书写提示：第一笔写竖，第二、三笔点的写法有所不同。

Writing tips：The first stroke should be 竖(shù). The following two strokes 点 (diǎn) are different.

（十六）几 jǐ

词语：几个(a few)　几天(a few days)

析字：小篆写作"𠘧"，楷书写作"几"。像古代家里用的小而矮的桌子。汉语中借用这个字来询问数量"多少"。

Analysis of the character：It had been written as "𠘧" and "几" in Seal Script(Xiaozhuan) and Regular Script(Kaishu) respectively to refer to "how many". Its form was similar to the short desk used at home in ancient times.

田字格书写 Writing in Tin Word Format：

丿 几

书写提示：第一笔是撇，不能写成竖。

Writing tips：The first stroke is 撇(piě), not 竖(shù).

（十七）天 tiān

词语：白天(daytime)　每天(everyday)

析字：金文写作"🚶""夭"，像人的形状。隶书写作"天"，楷书写作"天"。本义是"人的头顶"，后来字义引申，演变出"天空""日""天气""季节"等意思。

Analysis of the character：It had been written as "🚶" and "夭" in Bronze Script(Jinwen)，similar to the image of a person. Then it had been written as "天" and "天" in Clerical Script(Lishu) and Regular Script(Kaishu) respectively. The original meaning of the form was "the top of a person" but it had been extended as "sky" "day" "weather" "season".

田字格书写 Writing in Tin Word Format：

一 二 于 天

书写提示：上面的横稍短一些。

Writing tips：The upper 横(héng) should be a little shorter.

（十八）个 gè

词语：一个(one)　个人(individual)

析字：古代汉字写作"个"，楷书写作"个"。古代汉语本来用这个字表示竹子的数量单位，后来在汉语中被通用为个体量词，如"三个月""十个人"。又引申表示"单独的"，如"个别""个体""个人"。

Analysis of the character：It had been written as "个" and "个" in ancient Chinese character and Regular Script(Kaishu) respectively. In ancient Chinese，the form was similar to the image of bamboo leaves and was used as numerical unit for bamboos. Then it was commonly used as an individual measure word in phrase like "三个月" and "十个人". The meaning had been extended to refer to "individual"，like "个别""个体""个人".

田字格书写 Writing in Tin Word Format：

丿 人 个

书写提示：撇和捺应在上端相接，写成"入"，不能写成"人"。

Writing tips：The 撇（piě）and the 捺（nà）should be connected to form "入", not "人".

（十九）人 rén

词语：每个人（every one） 人们（people）

析字：象形字。甲骨文写作"" ，金文写作"" ，隶书写作"" ，楷书写作"人"。字的本义是"人类""个人"。

Analysis of the character：It is a pictographic character. It had been written as "" "" "" and "人" in Oracle Bone Script（Jiaguwen）, Bronze Script（Jinwen）, Clerical Script（Lishu）and Regular Script（Kaishu）respectively. The original meanings are "human beings" "a person".

田字格书写 Writing in Tin Word Format：

丿 人

书写提示：不能写成"入"。

Writing tips：It should not be written as "入".

（二十）系 xì

词语：关系（relationship） 联系（connection）

析字：古代汉字写作"" ，像一只手抓着下面几股丝线，字的本义是"连接"。

小篆写作"系"(只保留了一股丝线),楷书写作"系"。在本义的基础上,后来产生了"关系""联系"的意思。

Analysis of the character: It had been written as "系" in ancient Chinese character, like holding some strand of silk threads, its original meaning was "connection". It also had been written as "系"(only one strand of silk thread left) in Seal Script(Xiaozhuan),"系"in Regular Script(Kaishu). On the basis of original meaning, then it generated the meanings of "relationship" and "connection".

田字格书写 Writing in Tin Word Format:

丿 乙 玉 玄 系 系 系

系 系 系 系 系 系 系 系 系 系 系 系 系 系

书写提示:第一笔是撇,不能写成横。

Writing tips: The first stroke is 撇(piě), and should not be written as 横(héng)。

三、词语练习 Phrase Practice

1. 找出方框B中由方框A中的每个汉字构成的词语,同学们互相检查正确与否。

Find out the phrase in Table B formed by each Chinese character in Table A and check with your classmates.

A
一 二 三 六 八 九 十 百 千 多 少 天 人

> B
>
> 很多　每天　三百六十五天　每个人　八十八　星期四　十二　三个　第九课　第二课　一天　五个人　七天　两个　十六　八百　十六　二十三　七十　四天　六　五千　一百　不少　天气　人人　几个人

2. 将词语与对应的拼音连起来。
Link the phrases with corresponding pinyin.

多少人　　　　　　（xīng qī liù）

天气　　　　　　　（dì yī kè）

很多人　　　　　　（duō shǎo rén）

九十八　　　　　　（tiān qì）

星期六　　　　　　（hěn duō rén）

第一课　　　　　　（jiǔ shí bā）

四、综合练习 Comprehensive Practice

1. 按照笔画的拼音写出对应的笔画。
Write out the corresponding strokes according to the pinyin of the strokes.

héng ＿＿＿　　diǎn ＿＿＿　　shù ＿＿＿　　tí ＿＿＿　　piě ＿＿＿　　nà ＿＿＿

2. 试着给下面的汉字加上一个笔画，使其变成一个不同的汉字。
Add one stroke to each of the following characters to change it into another character.

一：　　　二：　　　十：　　　人：　　　大：

3. 按要求写出相应笔顺的笔画。
Write out the required stroke following stroke orders.

例：天（3）：丿（按笔顺写出第3笔）

Example：天（3）：丿（write out the third stroke of the character following stroke orders)

少(1)： 个(3)： 五(2)： 四(5)： 天(4)： 千(1)：

4. 比较下面每组汉字,指出它们的区别。

Compare the following pairs of characters and point out the differences.

大—天 小—少 人—个 六—大 每—母 十—千 七—十

五、课外任务 After-class Task

1. 用拼音在电脑或手机上打出下面的词语。

Type out the following phrases on your computer or mobile phone with pinyin.

多少 星期天 每个人 天气 八十九 中国人

2. 调查朋友们或同学们电话号码的后四位数字,填写下面的表格。

Collect the last four numbers of your friends' or classmates' cellphone number and fill them in the following table.

	电话号码后四位数字 The last four numbers of cellphone number	写出数字相应的汉字 Corresponding Chinese characters
A		
B		
C		
D		
E		

第二课 象 形 字
Lesson Two Pictographic Characters

一、汉字知识 Knowledge of Chinese Characters

(一) 笔画和笔顺 Strokes and Stroke Orders

1. 笔画的变形 Deformation of Strokes

每一种笔画都有可能因为汉字构形和书写美观的需要,在具体的汉字中进行适当的变形。例如,写在上面的点,一般比写在下面的点短一些(如"六");写在上面的横,一般比下面的横短一些(如"二""三");字形左侧的撇一般比写在上面的长一些(如"人""天"),字形上部的撇一般写得比较平、比较短(如"千""每")。

Each kind of stroke may be appropriately deformed in specific Chinese characters because of the needs of Chinese character configuration and beautiful writing. For example, 点(diǎn) written above are generally shorter than 点(diǎn) written below (such as "六"); the 横(héng) written above is generally shorter than the 横(héng) below (such as "二" and "三"); the 撇(piě) in the left part is generally longer than that written above (such as "人" and "天"), while the 撇(piě) in the upper part is generally written flatter and shorter (such as "千" and "每").

2. 复合笔画 Compound Strokes

除了第一课学过的6种基本笔画,汉字还有20多种在基本笔画的基础上加以变化而来的复合笔画,主要包括以横起笔、以竖起笔、以撇起笔等。复合笔画也都应一笔写完。以横起笔的复合笔画见表2.1。

In addition to the 6 basic strokes learned in Lesson One, there are more than 20 compound strokes which are changed from basic strokes, mainly including strokes starting with 横(héng), 竖(shù), 撇(piě), etc. Compound strokes should also be written in one stroke. Compound strokes starting with 横(héng) see Table 2.1.

表2.1　以横起笔的复合笔画 Compound Strokes Starting with 横(héng)

复合笔画 Compound strokes	名称(拼音) Names(Pinyin)	字例 Examples	书写练习 Practice
ㄱ	横折(héng zhé)	四 书	
フ	横撇(héng piě)	又 水	
⼀	横钩(héng gōu)	写 买	
ㄇ	横折钩(héng zhé gōu)	月 为	
ㄱ	横折提(héng zhé tí)	语 话	
ㄟ	横折斜钩(héng zhé xié gōu)	风 飞	
ㄟ	横折弯钩(héng zhé wān gōu)	九 几	
ㄋ	横撇弯钩(héng piě wān gōu)	队 部	
ㄋ	横折折撇(héng zhé zhé piě)	及 建	
ㄋ	横折折折钩(héng zhé zhé zhé gōu)	奶 仍	

练一练 Practice

找出下面汉字中以横起笔的复合笔画,并与相应的拼音名称连起来。
Find out the compound strokes starting with 横(héng) in the following Chinese characters, and connect them with the corresponding pinyin names.

五　九　飞　买　水　认

héng zhé tí　　héng piě　　héng zhé　　héng zhé xié gōu　　héng gōu

héng zhé wān gōu

3. 基本笔顺 Basic Stroke Orders

除了前面学的4种笔顺,还有另外4种基本笔顺规则(见表2.2):

In addition to the 4 stroke orders learned, there are 4 other basic stroke order rules (see Table 2.2):

表 2.2　基本笔顺规则 Basic Stroke Order Rules

	笔顺规则 Stroke order rules	字例 Examples	仿写 Imitate to write
1	先中后旁 first middle, then side	小：亅 亅 小	
2	先外后内 first outside, then inside	同：丨 冂 冂 同	
3	先进后关 first inside, then close	因：丨 冂 囙 因	
4	逐部分写 write component by component	认：讠 认	

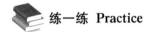
练一练 Practice

按照正确的笔顺写笔画。
Write strokes in correct order.
"水"的第二笔是（the second stroke of "水" is）_____
"四"的第三笔是（the third stroke of "四" is）_____
"口"的第三笔是（the third stroke of "口" is）_____
"多"的第四笔是（the fourth stroke of "多" is）_____

（二）汉字的结构类型 The Structural Types of Chinese Characters

　　古代汉字按照构造的方法来分，可以分为 4 种主要类型：象形字、指事字、会意字和形声字。经历了几千年的发展演变，现代汉字的结构已变得十分复杂多样，不像古代汉字那样清晰、简单，但是这 4 种基本的结构类型仍然保存了下来。了解汉字的结构类型，对于深入学习和了解汉字十分重要。

　　Ancient Chinese characters can be divided into 4 main types according to the construction methods: pictographic characters, indicative characters, associative characters and pictophonetic characters. After thousands of years of evolution, the structure of modern Chinese characters has become very complex and diverse, which is not as clear and simple as ancient Chinese characters, but these 4 basic structural types have still been preserved. Understanding the structural types of Chinese characters is very important for in-depth study and understanding of Chinese characters.

这一课我们先来介绍象形字。

In this lesson, let's first introduce pictographic characters.

古人最早在构造某个汉字时,按照这个汉字所代表的事物的特征或典型的形象来构造字形,这样的汉字是象形字。在古代汉字中,象形字的总数量不是很多,大约有300个,但是它们是汉字系统中最基础的部分,所表示的多是人类社会、自然界中最为常见、最基本的事物。例如,"人"古代汉字写作"𠆢",字形像侧立的人形。

When the ancients first constructed a Chinese character, they constructed the form according to the characteristics or typical images of the things represented by the Chinese character, and such Chinese characters were pictographic characters. In ancient Chinese characters, the total number of pictographic characters was not many, about 300, but they were the most basic part of the Chinese character system, which mostly represented common and basic things in human society and nature. For example, "人" was written as "𠆢" in ancient Chinese character, and it is like a human figure standing sideways.

二、汉字形音义 The Form, Pronunciation and Meaning of Chinese Characters

 目标汉字 Learning Objective

女 子 儿 身 老 来 见 干 手 大 日 月 雨 水 火 中 车 文 口 牛

(一) 女 nǔ

词语:女儿(daughter)　女孩(girl)

析字:象形字。甲骨文写作"𛀀",像女人盘腿而坐。小篆变为"𗊠",秦代隶书再变为"𠁣",楷书变成"女"。本义是"女人",后来也引申表示"女性""女儿",如"女学生""独生女"。

Analysis of the character: It's a pictographic character. In Oracle Bone Script(Jiaguwen), "𛀀" was like a woman sitting cross-legged. Seal Script (Xiaozhuan) became "𗊠", in Clerical Script(Lishu) of Qin Dynasty, the form became "𠁣", and in Regular Script(Kaishu), it became "女". The original meaning was "woman", and later it was extended to mean "female" and "daughter", such as "female student" "only daughter".

田字格书写 Writing in Tin Word Format:

く女女

女	女	女	女	女	女	女	女	女	女	女	女	女

书写提示:注意第一笔是撇折,不是横。

Writing tips: Pay attention to the first stroke, it is 撇折(piě zhé), not 横(héng).

 汉字锦囊 Idea Box of Chinese Characters

来源于人体形状的汉字

The Characters Derived from the Shape of the Human Body

汉字中有很多字形来源于人体的形状,这是因为古人造字时,常常依照人体的形状创造相应意思的汉字。例如,"女"像女人盘腿坐着的样子,"子"像小孩的样子,"老"像老人拄着拐杖。学习汉字时,要注意总结这些汉字的特点。

Many forms of Chinese characters come from the shape of human body, because when the ancients created Chinese characters, they often created characters of corresponding meanings according to the shape of human body. For example, "女" looks like a woman sitting cross-legged, "子" looks like a child, and "老" looks like an old man on crutches. When learning Chinese characters, we should pay attention to summarizing the features of these Chinese characters.

(二) 子 zǐ

词语:儿子(son)　孩子(child)

析字:小篆写作"𐅀",像襁褓中的婴儿,楷书写作"子"。本义是"幼小的孩子",现在也可表示"儿子"的意思。现代汉语中可以在名词后面作为后缀,如"桌子""房子"。

Analysis of the character: Seal Script(Xiaozhuan) was written as "𐅀", like a baby in swaddling clothes, and Regular Script(Kaishu) was written as "子". The original meaning was "young children", and now it can also mean "son". In modern Chinese, it can be used as suffixes after nouns, such as "table" "house".

田字格书写 Writing in Tin Word Format:

`フ了子`

子	子	子	子	子	子	子	子	子	子	子	子	子

书写提示:第一笔是横撇。

Writing tips: The first stroke is 横撇(héng piě).

(三) 儿 ér

词语:儿童(children)　女儿(daughter)

析字:甲骨文写作"𢎁",小篆写作"𦥑",楷书写作"兒",像小孩子张口哭笑的样子。简化字写作"儿"。本义是"小孩",后来也表示"儿子"。普通话中常用在名词后作为后缀,如"小狗儿""花儿"。

Analysis of the character: In Oracle Bone Script(Jiaguwen) it was written as "𢎁", in Seal Script(Xiaozhuan) it was written as "𦥑", and in Regular Script (Kaishu) it was written as "兒", like a child opening his mouth and crying. In simplified characters, it was written as "儿". The original meaning was "child", and later it also meant "son". In mandarin Chinese it is often used as a suffix after nouns, such as "puppy" "flower".

田字格书写 Writing in Tin Word Format:

丿 儿

儿 儿 儿 儿 儿 儿 儿 儿 儿 儿 儿 儿 儿 儿 儿

书写提示:左右笔画要分开。
Writing tips: The left and right strokes should be separated.

(四) 身 shēn

词语:身体(body) 全身(whole body)

析字:甲骨文写作"↑",金文写作"ᔔ",字形像突出腹部特征的人的身体,小篆写作"ᔕ",隶书写作"身",楷书变为"身"。本义为"人的身躯",后来引申出"自身""亲自"的意思。

Analysis of the character: In Oracle Bone Script (Jiaguwen) it was written as "↑", in Bronze Script (Jinwen) it was written as "ᔔ", the form was like a human body with prominent abdominal features. In Seal Script (Xiaozhuan), it was written as "ᔕ", and in Clerical Script (Lishu), it was written as "身". In Regular Script (Kaishu) it became "身". Its original meaning was "human body". Later, the meanings of "self" and "personally" were extended.

田字格书写 Writing in Tin Word Format:

丿 亻 冂 自 自 身 身

身 身 身 身 身 身 身 身 身 身 身 身 身

书写提示:倒数第二笔横,左侧稍伸出一点儿,右侧不伸出。
Writing tips: For the penultimate stroke 横(héng), a little reach out on the

left side and not on the right side.

(五) 老 lǎo

词语：老人（old people）　老师（teacher）

析字：甲骨文写作"𧮫"，像一个手里拿着拐杖的老人。金文变为"𠄎"，秦代隶书写作"老"。本义是"老人"，后来引申为"年老""旧""时间久"等意思。

Analysis of the character：In Oracle Bone Script(Jiaguwen)，"𧮫" was like an old man with a crutch in his hand. Its Bronze Script(Jinwen) form became "𠄎"，and its Clerical Script(Lishu) form in Qin Dynasty was written as "老". The original meaning was "old man"，which was later extended to "old" and "long time".

田字格书写 Writing in Tin Word Format：

一 十 土 尹 耂 老

书写提示：最后一笔撇不能出头。

Writing tips：Don't make the last stroke 撇(piě) reach out.

(六) 来 lái

词语：上来（come up）　快来（come on）

析字：甲骨文写作"来"，像麦株的形状。秦代隶书写作"来"，楷书变成"來"，简化字写成"来"。自古至今，汉语中都是借用原本表示麦子的"来"表示"来去"的"来"。

Analysis of the character：In Oracle Bone Script(Jiaguwen)，"来" was like the shape of wheat. The Clerical Script(Lishu) form in Qin Dynasty was written as "来"，its Regular Script(Kaishu) form became "來"，and its simplified character form was abbreviated as "来". Since ancient times, in Chinese language, the character which means "come and go", has been borrowed from

"𝒳", which originally meant wheat.

田字格书写 Writing in Tin Word Format：

一 ㄈ ㄈ 五 平 来 来

书写提示：中间的竖笔不是第二笔，而是第五笔。

Writing tips：The stroke 竖(shù) in the middle is not the second stroke，but the fifth one.

（七）见 jiàn

词语：看见(see)　听见(hear)

析字：甲骨文写作"𦣻"，像跪着的人形而突出其大大的眼睛，以表示"看见"的意思。金文写作"𦣻"，后来上面的眼睛变成"目"，下面的人形变成"儿"，楷书写成"見"，简化字变成"见"。本义是用眼睛"看"，后来也可以表示"听"的结果，如"听见"。

Analysis of the character：Its Oracle Bone Script(Jiaguwen) form was "𦣻", like a kneeling human figure，highlighted its big eyes to show the meaning of "seeing". Its Bronze Script(Jinwen) form was written as "𦣻"，and later the upper eyes became "目"，the lower human figure became "儿"，the Regular Script(Kaishu) form was written as "見"，and the simplified character form became "见". The original meaning was to "see" with the eyes，and later it can also mean the result of "listen".

田字格书写 Writing in Tin Word Format：

丨 冂 贝 见

书写提示：不能与"贝"混淆。

Writing tips：Don't confuse it with "贝".

（八）干 gàn/gān

词语：干什么（what to do） 干净（clean）

析字：古代汉字写作"❣"或"丫"，像古代军队使用的盾牌。小篆写作"丫"，楷书写作"干"。由"盾牌"的意思引申出"打扰""做事情"等意思。

Analysis of the character：It had been written as "❣" and "丫" in ancient Chinese character，like a shield used in ancient army. Then it had been written as "丫" and "干" in Seal Script(Xiaozhuan) and Regular Script(Kaishu) respectively. The meaning was extended from "shield" to "interrupt" "do things" and so on.

田字格书写 Writing in Tin Word Format：

一 二 干

干 干 干 干 干 干 干 干 干 干 干 干 干 干

书写提示：注意细小的差别，不能写成"千"。

Writing tips：Please pay attention to the slight difference，don't write it as "千".

（九）手 shǒu

词语：左手（left hand） 右手（right hand）

析字：金文写作"ϟ"，像五指张开的人手的样子。小篆写作"ϟ"，楷书变为"手"，从古至今，字形几乎没有太大变化。本义是"人的手"，后来引申出"用手做""做事情的人"等意思，如"手写""手工""新手"等。

Analysis of the character：The Bronze Script(Jinwen) form was written as "ϟ"，like a hand with five fingers open. Its Seal Script(Xiaozhuan) form was written as "ϟ"，its Regular Script(Kaishu) form became "手"，and the form has hardly changed since ancient times. The original meaning was "human hand".

Later, the meanings of "doing things by hand" and "the person who does things" were extended, such as "handwriting" "manual" "novice" and so on.

田字格书写 Writing in Tin Word Format：

书写提示：第一笔是撇，不能写成提，也不能写成横。

Writing tips：The first stroke is 撇(piě), not 提(tí) or 横(héng).

（十）大 dà

词语：大人(adult)　大学(university)

析字：甲骨文写作"↑"，像正面站立的人形。小篆写作"大"，楷书写作"大"。从古至今，字形没有很大变化。字形以"成年人的外形"来表示抽象意义的"大"。

Analysis of the character：The Oracle Bone Script（Jiaguwen）form was "↑", like a human figure standing on the front. In Seal Script（Xiaozhuan），it was written as "大", while its Regular Script（Kaishu）form was "大". Since ancient times, the form has not changed much. The form expresses the abstract meaning of "big" with "the shape of an adult".

田字格书写 Writing in Tin Word Format：

书写提示：不能写成"天"。

Writing tips：It should not be written as "天".

汉字锦囊 Idea Box of Chinese Characters

只差一点点

Only a Little Difference

汉字中有些字区别很小,有的只差一两个笔画。例如,"大—太""日—白""白—百""天—夫""七—十"等。学习汉字,要注意明白字理,认真比较,及时总结,反复练习。

The differences between some Chinese characters are very small, and some of them are only one or two strokes, such as "大—太""日—白""白—百""天—夫""七—十" and so on. To learn Chinese characters, we should understand the theory of characters, compare carefully, summarize in time, and practice repeatedly.

(十一) 日 rì

词语:生日(birthday) 星期日(Sunday)

析字:甲骨文写作"⊙",像太阳的形状(中间的点只是起装饰或区别的作用),小篆写成"日",与现在的楷书字形没有太大区别。本义是"太阳",后来引申为表示与时间有关的意思,如"日期""今日"。

Analysis of the character: The Oracle Bone Script(Jiaguwen) form was "⊙", like the shape of the sun (the middle point was just the function of decoration or difference), and its Seal Script(Xiaozhuan) form was written as "日", which was not much different from the current Regular Script(Kaishu). The original meaning was "the sun", and later it can be extended to mean something related to time, such as "date" and "today".

田字格书写 Writing in Tin Word Format：

书写提示：中间的横稍短，不与右侧相连；下面的横最后写。

Writing tips：The middle 横（héng）is slightly shorter and not connected with the right side；the 横（héng）at the bottom is the last stroke.

（十二）月 yuè

词语：九月（September） 月亮（moon）

析字：金文写作"𝔇"，像半月形状，小篆写作"☾"，楷书写作"月"。本义是"月亮"，后来也用作表示时间的名词，如"这个月"。

Analysis of the characters：Its Bronze Script（Jinwen）form was written as "𝔇", which was like a half-moon shape. In Seal Script（Xiaozhuan）, it was written as "☾" and its Regular Script（Kaishu）form was written as "月". The original meaning was "moon", which was later used as a noun to express time, such as "this month".

田字格书写 Writing in Tin Word Format：

书写提示：中间的短横，与左侧竖撇相连，与右侧笔画不连。

Writing tips：The short 横（héng）in the middle is connected with the left 竖撇（shù piě）, but not with the right stroke.

(十三) 雨 yǔ

词语:下雨(rain)　大雨(heavy rain)

析字:甲骨文写作"⾬",小篆写作"⾬",像雨水从天空落下。楷书写作"雨",字形变化不大。本义是"雨水"。

Analysis of the character：Its Oracle Bone Script(Jiaguwen) form was "⾬", Its Seal Script(Xiaozhuan) form was "⾬", like rain falling from the sky. Its Regular Script(Kaishu) form was written as "雨", the form changed not much. The original meaning was "rain".

田字格书写 Writing in Tin Word Format：

一丆冂币币雨雨雨

雨 雨 雨 雨 雨 雨 雨 雨 雨 雨 雨 雨 雨

书写提示:中间的四个点,应最后书写。

Writing tips：The four 点(diǎn) in the middle should be written last.

(十四) 水 shuǐ

词语:喝水(drink water)　中文水平(Chinese level)

析字:甲骨文写作"水",像河流中水流动的样子,秦代隶书写作"水",楷书变成"水"。字的本义是"水流"或"水"。

Analysis of the character：Its Oracle Bone Script(Jiaguwen) form was "水", like water flowing in a river. The Clerical Script(Lishu) form in Qin Dynasty was written as "水", its Regular Script(Kaishu) form became "水". The original meanings of the character were "flow" or "water".

田字格书写 Writing in Tin Word Format：

丨 刁 才 水

水	水	水	水	水	水	水	水	水	水	水	水	水	水	水

书写提示：第一笔写中间的竖钩，不是左边的横撇。

Writing tips：The first stroke is 竖钩（shù gōu）in the middle, not 横撇（héng piě）on the left.

(十五) 火 huǒ

词语：火车（train） 火锅（hotpot）

析字：甲骨文写作"🔥"，像燃烧的火苗的形状，小篆写作"火"，楷书变为"火"，从古至今，字形没有很大变化。本义是"物体燃烧所发的光、焰和热"，后来引申为"发怒"（如"发火"）、"火一样的颜色"（如"火红"）等意思。

Analysis of the character：Its Oracle Bone Script(Jiaguwen) form was "🔥", like a burning flame shape, its Seal Script(Xiaozhuan) form was "火", its Regular Script(Kaishu) form became "火", and the form has not changed much since ancient times. The original meaning was "light, flame and heat from the burning of an object", which was later extended to mean "angry"(such as "get angry"), "fire-like color"(such as "flaming red"), etc.

田字格书写 Writing in Tin Word Format：

丶 丷 少 火

火	火	火	火	火	火	火	火	火	火	火	火	火	火	火

书写提示：第一笔是点，第二笔是撇。

Writing tips：The first stroke is 点（diǎn）, the second stroke is 撇（piě）.

（十六）中 zhōng

词语：中国（China）　中间（middle）

析字：甲骨文写作"🀄"，像旗杆的上下有飘带之形，旗杆表示正中的意思，字的本义是"中心""中间"。战国时期字形写作"中"，省去了旗杆上下的飘带。楷书写作"中"，本义是"中间"。

Analysis of the character：Its Oracle Bone Script（Jiaguwen）form was "🀄", like ribbons above and below the flagpole，which meant the center. The original meanings of this character were "center" and "middle". In Warring States Period，the writing form was "中"，which omitted the ribbons above and below the flagpole. Its Regular Script（Kaishu）form was "中". The original meaning was "middle".

田字格书写 Writing in Tin Word Format：

丿 口 口 中

中	中	中	中	中	中	中	中	中	中	中	中

书写提示：中间的竖笔应最后写，位置在正中间。

Writing tips：The stroke 竖（shù）in the middle should be written last.

（十七）车 chē

词语：汽车（automobile）　车站（station）

析字：金文写作"🚗"，像古代的车辆，突出显示左右两个车轮。后来为了书写简便，写为"车"，只用一个车轮表示。楷书繁体字写成"車"，简化字变为"车"。本义是"有轮子的交通工具"。

Analysis of the character：Its Bronze Script（Jinwen）form was written as "🚗", like ancient vehicles，highlighting the left and right wheels. Later，for the sake of writing simplicity，it was written as "车"，which was represented by only one wheel. Its traditional Chinese character in Regular Script（Kaishu）was written as "車", and its simplified character form was changed into "车". The original meaning was "vehicles with wheels".

田字格书写 Writing in Tin Word Format：

一 𠂇 车 车

车	车	车	车	车	车	车	车	车	车	车	车	车

书写提示：上面的横稍短，下面的横稍长。

Writing tips：The above 横（héng）is slightly short，while the below 横（héng）is slightly long.

（十八）文 wén

词语：中文（Chinese） 文化（culture）

析字：甲骨文写作"𡥀"，像人的身体上有纹身的样子，字的本义是"花纹""纹理"。小篆写作"𡥀"，楷书变成"文"。后来由"花纹""纹理"的意思，引申、变化出其他新的意思，如"文采""文字""文章"等。

Analysis of the character：It had been written as "𡥀" in Oracle Bone Script (Jiaguwen)，the shape of this character was like the tattoo figures on human body. Its original meaning was "pattern" "texture". It also had been written as "𡥀" in Seal Script(Xiaozhuan)，and "文" in Regular Script(Kaishu). Later the meaning was extended from "pattern" or "texture" into those new contents，like "literary grace" "words" "articles" and so on.

田字格书写 Writing in Tin Word Format：

丶 一 ナ 文

文	文	文	文	文	文	文	文	文	文	文	文	文

书写提示：点下面的横、撇、捺，不能写成"又"。

Writing tips：The strokes beneath the 点（diǎn）are 横（héng），撇（piě），捺

(nà), and should not be written as "又".

(十九) 口 kǒu

词语：门口(doorway)　入口(entrance)

析字：象形字。古代汉字写作"㕣"，像人的口形，小篆写作"㕣"，楷书写作"口"。字的本义是"人或动物的口"，后来表示"出入通过的地方"，如"门口""路口"。

Analysis of the character：It's a pictographic character. The ancient Chinese character form "㕣" was like a human mouth. Then the character had been written as "㕣" and "口" in Seal Script (Xiaozhuan) and Regular Script (Kaishu) respectively. The original meaning of the character was "the mouth of human or animal", later it was extended to mean "a place to go in and out", such as "doorway" "junction".

田字格书写 Writing in Tin Word Format：

丨 冂 口

书写提示：按照竖、横折、横的顺序书写。

Writing tips：Please notice the stroke orders 竖(shù)、横折(héng zhé)、横(héng)。

(二十) 牛 niú

词语：牛肉(beef)　牛奶(milk)

析字：甲骨文写作"牛"，像牛头的形状，秦代字形写作"牛""牛"，楷书写作"牛"。

Analysis of the character：Its Oracle Bone Script (Jiaguwen) form "牛" was like a cow's head shape, in Qin Dynasty it was written as "牛""牛", and its Regular Script (Kaishu) form was "牛".

田字格书写 Writing in Tin Word Format：

丿 匕 二 牛

牛	牛	牛	牛	牛	牛	牛	牛	牛	牛	牛	牛	牛	牛	牛

书写提示：不能写成"午"或者"生"。

Writing tips：It should not be written as "午" or "生".

练一练 Practice

1. 说一说下面每组汉字的区别。

Talk about the differences between two Chinese characters in the following groups.

小—水　牛—午　日—目

大—火　日—月　儿—人

2. 把下面象形字与其对应的汉字连起来。

Match the Chinese characters and the pictographs below.

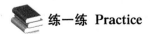

牛　水　火　女　羊　身　手　车　见

三、词语练习 Phrase Practice

1. 找出方框 B 中由方框 A 中的每个汉字构成的词语，同学们互相检查正确与否。

Find out the phrase in Table B formed by each Chinese character in Table A and check with your classmates.

第二课 象形字

A

女 子 儿 老 长 大 日 月 雨 水 中 车 羊 牛

B

老师 喝水 牛奶 车站 大人 十月 下雨 孩子 儿子 中国 儿歌
老人 长江 星期日 长大 羊肉 女孩 桌子 水平 中心 汽车 女人
山羊 公牛 校长

2. 将词语与对应的拼音连起来。

Link the phrases with the corresponding pinyin.

牛奶　　　　　　ér zi

老师　　　　　　chē zhàn

女生　　　　　　niú nǎi

儿子　　　　　　nǚ shēng

车站　　　　　　lǎo shī

3. 读出下面的句子。

Read out the following sentences.

① 你是中国人吗？

② 外面在下雨。

③ 学校离火车站不远。

④ 明天是星期日。

⑤ 我没见过山羊。

⑥ 今天天气很好。

⑦ 长大后，他想当老师。

四、综合练习 Comprehensive Practice

1. 按照笔画的拼音写出对应的笔画。

Write out the corresponding strokes according to the pinyin of the strokes.

héng piě　　héng zhé　　héng zhé wān gōu　　héng gōu　　héng zhé gōu

(　　)　　(　　)　　(　　)　　(　　)　　(　　)

2. 找出下面汉字中的复合笔画，并写出来。

Find out the compound strokes in the following characters and write them out.

中(　　)

水(　　)

飞(　　)

乃(　　)

队(　　)

3. 选字组词。

Choose characters to make out words.

① (A. 牛　B. 午　C. 土)奶

② 明(A. 天　B. 夫　C. 大)

③ 看(A. 见　B. 贝　C. 儿)

④ (A. 者　B. 老　C. 考)师

⑤ 下(A. 雨　B. 月　C. 日)

⑥ 星期(A. 中　B. 日　C. 子)

五、课外任务 After-class Task

1. 用下面所给的古代汉字制作字词卡片，每张卡片上写出：古代汉字、现代汉字、拼音、由其组成的两个词语。

Make character cards with the ancient Chinese characters given below, and write on each card: ancient Chinese characters, modern Chinese characters, pinyin and two words composed by the character.

例 Example：

> 雨
>
> 雨 yǔ
>
> 雨水　　下雨
> yǔ shuǐ　xià yǔ

2. 用拼音在电脑或手机上打出下面的词语。

Type out the following phrases on your computer or mobile phone with pinyin.

中国　长江　老师　儿子　女儿　金鱼　听见　火车　身体　水果

第三课　独体字与合体字
Lesson Three　Single Characters and Compound Characters

一、汉字知识 Knowledge of Chinese Characters

(一) 复合笔画 Compound Strokes

以竖起笔的复合笔画、以撇起笔的复合笔画、两个特殊钩笔分别见表3.1、表3.2、表3.3。

Compound strokes starting with 竖(shù), compound strokes starting with 撇(piě) and two special 钩(gōu) strokes see Table 3.1, Table 3.2 and Table 3.3 respectively.

表 3.1　以竖起笔的复合笔画 Compound Strokes Starting with 竖(shù)

复合笔画 Compound strokes	名称(拼音) Names (Pinyin)	字例 Examples	仿写 Imitate to write
ㄴ	竖折(shù zhé)	山　亡	
㇗	竖提(shù tí)	长　民	
亅	竖钩(shù gōu)	水　利	
ㄴ	竖弯钩(shù wān gōu)	已　儿	
ㄇ	竖折折钩(shù zhé zhé gōu)	马　鸟	
㇄	竖折撇(shù zhé piě)	专　传	

表3.2 以撇起笔的复合笔画 Compound Strokes Starting with 撇(piě)

复合笔画 Compound strokes	名称（拼音） Names（Pinyin）	字例 Examples	仿写 Imitate to write
㇊	撇点(piě diǎn)	女 妈	
㇌	撇折(piě zhé)	车 红	

表3.3 两个特殊钩笔 Two Special 钩(gōu) Strokes

复合笔画 Compound strokes	名称（拼音） Names（Pinyin）	字例 Examples	仿写 Imitate to write
㇂	斜钩(xié gōu)	代 我	
㇁	弯钩(wān gōu)	家 狗	

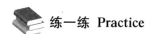 练一练 Practice

1. 找出下面汉字中的复合笔画，并说出名称。
Find out compound strokes in the following characters, and say their names.

去 与 出 以 老 东 妹 了 七 狂

2. 请把复合笔画的名称与笔画连起来。
Link the names of compound strokes with corresponding strokes.

撇折　　竖弯钩　　竖钩　　竖提　　弯钩　　斜钩

㇁　　　㇂　　　亅　　　㇌　　　乚　　　丨

（二）汉字的结构类型 The Structure Types of Chinese Characters

这一课，我们来介绍独体字与合体字。
In this lesson, let's introduce single characters and compound characters.

按照形体结构是否可以分解来划分，汉字可以分为独体字和合体字两部分。独体字是形体构造具有独立性、一般不能拆分（如果再拆分的话，就只剩下笔画）的汉字。例如，"人""大""水""土""四""飞""火"等。合体字是由两个或两个以上构字成分组合而成的汉字。例如，"汉""语""国""分""体""字"等。独体字一般笔画数较少，形体比较简单。

According to whether the structure of Chinese characters can be decomposed or not, Chinese characters can be divided into two parts: single characters and compound characters. The single characters have independent structure, which cannot be split (if this kind of characters are split, there are only strokes remained). For example, "人""大""水""土""四""飞""火", etc. Compound characters are combined by two or more components. For example, "汉""语""国""分""体""字", etc. In general, the stroke number of single characters is small, the form is simple.

在常用汉字中，独体字的数量只有200多个，但是它们是构成全部合体字的基础。因此，掌握好独体字十分重要。

In commonly-used Chinese characters, the number of single characters is only about 200, but they are the basis for forming compound characters. Thus, it is vital to master single characters.

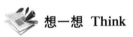
想一想 Think

指出下列汉字中的独体字和合体字。

Please point out which are the single characters and which are the compound characters in the following characters.

你　上　好　用　中　姓　五　名　牛　吗　快　小　多

二、汉字形音义 The Form, Pronunciation and Meaning of Chinese Characters

 目标汉字 Learning Objective

飞 书 不 了 么 再 太 白 住 作 做 什 们 你 他 体 休 从 方 候

（一）飞 fēi

词语：飞机(airplane)　飞快(very fast)

析字：古代汉字写作"𠇎""𦐇"，像鸟儿展开双翼飞翔，楷书繁体写作"飛"，简化字写成"飞"。

Analysis of the character：It had been written as "𠇎" "𦐇" in ancient Chinese character. The form of this character just like a bird spreads its wings when flies. The traditional Chinese character had been written as "飛" in Regular Script(Kaishu), and then simplified as "飞".

田字格书写 Writing in Tin Word Format：

书写提示：注意第一笔横折斜钩的写法。

Writing tips：Please notice the first stroke 横折斜钩(héng zhé xié gōu).

(二) 书 shū

词语：看书(read books)　图书馆(library)

析字：古代汉字写作"🖋"，古代字形的上面像人手拿着毛笔写字，下面是表示字音的"者"，秦代隶书写作"書"，楷书写作"書"，后来简化为"书"。

Analysis of the character：It had been written as "🖋" in ancient Chinese character. The upper part of this character just like a man whose hands have a Chinese brush, the below part is "者", which represents this character's pronunciation. Then it had been written as "書" and "書" in Clerical Script (Lishu) in Qin Dynasty and Regular Script(Kaishu) respectively, and then simplified as "书".

田字格书写 Writing in Tin Word Format：

フ コ 书 书

书 书 书 书 书 书 书 书 书 书 书 书 书 书 书 书

书写提示：第二笔横折钩要写得稍微宽一点，点最后写。

Writing tips：The second stroke 横折钩(héng zhé gōu) should be written slightly wider, and the 点(diǎn) should be written at last.

(三) 不 bú/bù

词语：不是(not)　不能(cannot)

析字：古代汉字写作"🌱""🌱"，现代学者一般认为，字形上面像花蒂的子房，下面像花蕊下垂的样子。自古以来，"不"都被借用作为否定的副词，用在动词、形容词前面。

Analysis of the character：It had been written as "🌱" and "🌱" in ancient Chinese character. Modern scholars generally believe that, the upper part of this character just like the ovary of flower, the below part is similar to a drooping stamen. From ancient times to present, "不" is borrowed as a negative adverb, which is used in front of verb and adjective.

田字格书写 Writing in Tin Word Format：

书写提示：最后一笔是长点，不能写成捺。

Writing tips：The last stroke is long 点（diǎn），it should not be written as 捺（nà）.

（四）了 le/liǎo

词语：走了（went）　了解（understand）

析字：古代汉字写作"了"，楷书写作"了"，字形像包裹起来的婴儿。在汉语中，"了"是多音字，有两个读音。被借用来表示"知道""明白""结束"的意思时，读"liǎo"；在现代汉语中，被借用来作为句尾的语气助词和时态助词时读"le"，如"下雨了！""雨已经下了三天。"

Analysis of the character：It had been written as "了" in ancient Chinese character. Then it had been written as "了" in Regular Script（Kaishu）. The form of this character was similar to a wrapped baby. In Chinese,"了" is a polyphonic character, which has two pronunciations. When "了" is borrowed to refer to "know" "understand" "end", its pronunciation is "liǎo". In modern Chinese, when it is borrowed as the modal particle or tense-aspect particle in the end of a sentence, its pronunciation is "le", for example, "It is raining!" "It has been raining for three days."

田字格书写 Writing in Tin Word Format：

书写提示：第二笔是竖钩，不能写成竖。

Writing tips：The second stroke is 竖钩(shù gōu), it should not be written as 竖(shù).

（五）么 me/mó

词语：什么（what）　怎么（how）

析字：小篆写作"麼"，楷书写作"麼""麽"，简化字写成"么"。在古代汉语中，"么"表示"小"的意思。现代汉语中，只用为后缀，构成"多么""什么""那么"这样的词语。

Analysis of the character：It had been written as "麼" and "麼" "麽" in Seal Script(Xiaozhuan) and Regular Script(Kaishu) respectively, and then simplified as "么". In ancient Chinese, the meaning of this character was "small". In modern Chinese, it is used as suffix only, constituting phrases such as "how" "what" "so".

田字格书写　Writing in Tin Word Format：

丿 厶 么

么	么	么	么	么	么	么	么	么	么	么	么

书写提示：不能写成"公"。

Writing tips：It should not be written as "公".

（六）再 zài

词语：再见（goodbye）　再说一遍（say it again）

析字：甲骨文写作"𠕇"，像两部分重叠的样子，本义为"第二次"。后来写作"再""再"。汉语中，用作副词，表示"又一次""更加"等意思。

Analysis of the character：It had been written as "𠕇" in Oracle Bone Script (Jiaguwen), which just like two same parts overlap together. The original meaning of this character was "second time". Then it had been written as "再"

"再". In Chinese, it is used as adverb, which refers to "once again" "even more".

田字格书写 Writing in Tin Word Format：

一 厂 ñ 币 再 再

书写提示：最后一横长一些。

Writing tips：The last stroke 横(héng) should be written longer.

(七) 太 tài

词语：太好了(wonderful)　太阳(sun)

析字：在古代汉字中，写法跟"大"是一样的。后来在"大"下面加点，分化出"太"，写成"", 楷书变成"太"。本义是"极大"，后来表示"过于""过分"。

Analysis of the character：It had been written as the same as "大" in ancient Chinese character. Later, the below part of "大" was added a 点 (diǎn), forming the character of "太". It had been written as "", then it had been written as "太" in Regular Script(Kaishu). The original meaning of this character was "extremely big", later it referred to the meanings of "too" "excessive".

田字格书写 Writing in Tin Word Format：

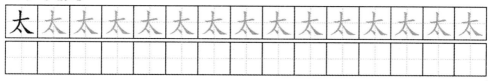

书写提示：最后一笔是点，不能写成捺。

Writing tips：The last stroke is 点(diǎn), it should not be written as 捺(nà).

(八) 白 bái

词语：白天（daytime） 白色（white）

析字：古代汉字写作"θ"，现代学者认为字形像人的面孔，跟"皃"（意思是"面貌"）应该是一个字，后来借用来表示"白色"。小篆写作"白"，楷书写作"白"。

Analysis of the character：It had been written as "θ" in ancient Chinese character, modern scholars generally believe that, this character is similar to the shape of people's face, which should be the same character as "皃"（means people's face）. Later, it was borrowed to represent the meaning of "white". It had been written as "白" and "白" in Seal Script（Xiaozhuan）and Regular Script（Kaishu）respectively.

田字格书写 Writing in Tin Word Format：

丿 亻 白 白 白

书写提示：中间的横与左侧笔画相连，不与右侧笔画相连。

Writing tips：The middle 横（héng）should be connected with the left stroke and isolated from the right stroke.

(九) 住 zhù

词语：居住（dwell） 站住（keep one's feet）

析字：合体字，左边的"亻"与字义有关，右边的"主"表示字的读音。

Analysis of the character：It is a compound character, the left stroke "亻" is related to this character's meaning, the right stroke "主" represents this character's pronunciation.

田字格书写 Writing in Tin Word Format：

丿 亻 亻 亻 亻 住 住

住	住	住	住	住	住	住	住	住	住	住	住	住

书写提示：右边的"主"不能写成"王"。

Writing tips："主" on the right should not be written as "王"。

 汉字锦囊 Idea Box of Chinese Characters

常用偏旁——单人旁（亻）

Commonly-used Components — Danrenpang（亻）Component

汉字偏旁"亻"是由"人"字演变而来，一般在合体字的左侧，称为"单人旁"。"亻"是合体字中常用的偏旁，可以构成很多汉字，如"作""做""你""他""们""休""体"等。"亻"一般表示与"人"或"人体"相关的意思，有时也表示某种抽象的意思。

The component "亻" is evolved from the character "人", which is usually used in the left side of compound characters, and named "Danrenpang". This component is commonly-used, which can form many characters, such as "作""做""你""他""们""休""体", etc. "亻" represents the meanings that are related to "human being" or "the body of human" in general, it also represents some abstract meanings sometimes.

（十）作 zuò

词语：作业（homework）　工作（work）

析字：合体字，左边的"亻"和右边的"乍"都与字的意思有关（"乍"表示"突然"的意思）。"作"的本义是"人突然站起来"，后来引申出"工作""起来"的意思。

Analysis of the character：It is a compound character, the left stroke "亻" and the right stroke "乍" are both related to this character's meaning（the meaning of "乍" is sudden). The original meaning of "作" was "a person who stand up suddenly". Later, it generated meanings of "work" "get up".

田字格书写 Writing in Tin Word Format：

ノ 亻 仁 仨 竹 作 作

书写提示：左侧的"亻"不能写成"彳"。

Writing tips：The left side "亻" should not be written as "彳".

(十一) 做 zuò

词语：做朋友（make friends） 做饭（cook）

析字：合体字，"亻"与字的意思有关，"故"与字的读音有关。"做"是从"作"分化出来的。

Analysis of the character：It is a compound character, the stroke "亻" is related to this character's meaning, "故" is related to this character's pronunciation. "做" is differentiated from "作".

田字格书写 Writing in Tin Word Format：

ノ 亻 亻 什 仕 估 估 做 做 做 做

书写提示：字形左、中、右三部分的比例要大体均等。

Writing tips：The proportion of the left, middle and right part should be equal.

(十二) 什 shén/shí

词语：什么（what） 做什么（what to do）

析字:"亻"在字形中不表示实在的意思,右边的"十"与读音有关。

Analysis of the character: In this character, "亻" doesn't represent indeed meaning, the right stroke "十" is related to this character's pronunciation.

田字格书写 Writing in Tin Word Format:

丿 亻 仁 什

书写提示:左侧"亻"略微窄一些。

Writing tips: The left stroke "亻" should be written slightly narrow.

(十三) 们 mén/men

词语:我们(we) 你们(you) 他们(they)

析字:左边的"亻"表示字义与人相关,右边的"门"表示读音,不能单独使用,只作为后缀,用在代词或指人的名词后面,表示复数。

Analysis of the character: The left stroke "亻" represents this character's meaning is related to people, the right stroke "门" represents this character's pronunciation, which is used behind pronoun or noun that refers to people as suffix only, representing plural, cannot be used alone.

田字格书写 Writing in Tin Word Format:

丿 亻 亻 们 们

书写提示:右边的"门"先写点。

Writing tips: The 点(diǎn) in right part "门" should be written firstly.

(十四) 你 nǐ

词语：你们（you）　你好（hello）

析字：左边的"亻"与字义有关，右边的"尔"原来可以表示字音，但是现代汉字中由于语音变化，现在已经不能表示字音。

Analysis of the character：The left stroke "亻" is related to this character's meaning, the right stroke "尔" can represent this character's pronunciation originally. However, with the change of modern Chinese character's pronunciation, "尔" can't represent pronunciation anymore.

田字格书写 Writing in Tin Word Format：

丿 亻 亻 你 你 你 你

书写提示：右边第二笔是横钩，不能写成横折钩。

Writing tips：The second stroke in right part is 横钩（héng gōu）, it should not be written as 横折钩（héng zhé gōu）.

(十五) 他 tā

词语：他们（they）　他人（other people）

析字：左边的"亻"与字义有关。由于语音变化，右边的"也"现已不表示字音。

Analysis of the character：The left stroke "亻" is related this character's meaning. With the change of Chinese character's pronunciation, the right stroke "也" can't represent pronunciation anymore.

田字格书写 Writing in Tin Word Format：

ノ 亻 亻 仂 他

他	他	他	他	他	他	他	他	他	他	他	他	他

书写提示：右边"也"第一笔的横略微向上倾斜。

Writing tips：The first stroke 横（héng）in right part "也" should be written upward-sloping slightly.

（十六）体 tǐ

词语：身体（body） 体育场（stadium）

析字：古代汉字写作"軆"，楷书写作"體"，左边的"骨"与意思有关，右边的部分表示读音。简化字变成"体"，"亻"和"本"两部分都是与字义相关的。

Analysis of the character：It had been written as "軆" in ancient Chinese character, then it had been written as "體" in Regular Script（Kaishu），the left stroke "骨" was related to this character's meaning, the right part represented this character's pronunciation. Then it was simplified as "体", the two parts "亻" and "本" were both related to the meaning of this character.

田字格书写 Writing in Tin Word Format：

ノ 亻 亻 仁 什 仕 休 体

体	体	体	体	体	体	体	体	体	体	体	体	体

书写提示：最后一笔短横，不能与左侧和右侧笔画相连。

Writing tips：The last stroke short 横（héng）should be written shorter and isolated from the left and the right strokes.

（十七）休 xiū

词语：休息（have a rest）　休学（suspension of schooling）

析字：古代汉字写作"𠆢木"，像一个人靠着一棵树休息的样子，本义为"休息"。

Analysis of the character：It had been written as "𠆢木" in ancient Chinese character, which was similar to a person who is leaning a tree for resting, the original meaning of this character was "resting".

田字格书写 Writing in Tin Word Format：

丿 亻 仁 什 什 休

书写提示：注意与"体"的区别。

Writing tips：Please notice the difference from another character "体".

（十八）从 cóng

词语：从来（at all times）　从北京到上海（from Beijing to Shanghai）

析字：甲骨文写作"𠈌"，像两个人前后随行，字的本义是"跟从"。后来小篆写作"从"，楷书写作"从"。

Analysis of the character：It had been written as "𠈌" in Oracle Bone Script (Jiaguwen), which was similar to two people walking one by one. The character's original meaning was "following". Later, it had been written as "从" and "从" in Seal Script(Xiaozhuan) and Regular Script(Kaishu) respectively.

田字格书写 Writing in Tin Word Format：

丿 人 从 从

书写提示：左边的"人"可稍微写得小一些，而且第二笔不能写成捺，应写成点。

Writing tips：The left stroke "人" should be written slightly small, and the second stroke should not be written as 捺(nà), but 点(diǎn).

（十九）方 fāng

词语：方法(method)　方向(direction)

析字：甲骨文写作"𣂚"，像两个人合力耕田，古代汉语中借用这个字形来表示"方向"的意思。小篆写作"𣂑"，楷书写作"方"。由"方向"的意思又引申出"方法"的意思。

Analysis of the character：Its Oracle Bone Script(Jiaguwen) form "𣂚" was like two men ploughing together. The form of the character had been borrowed to express the meaning of "direction" in ancient Chinese. The character had been written as "𣂑" and "方" in Seal Script（Xiaozhuan）and Regular Script（Kaishu）respectively. Later, the meaning of the character was extended to "method" from the meaning of "direction".

田字格书写 Writing in Tin Word Format：

丶一亍方

书写提示：下面的部分不能写成"刀"。

Writing tips：The lower part should not be written as "刀".

（二十）候 hòu

词语：时候(time)　等候(wait)

析字：小篆写作"𠊱"，左边的"亻"表示字义，右边的"侯(hóu)"表示字音，楷书写作"候"。本义是"守候""等候"，后又从"等候"的意思引申出名词"时候"的意思。

Analysis of the character：It had been written as "𠊱" in Seal Script（Xiaozhuan）. The left side "亻" is related to the character's meaning and the right side "侯(hóu)" represents its pronunciation. It had been written as "候" in Regular Script(Kaishu). The original meanings of the character were "expect" and "wait". Then the meanings were extended to "time", as a noun.

田字格书写 Writing in Tin Word Format：

丿 亻 亻 伫 伫 俨 俨 俨 候 候

候 候 候 候 候 候 候 候 候 候 候 候 候

书写提示：中间的短竖"丨"不能丢。

Writing tips：The short 竖(shù) "丨" in the middle should not be omitted.

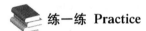 练一练 Practice

1. 说一说下面每组汉字的区别。

Talk about the differences between two Chinese characters in the following groups.

百—白 往—住 休—体

他—她 么—公 太—大

2. 根据示例，填写部件、汉字及词语。

According to the example, fill the missing parts, characters and words.

例 Example：亻＋乍→作→作业

亻＋（　　）→（　　）→（条件）

亻＋（　　）→（便）→（　　）

（　　）＋人→（从）→（　　）

（　　）＋故→（　　）→（做饭）

亻＋（　　）→（　　）→（休息）

（　　）＋本→（体）→（　　）

三、词语练习 Phrase Practice

1. 找出方框 B 中由方框 A 中的每个汉字构成的词语,同学们互相检查正确与否。

Find out the phrase in Table B formed by each Chinese character in Table A and check with your classmates.

```
A
飞 书 不 么 白 住 作 做 什 们 他 体 休 从 便
```

```
B
看书 不去 什么 做作业 我们 便宜 体育 住址 白色 起飞 休息
为什么 书本 居住 他们 午休 身体 做饭 写作 从来 飞机 从前
雪白 不可能 作为
```

2. 将词语与对应的拼音连起来。

Link the phrases with corresponding pinyin.

信件　　　　　　（fāng biàn）

太阳　　　　　　（xiū xué）

再见　　　　　　（xìn jiàn）

方便　　　　　　（tài yáng）

休学　　　　　　（zài jiàn）

3. 读出下面的句子。

Read out the following sentences.

① 你做完作业了吗?

② 坐地铁去学校很方便。

③ 中药太苦了。

④ 他住在哪儿?

⑤ 你休息一会儿吧。

⑥ 我喜欢体育课。

四、综合练习 Comprehensive Practice

1. 按照笔画的拼音写出对应的笔画。

Write out the corresponding strokes according to the pinyin of the strokes.

shù tí _____   shù wān gōu _____   shù zhé _____   shù zhé piě _____

piě diǎn _____   piě zhé _____   xié gōu _____   wān gōu _____

2. 找出下面汉字中的复合笔画，并写出来。

Find out the compound strokes in the following characters and write them out.

小（　　）

儿（　　）

乌（　　）

女（　　）

我（　　）

3. 选字组词。

Choose characters to make out words.

①（A. 白　B. 日　C. 甜）天

② 什（A. 玄　B. 么　C. 宏）

③（A. 木　B. 体　C. 休）息

④（A. 伸　B. 便　C. 们）宜

⑤（A. 舟　B. 冉　C. 再）见

⑥（A. 书　B. 夹　C. 马）本

五、课外任务 After-class Task

1. 用拼音在电脑或手机上打出下面的词语。

Type out the following phrases on your computer or mobile phone with pinyin.

为什么　飞行　居住　从来　做作业　吃饭了　怎么　工作

2. 姓名卡片趣味练习。

Interesting Chinese name card.

制作自己的中文姓名卡片，向你的同学们提问自己的姓名里有哪些笔画，看谁找到的笔画又对又多。

Make your own Chinese name card, then ask your classmates what strokes are in your name. See whose answers are both right and well.

第四课 指事字
Lesson Four　Indicative Characters

一、汉字知识 Knowledge of Chinese Characters

(一) 汉字的结构单位 The Structural Units of Chinese Characters

这一课，我们来介绍偏旁与部件。

In this lesson, let's introduce components and parts.

偏旁和部件都是汉字结构的中介性结构单位。偏旁是指用来构成合体字的直接构字单位，多数偏旁能独立表示完整音义。例如，"休"字左边的"亻"和右边的"木"都是偏旁；"语"字左边的"讠"和右边的"吾"也都是偏旁。

The components and parts are both medium structure units of Chinese characters. The components are the direct units of forming compound characters, most of them can represent complete pronunciation and meaning independently. For example, the left and right parts of "休" and "语" are components.

部件是现代汉字中由笔画或笔画组合构成的、能够独立运用且形式上相对独立的结构单位。例如，"点"字上面的"占"和下面的"灬"，构成"语"字的"讠""五""口"都是部件。偏旁和部件既有联系，也有区别。偏旁和部件的特点见表4.1。

The parts are combined by strokes or stroke combinations, whose forms are relatively independent and can be used independently. For example, the upper stroke of "占" and below part "灬" of "点", the "讠""五""口" of "语" are all

第四课　指　事　字

parts. There are both links and also differences between components and parts. The distinguishing features of components and parts see Table 4.1.

表 4.1　偏旁和部件的特点　The Distinguishing Features of Components and Parts

特点 Distinguishing features	直接构成汉字 Form Chinese characters directly	传统汉字学使用的概念 The concept is used in traditional Chinese characters' study	现代汉字使用的概念 The concept is used in modern Chinese characters' study	多数可表示完整音义 Most can represent complete pronunciation and meaning	有层次性 Have the characteristic of layered
偏旁 Components	+	+	+/−	+	−
部件 Parts	+/−	−	+	+/−	+

Note："+" indicates components or parts have this feature."−" indicates components or parts don't have this feature.

 练一练　Practice

分析下列偏旁并填写表格中的空白处。
Analyse the following components and fill in the blank.

偏旁及名称 Components and its names	经常出现的位置 Frequent locations	字例 Examples
口	左边（left）	吃
日		
木		
氵		
扌		
艹		
亻		
土		

· 67 ·

续表(Continued)		
偏旁及名称 Components and its names	经常出现的位置 Frequent locations	字例 Examples
忄		
宀		
火		
辶		
贝		
刂		
礻		

(二)汉字的结构类型 The Structural Types of Chinese Characters

这一课,我们来介绍指事字。

In this lesson, let's introduce indicative characters.

指事字包括纯抽象符号的字,以及在象形字上添加指事符号以表示字义的字。例如,甲骨文"亖",画四条横线,表示数词"四";古代汉字在"木"字下部加条短横,以表示"本"字的意义;"刀"在"刀"口处加一个点,以表示刀刃的意思。与其他结构类型的汉字相比,汉字中的指事字数量不多。

Indicative characters contain the characters of pure abstract symbols, and adding indicative symbols into pictographic characters for representing meanings. For example, the Oracle Bone Script(Jiaguwen) form "亖", which drew four horizontal lines to refer to number "four". In ancient Chinese character, "木" had been added a short 横(héng) in below part to refer to the meaning of "本". "刀" had been added a 点(diǎn) in left part of the stroke "丿" to represent the meaning of knife's edge. Compared to other types' Chinese characters, the number of indicative characters is small.

二、汉字形音义 The Form, Pronunciation and Meaning of Chinese Characters

 目标汉字 Learning Objective

上 下 本 也 我 小 里 午 年 弟 第 山 页 包 备 姐 妹 妈 奶 她

（一）上 shàng

词语：上课（attend a class） 上午（morning）

析字：古代汉字写作"⼆"，上面的"⼀"是指事符号，标指抽象的字义"上"。到战国时期写作"上"。字的本义是"高处""上面"。

Analysis of the character: It had been written as "⼆" in ancient Chinese character, the upper part "⼀" was indicative symbol, referring to the abstract meaning of "up". By the period of the Warring States Period, it had been written as "上". The original meanings of this character were "highland" "upside".

田字格书写 Writing in Tin Word Format：

丨 卜 上

上	上	上	上	上	上	上	上	上	上	上	上	上	上	上

书写提示：先写竖，再写短横和下面的长横。

Writing tips: Write 竖(shù) firstly, then write short 横(héng) and long 横(héng) in the below part.

（二）下 xià

词语：下课（after class） 下午（afternoon）

析字：古代汉字写作"⌒"，下面的"一"是指事符号，标指抽象的字义"下"。战国时期写作"下"，与今天没有什么差别。字的本义是"下面""位置在下"。

Analysis of the character：It had been written as "⌒" in ancient Chinese character, the below part "一" was an indicative symbol, representing the abstract meaning of "下". By the period of the Warring States Period, it had been written as "下", there was no difference from nowadays. The original meanings of this character were "underside" "the position is in under".

田字格书写 Writing in Tin Word Format：

一丁下

下	下	下	下	下	下	下	下	下	下	下	下

书写提示：最后一笔是点，不能写成横。

Writing tips：The last stroke is 点（diǎn）, it should not be written as 横（héng）.

（三）本 běn

词语：本来（originally） 作业本（exercise books）

析字：古代汉字写作"木"，在"木"字的下面加指事符号"•"，表示"树木的根部"，秦代写作"本"，楷书写作"本"。字义引申有"根本""本来"的意思。

Analysis of the character：It had been written as "木" in ancient Chinese character, adding an indicative symbol "•" in the below part of "木", representing the meaning of "root of tree". It had been written as "本" and "本" in Qin Dynasty and Regular Script（Kaishu）respectively. It has the extended meanings of "root" "originally".

田字格书写 Writing in Tin Word Format：

一十才木本

本本本本本本本本本本本本本本本本

书写提示：最后一笔短横，不能写得过长。

Writing tips：The last stroke is short 横（héng），it should not be written too long.

（四）也 yě

词语：也是（as well） 也去（go as well）

析字：古代汉字写作"㠯"，秦代写作"也"，后来的楷书写作"也"。可见古代汉字上面的"凵"（口）表示人说话，下面的"乁"表示说话的停顿。古代汉语中用作语气助词，现代汉语中用作副词，通常表示"同样"的意思，例如，"你去，我也去"。

Analysis of the character：It had been written as "㠯" in ancient Chinese character, and then it had been written as "也" and "也" in Qin Dynasty and Regular Script（Kaishu） respectively. The upper part "凵"（口） means people is speaking, and the below part "乁" refers to the pause of speaking. It was used as a modal particle and adverb in ancient and modern Chinese relatively, representing the meaning of "as well", for example, "if you go, I will go as well".

田字格书写 Writing in Tin Word Format：

㇈𠃋也

也也也也也也也也也也也也也也也也

书写提示：第一笔横折钩起笔位置稍低，折笔的位置要稍高一些。

Writing tips：The starting point of the first stroke 横折钩（héng zhé gōu） should be written slightly lower, and the stroke 折（zhé） should be written higher.

(五) 我 wǒ

词语:我们(we)　自我(ego)

析字:甲骨文写作"𢆉",像古代兵器的形状,金文写作"𢆉",秦代写作"我""𢆉",楷书写作"我"。在古代,人们借用本来表示兵器的"我"来表示自称的代词,直到今天都是如此。

Analysis of the character：It had been written as "𢆉" in Oracle Bone Script (Jiaguwen), whose form was similar to the shape of ancient Chinese weapon. It had been written as "𢆉" and "我""𢆉" in Bronze Script (Jinwen) and Qin Dynasty respectively, and then it has been written as "我" in Regular Script (Kaishu). In ancient times, the character "我" was borrowed to use as the self-described pronoun.

田字格书写　Writing in Tin Word Format:

ノ 一 二 手 手 我 我 我

书写提示:第五笔斜钩的起笔位置比第一笔短撇应稍高,最后一笔是点。

Writing tips：The starting point of the fifth stroke 斜钩(xié gōu) should be written higher than the first stroke short 撇(piě). The last stroke is 点(diǎn).

(六) 小 xiǎo

词语:小时(hour)　小学(primary school)

析字:甲骨文写作"小",秦代写作"小",后来的楷书写作"小"。古代字形像细小的沙粒形状,以此表示"细小""微小"的意思。

Analysis of the character：It had been written as "小" and "小" in Oracle Bone Script(Jiaguwen) and Qin Dynasty respectively. Then it has been written as "小" in Regular Script(Kaishu). The form of this character was similar to the shape of tiny sand. Thus, it represented the meanings of "tiny" "little".

田字格书写 Writing in Tin Word Format：

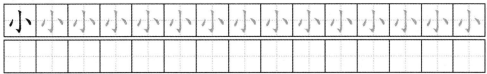

书写提示：先写中间的竖钩，再写左右两边的点。

Writing tips：The middle stroke 竖钩（shù gōu）should be written firstly, and then wrote the left and right stroke 点（diǎn）.

（七）里 lǐ

词语：里面（inside） 这里（here）

析字：古代汉字写作"里""里"，上面是"田"，下面是"土"，合在一起表示"居住的地方"的意思，这是"里"字的本义。后来引申出"地方""内部"等意思，如"这里""那里""心里"等。

Analysis of the character：It had been written as "里""里" in ancient Chinese character. The upper part was "田", the below part was "土", the two parts meant "the place of residence" together, here was the original meaning of "里". Later, it generated the meanings of "locality" "interior". For example, "这里""那里""心里".

田字格书写 Writing in Tin Word Format：

丨 冂 冋 日 甲 甲 里

里	里	里	里	里	里	里	里	里	里	里	里	里	里

书写提示：下面的两横应后写，上面的横稍短，下面的横稍长。

Writing tips：The two 横（héng）in below part should be written lastly, the upper 横（héng）should be written slightly short, and below 横（héng）should be written longer.

(八) 午 wǔ

词语:中午(noon) 下午(afternoon)

析字:古代汉字写作"𠂤""丨",本来是"杵"(古人用来在石臼中捣碎谷粒的一种工具)的象形字。金文字写作"↑",秦代写作"午",楷书写作"午"。"午"最早的字义在古代早就不用了,后来人们借用这个字来表示"时间"或"顺序"。

Analysis of the character: It had been written as "𠂤" "丨" in ancient Chinese character. The form was "杵"(a tool used by the ancients to mash grains in the stone mortar), which was a pictographic character. It had been written as "↑" and "午" in Bronze Script(Jinwen) and Qin Dynasty respectively, and then it had been written as "午" in Regular Script(Kaishu). The original meaning of "午" was abandoned in ancient times, later it was borrowed to refer to "time" or "order".

田字格书写 Writing in Tin Word Format:

丿 ⺧ ⺧ 午

午	午	午	午	午	午	午	午	午	午	午	午	午	午

书写提示:竖最后写,不能出头。

Writing tips: The stroke 竖(shù) should be written lastly, which should not be written over upper 横(héng).

(九) 年 nián

词语:今年(this year) 去年(last year)

析字:甲骨文"年"字写作"𠂇",上面是"禾",下面是"人",像一个人头顶着禾谷的样子,表现的是古人庆贺丰收的舞蹈:当禾谷丰收后,人们头顶着禾谷翩翩起舞,可见"年"的本义是"粮食丰收"。秦代写作"秊",楷书写成"年"。汉语中经常用"年"作为时间词语,还引申出"岁数""年纪"等意思,如"年轻""年龄"等。

Analysis of the character: It had been written as "𠂇" in Oracle Bone Script

(Jiaguwen), the upper part was "禾", below part was "人". It was similar to a person whose overhead had cereal, which represented that ancients were dancing for celebrating harvest. The original meaning of "年" was "harvest". It had been written as "秊" and "年" in Qin Dynasty and Regular Script(Kaishu). "年" is often used as a time word, and generated the meaning of "age", such as "young" "age" and so on.

田字格书写 Writing in Tin Word Format：

丿 ㇒ 𠂉 午 年 年

书写提示：下面的横要稍微长一些，中间的竖最后写。

Writing tips：The below 横(héng) should be written slightly longer, and the middle 竖(shù) should be written lastly.

（十）弟 dì

词语：弟弟(younger brother)　兄弟(brothers)

析字：古代汉字写作"弟"，像绳索缠绕在有权的短木桩上，合在一起表示"一圈一圈的次序""顺序"的意思，后来引申出"兄弟"的意思。

Analysis of the character：It had been written as "弟" in ancient Chinese character, which was similar to a rope twine in a short branch's fork, representing the meanings of "sequence" "order". Then, it generated the meaning of "brothers".

田字格书写 Writing in Tin Word Format：

丶 丷 䒑 뇌 弟 弟

书写提示：先写上面的点、撇，再写中间的"弓"，最后写竖、撇。

Writing tips：The writing order of this character is upper stroke 点（diǎn）and 撇（piě）firstly, middle stroke "弓" secondly, the stroke 竖（shù）and 撇（piě）should be written lastly.

（十一）第 dì

词语：第一课（the first lesson）　第二次（the second time）

析字：形声字。上面的"⺮"表示字义（古人把字写在竹简上，写好后按照次序编起来），下面的"弔"表示读音。字的本义是"顺序"。

Analysis of the character：It is a pictophonetic character. The "⺮" on the top represents its meaning（the ancient Chinese wrote on the bamboo slips, and then placed them in certain orders）, the "弔" at the bottom indicates its pronunciation. The original meaning of this character was "sequence".

田字格书写　Writing in Tin Word Format：

书写提示：下面的"弔"不能写成"牙"。

Writing tips：The "弔" at the bottom should not be written as "牙".

（十二）山 shān

词语：高山（high mountain）　山头（the top of a mountain）　爬山（climb a mountain）

析字：象形字。古代汉字写作"⛰"，像几座山峰并立的形状，小篆写作"山"，楷书写作"山"。自古至今，"山"的字形变化不大，字义也没有改变。

Analysis of the character：It is a pictographic character. It had been written as "⛰" in ancient Chinese character, like several mountain peaks stand together. It also had been written as "山" in Seal Script（Xiaozhuan）, and "山" in Regular Script（Kaishu）. Since ancient times, the shape of this character "山"

changed little, nor did its meaning.

田字格书写 Writing in Tin Word Format:

丨 山 山

书写提示:中间的竖稍长,左边和右边的竖稍短。

Writing tips: The stroke 竖(shù) in the middle is longer than those on each side.

(十三) 页 yè

词语:第一页(the first page) 页码(page)

析字:古代汉字写作"𩑋",字形的下面是人的身体,上面是突出显示的人的头部及面孔。字的本义是"人的头部"。楷书变成"頁",简化字写成"页"。汉字中很多以"页"为偏旁的汉字,字义都与人的头部有关,如"顶""项""顾""烦"等。在汉语中,很早就借用本来表示"人头"的"页"字,来表示"书的页码"。

Analysis of the character: It had been written as "𩑋" in ancient Chinese character, the lower part of this form was the human body, while the upper part was the emphasized human head and face. The original meaning of this character was "the head of the human being". It also had been written as "頁" in Regular Script(Kaishu), "页" in simplified character. When using "页" as their components, the meaning of many characters in Chinese can be all related to the head of the human being, like "head" "neck" "look" "annoying" and so on. In Chinese, there is a history that we borrowed the character "页" which means "the human head" to represent "the page number of the book".

田字格书写 Writing in Tin Word Format:

一 丆 丆 页 页

书写提示：下面的"人"不能写成"儿"。

Writing tips: The "人" at the bottom should not be written as "儿".

(十四) 包 bāo

词语：书包(schoolbag)　钱包(wallet)

析字：古代汉字写作"🅿"，外面的"🅿"表示包裹的外形，里面的"🅿"像母胎中的小孩，合在一起表示把东西包裹起来。后来引申出"把东西装起来、围起来"等意思，如"书包""包围"。

Analysis of the character: It had been written as "🅿" in ancient Chinese character, the "🅿" outer part meant the shape of a package, the "🅿" inner part was like a baby in mother's womb. The two parts mixed referred to wrap things up. Later the meaning was extended to "pack things up, enclose things" and so on, such as "schoolbag" "surround".

田字格书写 Writing in Tin Word Format：

丿 勹 匀 包 包

书写提示：下面的"巳"不能写成"巳"。

Writing tips: The "巳" in the lower part should not be written as "巳".

(十五) 备 bèi

词语：准备(prepare)　完备(complete)

析字：古代汉字写作"𤰞"，小篆写作"𤰞"，后来楷书写作"備"。左边的"亻"表示字义，右边的"𤰞"表示读音，简化字写成"备"。本义是"防备""准备"。

Analysis of the character: It had been written as "𤰞" in ancient Chinese character, then it turned into "𤰞" and "備" in Seal Script (Xiaozhuan) and Regular Script (Kaishu) respectively. The left stroke "亻" was related to this character's meaning, the right stroke "𤰞" represented this character's pronunciation. Then it was simplified as "备" with original meanings of "watching out" "preparation".

田字格书写 Writing in Tin Word Format：

丿 ク 夂 冬 各 各 备 备

书写提示：上面的部分不能写成"夕"。

Writing tips：The upper part should not be written as "夕".

(十六) 姐 jiě

词语：姐姐(sister) 大姐(eldest sister)

析字：左边的"女"与字的意思有关，表示字义与女性相关；右边的"且"表示读音(由于古代语音与现代语音的差异，许多形声字的声旁与字的读音有差异)。

Analysis of the character：The left stroke "女" represents this character's meaning is related to female. The right stroke "且" represents this character's pronunciation(due to the differences between ancient and modern pronunciations, many pictographic characters' parts that symbolize pronunciation differ in characters' pronunciation).

田字格书写 Writing in Tin Word Format：

乚 夊 女 如 如 姐 姐 姐

书写提示：注意左右两边结构匀称。

Writing tips：Notice that the left part and right part should be written equal.

(十七) 妹 mèi

词语：妹妹（younger sister）　姐妹（sisters）

析字：左边的"女"与字的意思有关，右边的"未"与字的读音有关。

Analysis of the character：The left stroke "女" is related to this character's meaning, the right stroke "未" is related to the pronunciation of this character.

田字格书写 Writing in Tin Word Format：

⺃ 𠃋 女 女⁻ 女⁻ 圹 妹 妹

书写提示：注意左右两边结构匀称。

Writing tips：Notice that the left and right part should be written equal.

(十八) 妈 mā

词语：妈妈（mother）　姑妈（father's sister; aunt）

析字：左边的"女"与字的意思有关，右边的"马"表示字的读音。

Analysis of the character：The left stroke "女" is related to this character's meaning, the right stroke "马" represents this character's pronunciation.

田字格书写 Writing in Tin Word Format：

⺃ 𠃋 女 女⁻ 妈 妈

书写提示：注意左右两边结构匀称。

Writing tips：Notice that the left part and right part should be written equal.

（十九）奶 nǎi

词语：牛奶（milk）　奶奶（grandmother）

析字：左边的"女"与字的意思有关，右边的"乃"与字的读音有关。

Analysis of the character：The left stroke "女" is related to this character's meaning, the right stroke "乃" is related to this character's pronunciation.

田字格书写 Writing in Tin Word Format：

书写提示：右边的"乃"不能写成"及"。

Writing tips：The right stroke "乃" should not be written as "及".

（二十）她 tā

词语：她们（they）　她俩（both of them）

析字：左边的"女"与字的意思有关，右边的"也"与字的读音有关。

Analysis of the character：The left stroke "女" is related to this character's meaning, the right stroke "也" is related to this character's pronunciation.

田字格书写 Writing in Tin Word Format：

书写提示：注意左右两边结构匀称。

Writing tips：Notice that the left part and right part should be written equal.

汉字锦囊 Idea Box of Chinese Characters

常用偏旁——女字旁（女）

Commonly-used Components — Nüzipang（女）Component

"女"是常用的汉字偏旁，一般用来标指字义，表示与女性有关的意思。常出现在字的左侧，有时也出现在字的下面。

"女" is a commonly-used component, which is related to characters' meaning, representing female. This component is usually used in the left of characters. Sometimes, it is also used in the below part of characters.

三、词语练习 Phrase Practice

1. 找出方框 B 中由方框 A 中的每个汉字构成的词语，同学们互相检查正确与否。

Find out the phrase in Table B formed by each Chinese character in Table A and check with your classmates.

A
上 下 也 小 里 午 年 弟 乐 姐 妹 妈 奶 姓 她

B
快乐 姐妹 兄弟 弟弟 奶奶 妈妈 新年 这里 中午 她们 小河 去年 午后 小学 也是 那里 姓名 上课 大小 下楼 音乐 您贵姓

2. 将词语与对应的拼音连起来。

Link the phrases with corresponding pinyin.

本来　　　　　　　（shàng xué）

上学　　　　　　（yǐ jīng）

姑姑　　　　　　（běn lái）

欢乐　　　　　　（gū gu）

已经　　　　　　（huān lè）

3. 读出下面的句子。

Read out the following sentences.

① 你们下课了吗?

② 我妈妈最喜欢听音乐。

③ 您贵姓?

④ 我是去年来中国学习汉语的。

⑤ 新年很快就要到了。

⑥ 我也是中国人。

四、综合练习 Comprehensive Practice

1. 按照偏旁名称的拼音写出相应的偏旁。

Write out the corresponding components according to the pinyin of the components.

sān diǎn shuǐ _____　　cǎo zì tóu _____　　kǒu zì páng _____

dān rén páng _____　　bǎo gài tóu _____　　lì dāo páng _____

shù xīn páng _____　　zǒu zhī páng _____

2. 写出下列汉字的两个组成部件。

Write out the two components of the following characters.

① 明:_____ + _____　　② 们:_____ + _____

③ 裙:_____ + _____　　④ 清:_____ + _____

⑤ 花:_____ + _____　　⑥ 远:_____ + _____

⑦ 字:_____ + _____　　⑧ 叶:_____ + _____

3. 写出你知道的带有下列偏旁的汉字,和同学比一比谁写得又多又对。

Write out the characters which have following components, and find out who can write more and better with your classmate.

① 忄:_____

② 木:_____

③ 扌:_____

④ 氵:_____

⑤ 土:_____

⑥ 刂:_____

五、课外任务 After-class Task

1. 用拼音在电脑或手机上打出下面的词语。

Type out the following phrases on your computer or mobile phone with pinyin.

下课　上学　哪里　下午　音乐　姐妹　姓名　已经　她们　今年

2. 使用上节课制作的中文姓名卡片,向同学们提问他们的中文名字是由哪些部件构成的,它们的偏旁又是什么。看谁回答得又对又快。

Use the Chinese name card made from last class, and ask your classmates what his/her Chinese name and character components are. Find out whose answers are both right and quick.

第五课 会 意 字
Lesson Five   Associative Characters

一、汉字知识 Knowledge of Chinese Characters

(一) 偏旁的位置关系 The Position Relations of Chinese Character Components

这一课,我们来介绍左右结构。

In this lesson, let's introduce the left-right structure.

在合体字中,汉字偏旁之间的位置关系主要有4种:左右结构、上下结构、包围结构和框架结构。了解汉字偏旁的位置关系,可以帮助我们更好地掌握汉字结构,正确书写汉字。在全部汉字中,左右结构的字最多,约占总数的三分之二。例如,"你""好""请""妈""林"等。根据左右部分大小不同,左右结构的汉字可以分为3种情况:

In the compound characters, there are 4 kinds position relations of Chinese character components: left-right structure, upper-lower structure, enclosure structure and frame structure. Having some understanding about the position relations of Chinese character components, we can grasp the structure of Chinese characters better and write them correctly. In all Chinese characters, the characters of left-right structure are the most, which accounts for about two-thirds of the total. For example, "你""好""请""妈""林" and so on. According to the size of the left and right parts, the characters of left-right structure can be divided into 3 situations:

1. 左边窄，右边宽。如"你""汉"。
Narrow left，wide right. Such as "你""汉".
2. 左边、右边一样宽。如"好""的"。
The left is as wide as the right. Such as "好""的".
3. 左边宽，右边窄。如"都""刚"。
Wide left，narrow right. Such as "都""刚".

（二）汉字的结构类型 The Structural Types of Chinese Characters

这一课，我们来介绍会意字。
In this lesson，let's introduce associative characters.

会意就是把两个或两个以上都表示意义的字符组合在一起构成一个新的字形，用来表示一个新的字义，这个新的字义一般和参与组合的各个字符都有一定的意义联系。

Associative characters are to combine two or more components that represent meaning together to form a new form，which is used to represent a new meaning. This new meaning is generally related to the meanings of each component involved in the character.

古代汉字中，"休"字写作"㑭"，像一个人倚靠着大树休息；"从"字写作"从"，表示一个人跟从另一人，字义是"跟从"；"炎"字写作"炎"，字义是"炎热"。在现代汉字中，也有一些通过字义组合构成的会意字。例如，"尖"字上面的"小"和下面的"大"组合成新的字义"尖"；"歪"字的字义由"不""正"组合而成；"看"字的字义由"手""目"组合而成。

In ancient Chinese character，"休" had been written as "㑭"，like a person resting on a tree. "从" had been written as "从" to refer to a person following another person，and it meant "follow". "炎" had been written as "炎"，and it meant "hot". In modern Chinese characters，there are also some associative characters formed by semantic combination. For example，the upper "小" and the lower "大" in "尖" are combined to form a new meaning. The meaning of the character "歪" is composed of the meaning of "不" and "正". The meaning of the character "看" is composed of the meaning of "手" and "目".

二、汉字形音义 The Form, Pronunciation and Meaning of Chinese Characters

 目标汉字 Learning Objective

```
会 去 比 走 图 非 米 衣 肉 毛 工 生 门 电 气 面
今 买 关 能
```

（一）会 huì/kuài

词语：开会（hold a conference） 一会儿（a little while）

析字：古代汉字写作"曾""會"，字形的上面和下面在一起是"合"，表示字的意义，中间是表示读音的部分，字的本义是"会合"。楷书写作"會"，简化字写作"会"。字义的发展线索大致为：会合→聚会、相遇→机会、符合→理解、能够。

Analysis of the character: It had been written as "曾" "會" in ancient Chinese character. The upper and lower parts of the character form together formed "合", refer to the meaning of the character. The middle part referred to the pronunciation of the character. The original meaning of the character was "congregation". It had been written as "會" in Regular Script(Kaishu), and simplified as "会". The development clues of meaning are as follows: congregation → gather, meet → opportunity, conformity → understanding, can.

田字格书写 Writing in Tin Word Format：

ノ 人 人 今 会 会

书写提示：下面的"云"不能写成"云"。

Writing tips：The lower part "云" should not be written as "云".

(二) 去 qù

词语：回去(go back)　去中国(go to China)

析字：甲骨文写作"🐘",金文写作"🐘",表示人离开所居住的地方。秦代以后，字形上面的"大"变成"土",楷书写成"去"。

Analysis of the character：It had been written as "🐘" and "🐘" in Oracle Bone Script(Jiaguwen) and Bronze Script(Jinwen) respectively, which referred to a person leaving the place where he lives. After Qin Dynasty, the upper "大" changed into "土", and the character had been written as "去" in Regular Script (Kaishu).

田字格书写　Writing in Tin Word Format：

一 十 土 去 去

去	去	去	去	去	去	去	去	去	去	去	去	去

书写提示：上面的横稍短,下面的横稍长。

Writing tips：The upper stroke 横(héng) is shorter than the lower one.

(三) 比 bǐ

词语：对比(contrast)　比赛(competition)

析字：甲骨文写作"𣥂",像两个"匕"["匕"(图 5.1)是古代一种长柄的取食器具]并列摆放的样子,秦代写作"比",汉代写作"比",楷书写作"比"。字的本义是"相邻""靠得近",后来字义引申出"比较"等意思,同时"匕"也提示字音。

Analysis of the character：It had been written as "𣥂" in Oracle Bone Script (Jiaguwen), like two "匕"["匕"(see Fig. 5.1) is an ancient long-handled eating utensil] placed in parallel. It had been written as "比" in Qin Dynasty, "比" in Han Dynasty, and "比" in Regular Script(Kaishu). The original meanings of the character were "adjacent" "close", then the meanings extended to "comparison" and so on. At the same time, "匕" suggested the pronunciation of the character.

图 5.1　匕(bǐ)

田字格书写 Writing in Tin Word Format：

一 匕 比 比

比	比	比	比	比	比	比	比	比	比	比	比	比	比	比

书写提示：左边是竖提，右边是竖弯钩。

Writing tips：The stroke on the left is 竖提(shù tí), and stroke on the right is 竖弯钩(shù wān gōu).

（四）走 zǒu

词语：走路(walk)　走开(go away)

析字：金文写作"𧺆"，像人扬起手臂奔跑的形状，下面是奔跑留下的脚印，小篆写作"𧺆"，楷书写作"走"。"走"的本义是"跑"（图 5.2），现在"走"字的意义已经发生变化，变为"行走"的意思。

图 5.2　跑 Run

Analysis of the character: It had been written as "㞢" in Bronze Script (Jinwen), like the shape of a man running up his arms, and the lower shape was the footprints left by running. It had been written as "走" and "走" in Seal Script(Xiaozhuan) and Regular Script(Kaishu) respectively. The original meaning of "走" was "run"(see Fig. 5.2), but now the meaning of "走" has changed into "walk".

田字格书写 Writing in Tin Word Format：

一 十 土 卡 丰 走 走

书写提示：下面的撇、捺要写得舒展一些。

Writing tips: The lower strokes 撇(piě) and 捺(nà) should be written extended.

(五) 图 tú

词语：图书馆(library) 地图(map)

析字：会意字。古代汉字写作"圖"，楷书写作"圖"。外面的"囗"表示范围，里面是"啚(bǐ)"字，表示边远地区的意思，两个部分合在一起表示把边远的地方都包括在内，"图"字本义是"地图"。现在简化字用"冬"代替里面复杂难写的"啚"。

Analysis of the character: It is an associative character. It had been written as "圖" in ancient Chinese character, and "圖" in the Regular Script(Kaishu). The peripheral "囗" represented the meaning of scope, and the "啚(bǐ)" inside meant the remote regions. Two parts were grouped together to extend the meaning that those remote regions are all included, the original meaning of the "图" was "map". The simplified character uses "冬" to replace "啚" which is more intricate.

田字格书写 Writing in Tin Word Format：

| 丨 冂 冂 囗 図 図 图 图 |

| 图 | 图 | 图 | 图 | 图 | 图 | 图 | 图 | 图 | 图 | 图 | 图 | 图 | 图 |

书写提示：正确的书写顺序是"丨、冂、冬、一"。

Writing tips：The correct writing order is "丨、冂、冬、一".

（六）非 fēi

词语：非常（very）　非洲（Africa）

析字：古代汉字写作"兆"，秦代隶书写作"兆"。字形表示"相违背"的意思，后引申出"错误"的意思。

Analysis of the character：It had been written as "兆" in ancient Chinese character. It had been written as "兆" in Clerical Script(Lishu) in Qin Dynasty to refer to "contrary", and then the meaning extended to "mistake".

田字格书写 Writing in Tin Word Format：

| 丨 丨 丿 刁 韭 非 非 非 |

| 非 | 非 | 非 | 非 | 非 | 非 | 非 | 非 | 非 | 非 | 非 | 非 | 非 | 非 |

书写提示：左边的竖稍短，右边的竖稍微长一些。

Writing tips：The left stroke 竖(shù) is a little shorter than the right one.

（七）米 mǐ

词语：米饭（cooked rice）　大米（rice）

析字：甲骨文写作"米"，像散开的米粒形，后来小篆写作"米"，楷书写作"米"。

Analysis of the character：It had been written as "米" in Oracle Bone Script (Jiaguwen), like the shape of scattered rice grain. Later, it had been written as

"𣲺" and "米" in Seal Script(Xiaozhuan) and Regular Script(Kaishu) respectively.

田字格书写 Writing in Tin Word Format：

丶丷业半米米

米	米	米	米	米	米	米	米	米	米	米	米	米	米

书写提示：中间的竖保持垂直，下面的撇和捺要写得舒展。

Writing tips：The middle stroke 竖(shù) should keep vertical. The lower strokes 撇(piě) and 捺(nà) should be written extended.

（八）衣 yī

词语：衣服(clothes)　大衣(coat)

析字：金文写作"𠆢"，小篆写作"𠘧"，像上衣的形状，隶书写作"衣"，楷书写作"衣"，失去了象形特点。

Analysis of the character：It had been written as "𠆢" and "𠘧" in Bronze Script(Jinwen) and in Seal Script(Xiaozhuan) respectively, like the shape of a coat. It had been written as "衣" and "衣" in Clerical Script(Lishu) and Regular Script(Kaishu) respectively, which lost the pictographic characteristic.

田字格书写 Writing in Tin Word Format：

丶一ㄣ产衣衣

衣	衣	衣	衣	衣	衣	衣	衣	衣	衣	衣	衣	衣	衣

书写提示：第四笔是竖提，不是短撇。

Writing tips：The fourth stroke is 竖提(shù tí), not short 撇(piě).

（九）肉 ròu

词语：牛肉(beef)　鸡肉(chicken)

析字:古代汉字写作"⺼""𠕎""𠕎",字的本义是"供食用的动物的肉"。隶书写作"宍",楷书写作"肉"。

Analysis of the character:It had been written as "⺼" "𠕎" "𠕎" in ancient Chinese character. The original meaning of the character was "meat of animals". It had been written as "宍" and "肉" in Clerical Script(Lishu) and Regular Script (Kaishu) respectively.

田字格书写 Writing in Tin Word Format:

丨 冂 冂 内 肉 肉

肉	肉	肉	肉	肉	肉	肉	肉	肉	肉	肉	肉	肉	肉

书写提示:注意第一笔是左侧的竖,第二笔是横折钩。

Writing tips:Notice the first stroke on the left is 竖(shù), and the second stroke is 横折钩(héng zhé gōu)。

(十) 毛 máo

词语:毛笔(brush)　羊毛(wool)　五毛钱(half yuan)

析字:象形字。古代汉字写作"⺉",像羽毛的形状,小篆写作"⺉",楷书写作"毛"。字的本义是"动物身上的毛",如"鸡毛"或"羊毛"。后来也表示"很小"的意思,如"小毛病"或"毛毛雨"。它也用来作为小的货币单位,如"一毛钱"。

Analysis of the character:It is a pictographic character. It had been written as "⺉" in ancient Chinese character, like the shape of a feather. It also had been written as "⺉" in Seal Script(Xiaozhuan), and "毛" in Regular Script (Kaishu). This character originally referred to "the feather or hair on the animal", like "chicken feather" or "wool". Later, it had the meaning of "tiny", like "small problem" "tiny little rain". It was also used as a monetary unit, like "one dime".

田字格书写 Writing in Tin Word Format：

书写提示：第一笔"撇"不能写成"横"。

Writing tips：The first stroke is 撇(piě), which should not be written as 横(héng).

(十一) 工 gōng

词语：工人(worker)　工厂(factory)

析字：古代汉字写作"⟂"，像曲尺的形状，小篆写作"工"，楷书写作"工"。后来字义引申为"工匠""劳动者""工作"等。

Analysis of the character：It had been written as "⟂" in ancient Chinese character, like the shape of a ruler. It had been written as "工" and 工 in Seal Script(Xiaozhuan) and Regular Script(Kaishu) respectively. And then the meaning extended to "craftsman" "laborer" "work" and so on.

田字格书写 Writing in Tin Word Format：

书写提示：上面的横稍短，下面的横稍长。

Writing tips：The upper stroke 横(héng) is a little shorter than the lower one.

(十二) 生 shēng

词语：学生(student)　出生(birth)　生活(life)

析字：甲骨文写作"⼭"，像小草刚刚从地面长出来的形状，金文写作"⽣"，隶书写作"±",楷书写作"生"。字的本义是"生长",后来引申出"生育""出生""发生"等意思。

Analysis of the character: It had been written as "↓" in Oracle Bone Script (Jiaguwen), like the shape of grass just growing from the ground. It had been written as "ϟ" and "±" and "生" in Bronze Script(Jinwen), Clerical Script (Lishu) and Regular Script(Kaishu) respectively. The original meaning of the character was "growth", then the meaning extended to "bear" "birth" "occurrence" and so on.

田字格书写 Writing in Tin Word Format:

丿 一 仁 牛 生

生	生	生	生	生	生	生	生	生	生	生	生	生	生

书写提示:第一笔是短撇;下面的横比上面的横稍长一些。

Writing tips: The first stroke is short 撇(piě). The lower stroke 横(héng) is a little longer than the upper one.

(十三) 门 mén

词语:门口(gate) 一门课(a course)

析字:甲骨文写作"閂",小篆写作"門",楷书写作"門",简化字写作"门"。字的本义是"房屋的门",后引申出"像门的东西""途径"的意思,如"闸门""一门课"等。

Analysis of the character: It had been written as "閂" "門" and "門" in Oracle Bone Script(Jiaguwen), Seal Script(Xiaozhuan) and Regular Script (Kaishu) respectively, and then simplified as "门". The original meaning of the character was "the door of the house", and then it had been extended to "something like a door" "approach" and so on.

田字格书写 Writing in Tin Word Format：

`丿门

书写提示：第一笔是点，第二笔是竖。

Writing tips：The first stroke is 点（diǎn），and the second stroke is 竖（shù）.

（十四）电 diàn

词语：电视（television） 电脑（computer）

析字：金文写作"🜲"，上面是"雨"，下面是闪电的形状，小篆写作"電"，楷书写作"電"。简化字省去上面的"雨"，写成"电"。字的本义是"闪电"，后引申表示物质中存在的一种能，如"电能""电子"。

Analysis of the character：It had been written as "🜲" in Bronze Script (Jinwen). The upper part was "雨", and the lower part was the shape of lightning. It had been written as "電" and "電" in Seal Script (Xiaozhuan) and Regular Script (Kaishu) respectively, and then simplified as "电". The original meaning of the form was "lightning", and then the meaning extended to an energy in matter, such as "electricity" "electron".

田字格书写 Writing in Tin Word Format：

丨冂日日电

书写提示：竖弯钩最后写，笔画书写要到位。

Writing tips：The last stroke is 竖弯钩（shù wān gōu），and the strokes should be written in place.

（十五）气 qì

词语：空气(air)　生气(angry)

析字：甲骨文写作"☰"，像云和空气流动的样子，字上面和下面的横比较长，中间的横较短，与"三"字有区别。在甲骨文中，"三"字写作"☰"，上面、下面和中间的横一样长。后来，为了使这两个字有所区别，"☰"(气)字上面的横弯曲上翘，下面的横往下弯曲，写成"气"。楷书写作"气"。

Analysis of the character：It had been written as "☰" in Oracle Bone Script (Jiaguwen), like the shape of flowing clouds and air. The upper and the lower strokes were longer, and the middle stroke was shorter, which was different from the character "三". In Oracle Bone Script (Jiaguwen), "三" had been written as "☰". The upper, lower and middle strokes 横(héng) were the same length. Later, in order to make these two characters had a distinction, the upper 横(héng) bent upward and the lower 横(héng) bent down in "☰"(气), and it was written as "气". It had been written as "气" in Regular Script (Kaishu).

田字格书写 Writing in Tin Word Format：

丿 二 乞 气

书写提示：注意横折斜钩的正确笔形。

Writing tips：Notice the right form of stroke 横折斜钩(héng zhé xié gōu).

（十六）面 miàn

词语：见面(meet)　对面(opposite)

析字：金文写作"🙾"，小篆写作"圙"，楷书写作"面"，字的本义是"人的脸面"。

注意："面条""面粉"等词语中的"面"，古代写作"麵"，汉字简化后写作"面"。

Analysis of the character：It had been written as "🙾" "圙" and "面" in

Bronze Script(Jinwen), Seal Script(Xiaozhuan) and Regular Script(Kaishu) respectively. The original meaning of the form was "the human's face". Note: The character "面" in "面条""面粉" had been written as "麵" in ancient times, and then simplified as "面".

田字格书写 Writing in Tin Word Format:

书写提示：第二笔是短撇，不能写成竖。

Writing tips: The second stroke is short 撇(piě), not 竖(shù).

(十七) 今 jīn

词语：今天(today)　今年(this year)

析字：甲骨文写作"△"，像"曰"(说话的意思)字的倒写形状，字的本义是"吟"。小篆写作"今"，楷书写作"今"。这个字后来一般被借用作为表示时间的词语，意思是"这个时候"，如"今天""今年"。

Analysis of the character: It had been written as "△" in Oracle Bone Script (Jiaguwen), like the inverted shape of "曰" (means speaking). The original meaning of the form was "chant". It had been written as "今" and "今" in Seal Script(Xiaozhuan) and Regular Script(Kaishu) respectively. Later, the character was generally borrowed as a word indicating time, which means "at this time", such as "today" "this year".

田字格书写 Writing in Tin Word Format:

书写提示:"今"不能写成"令"。

Writing tips:"今" should not be written as "令".

(十八) 买 mǎi

词语:买东西(buy things)　买书(buy books)

析字:甲骨文写作"🦴",小篆写作"𧵩",楷书写作"買"。上面是"网",下面是"贝"(古代的货币),合在一起表示"做生意网罗钱财,获得利润"的意思。后来专门指交易中"购买"的意思。简化字采用草书楷化的方法,简写成"买"。

Analysis of the character:It had been written as "🦴" "𧵩" and "買" in Oracle Bone Script(Jiaguwen), Seal Script(Xiaozhuan) and Regular Script(Kaishu) respectively. The upper part in the character is "网", and the lower part is "贝"(ancient currency), which meant "get profits from doing business" together. Later, it referred to the meaning of "purchase" in the transaction. It had been simplified as "买" by the method of cursive writing.

田字格书写 Writing in Tin Word Format:

フ ⁊ ⁊ 드 买 买

买	买	买	买	买	买	买	买	买	买	买	买	买	买

书写提示:第一笔横钩,注意其与平宝盖的区别。

Writing tips:The first stroke is 横钩(héng gōu). Pay attention to the difference with the stroke 平宝盖(píng bǎo gài).

(十九) 关 guān

词语:开关(switch)　关门(close the door)　关系(relationship)

析字:"关"字早期写作"𨳇",像门内有门闩,表示"关门"的意思。后来楷书写作"關"[外面的"門(门)"表示字义,里面的"𢇮"表示字音],后来这个字形简写成"関",简化字省去外边的"門",变成"关"。本义是"关门",后引申出"关口""重要的位置或部分"等意思。

Analysis of the character: The early Chinese character form "𨳇" was like a door with a bar inside with the meaning of "close the door". Later the character had been written as "關" in Regular Script (Kaishu) [the outer part "門(门)" was related to its meaning and the inner part "𢆶" represented its pronunciation], then the character was simplified into "关", and the outer part "門" was omitted, the character turned into "关". The original meaning of the character was "close the door", then the meaning was extended to "strategic pass" "important place or part" and so on.

田字格书写 Writing in Tin Word Format:

丶 丷 丷 兰 关 关

关	关	关	关	关	关	关	关	关	关	关	关	关	关

书写提示:上面不能写成"⺌"。

Writing tips: The upper part should not be written as "⺌".

(二十) 能 néng

词语:不能(unable)　能力(ability)

析字:金文写作"𦝈",像熊站立的样子,战国时期写作"𦝈"或"𦝈",隶书写作"能",后来的楷书写作"能"。字的本义是表示"熊"这种动物,在汉语中常借用来表示"能力""才能"的意思,也经常作为助动词使用。后又引申出"能量"的意思,如"电能""太阳能"。

Analysis of the character: It had been written as "𦝈" in Bronze Script (Jinwen), like the shape of a standing bear. It had been written as "𦝈" or "𦝈" in the Warring States Period. It had been written as "能" and "能" in Clerical Script (Lishu) and Regular Script (Kaishu) respectively. The original meaning was to express the animal "bear". In Chinese, it was often borrowed to express the meanings of "ability" "talent", and often used as a modal verb. Later, the meaning extended to "energy", such as "electric energy" "solar energy".

田字格书写 Writing in Tin Word Format：

㇄ ㇄ 厂 쉬 쉬 쉬 쉬 能 能 能

能	能	能	能	能	能	能	能	能	能	能	能	能	能

书写提示：按照字的结构单位顺序写：左上（厶）、左下（月）、右上（匕）、右下（匕）。

Writing tips：Write in the order of structural units：upper left(厶), lower left(月), upper right(匕), lower right(匕).

 汉字锦囊 Idea Box of Chinese Characters

字义的变化

The Changes in the Meaning of Characters

很多汉字有十分古老的来源，甚至有几千年的使用历史。汉字在最早使用的时候，字的意思与字的形体关系很密切，但是在后来的发展过程中，许多字都在原来本义的基础上按照一定的线索，引申、变化出新的意思。例如，"能"字的本义是"熊"，后来借用来表示"能力"，再后来又引申出"能源"的意思。

Many Chinese characters have very ancient sources, even thousands of years history. When Chinese characters were first used, the meaning of characters was closely related to their form. However, in the later development process, many characters extended and changed new meanings based on the original meaning according to certain clues. For example, the original meaning of the character "能" was "bear", which was later borrowed to express "ability" and later extended the meaning of "energy".

三、词语练习 Phrase Practice

1. 找出方框 B 中由方框 A 中的每个汉字构成的词语，同学们互相检查正确与否。

Find out the phrase in Table B formed by each Chinese character in Table A and check with your classmates.

A

会　去　比　米　衣　工　生　门　电　气　面　买　卖　能

B

开门　生字　打工　买单　可能　毛衣　工人　生活　能力　生气　比较
玉米　大衣　电池　外面　一会儿　下去　米饭　天气　买卖　回去　开会
比赛　电影　见面

2. 看拼音写汉字。

Read the following pinyin to write Chinese characters.

① huì(　　　)议　　② xué shēng(　　　)　　③ dà mǐ(　　　)
④ 开mén(　　　)　　⑤ 空qì(　　　)　　⑥ fēi cháng(　　　)

3. 读出下面的句子。

Read out the following sentences.

① 今天下午3点开会。
② 我周末去超市买牛肉和西瓜，你要一起去吗？
③ 最近的生活怎么样？
④ 服务员，我要买单。
⑤ 商店已经关门了。

四、综合练习 Comprehensive Practice

1. 给下列汉字加上一个偏旁，组成一个左右结构的新汉字。

Add one component to each of the following characters and change it into another left-right structure character.

第五课 会意字

① _____ +月→_____   ② _____ +水→_____
③ _____ +木→_____   ④ _____ +是→_____
⑤ _____ +昌→_____   ⑥ 禾+ _____ →_____
⑦ _____ +子→_____   ⑧ _____ +每→_____

2. 写出你知道的带有下列偏旁的左右结构的汉字,和同学们比一比,看谁写得又多又对。

Write down the left-right structure characters you know with the following components, and find out who can write more and better with your classmates.

① 亻：_____
② 女：_____
③ 讠：_____
④ 口：_____
⑤ 犭：_____

3. 选字组词。

Choose characters to make out words.

① (A. 从　B. 比　C. 匕)赛
② 开(A. 会　B. 令　C. 云)
③ (A. 士　B. 工　C. 王)厂
④ 出(A. 生　B. 牛　C. 丰)
⑤ (A. 田　B. 申　C. 电)视

五、课外任务 After-class Task

1. 用拼音在电脑或手机上打出下面的词语。

Type out the following phrases on your computer or mobile phone with pinyin.

一会儿　过去　电脑　共同　冬瓜　对面　买卖　不能　大门　空气

2. 走上街头,观察街道两侧商店的名字,请找出带有"日""亻""彳""扌""氵""木""刂"等偏旁的汉字。拍下来和同学们分享一下,看谁找得又多又好。

Please go to the street and observe the names of the Chinese shops on both sides of the street. Please find out the Chinese characters with the components "日""亻""彳""扌""氵""木""刂" and so on. Take a picture to share with your classmates. Find out who can find more and better.

第六课 形 声 字
Lesson Six Pictophonetic Characters

一、汉字知识 Knowledge of Chinese Characters

(一) 偏旁的位置关系 The Position Relations of Chinese Character Components

这一课我们来介绍上下结构。

In this lesson, let's introduce the upper-lower structure.

在合体字中,上下结构的字有很多,如"字""全""买"等。在汉字中,上下结构字的数量约占总数的23%,仅次于左右结构。按照上下两部分大小不同,上下结构主要可以分为3种情况:

In the compound characters, the upper-lower structure of the characters is so many, such as "字""全""买" and so on. In Chinese characters, the number of upper-lower structure characters accounts for about 23 percent of the total, which is second only to the left-right structure. According to the size of the upper and lower parts, the upper-lower structure characters can be divided into 3 situations:

1. 上面小,下面大。如"雷""花"。

The size of the upper part is smaller than the lower. Such as "雷" "花".

2. 上面和下面一样大。如"名""分"。

The size of the upper part is as big as the lower. Such as "名""分".

3. 上面大,下面小。如"点""想"。

The size of the upper part is bigger than the lower. Such as "点" "想".

(二) 汉字的结构类型 The Structural Types of Chinese Characters

这一课,我们来介绍形声字。

In this lesson, let's introduce pictophonetic character.

形声字就是由表示字义范围和类属的形符、指示汉字读音的声符两个部分组合而成的汉字,如"花""运""评"等。在汉字主要的4种结构类型中,形声字的数量最多,现代汉字中形声字约占总数的80%。

The pictophonetic character is composed of two parts: the component which indicates the scope of meaning and the category, and the component which indicates the pronunciation of the Chinese character. For example, "花" "运" "评" and so on. Among the 4 main structural types of Chinese characters, the number of pictophonetic characters is the largest, accounting for about 80 percent of the total in modern Chinese characters.

形声字形符和声符的组合方式多样,主要分为8种:

The combination of the forms and sounds of the pictophonetic characters is diverse, which are mainly divided into 8 kinds:

1. 左形右声,如"油""呼""铜""杆"。

The pictographic part is on the left side, and the phonetic part is on the right side, such as "油""呼""铜""杆".

2. 右形左声,如"飘""雌""刚""甥"。

The pictographic part is on the right side, and the phonetic part is on the left side, such as "飘""雌""刚""甥".

3. 上形下声,如"霏""花""竿""爸"。

The pictographic part is on the upper side, and the phonetic part is on the lower side, such as "霏""花""竿""爸".

4. 下形上声,如"架""慈""贡""凳"。

The pictographic part is on the lower side, and the phonetic part is on the upper side, such as "架""慈""贡""凳".

5. 外形内声,如"园""阁""阀""匾"。

The pictographic part is outside, and the phonetic part is inside, such as "园""阁""阀""匮".

6. 内形外声,如"辩""问""闷""衔"。

The pictographic part is inside, and the phonetic part is outside, such as "辩""问""闷""衔".

7. 形占一角,如"疆""载""颖""修"。

The pictographic part is in a corner, such as "疆""载""颖""修".

8. 声占一角,如"旌""旗""徒""近"。

The phonetic part is in a corner, such as "疆""载""颖""修".

上面8种类型中,最常见的是左形右声,约占形声字总数的67%。

Among the above 8 types, the most common situation is that the pictographic part is on the left side, and the phonetic part is on the right side, accounting for about 67 percent in the total pictophonetic characters.

二、汉字形音义 The Form, Pronunciation and Meaning of Chinese Characters

目标汉字 Learning Objective

学 好 孩 教 爷 睡 看 吃 喝 叫 和 号 吗 哪 吧 呢 知 唱 问 告

(一) 学 xué

词语:学生(student)　学习(study)

析字:金文写作"𭂁",是会意字,上面像两只手摆弄学习计数的工具,下面是房子和孩子,合在一起表示"教儿童学习"。小篆写作"𦥯",楷书写作"學",简化字写作"学"。"学"字的演变顺序为:𦥔甲骨文→𭂁金文→𦥯小篆→學隶书→學楷书→学简化字。

Analysis of the character: It had been written as "𭕊" in Bronze Script (Jinwen). It is an associative character. The upper part in the character was like the shape of playing a tool for learning to count with two hands, and the lower part was like the shape of house and children, which means "teach the children to learn" together. It had been written as "學" and "學" in Seal Script (Xiaozhuan) and Regular Script(Kaishu) respectively, and simplified as "学". The development order of its form is: 𭕊 Jiaguwen → 𭕊 Jinwen → 學 Xiaozhuan → 學 Lishu → 學 Kaishu → 学 Jianhuazi.

田字格书写 Writing in Tin Word Format:

丶 丶 丷 ⺍ 学 学 学 学

学	学	学	学	学	学	学	学	学	学	学	学	学	学

书写提示：前两笔的点，稍微往左侧倾斜，第四笔的点稍微往右侧倾斜。

Writing tips: The first two strokes 点(diǎn) are slightly tilted to the left, and the fourth stroke 点(diǎn) is slightly tilted to the right.

（二）好 hǎo/hào

词语：美好（beauty） 好看（good-looking）

析字：甲骨文写作"𡥀"，小篆写作"好"，楷书写作"好"。字形由"女""子"两部分组成，字的本义为"女子"，后引申为"美好""喜爱"的意思。

Analysis of the character: It had been written as "𡥀" "好" and "好" in Oracle Bone Script(Jiaguwen), Seal Script(Xiaozhuan) and Regular Script (Kaishu) respectively. The form was composed of two parts "女" and "子". The original meaning was "female", and then the meaning extended to "beauty" and "like".

田字格书写 Writing in Tin Word Format：

书写提示：注意左边的第三笔横，不能出头。

Writing tips：Pay attention to the third stroke 横（héng）on the left，don't reach out.

（三）孩 hái

词语：孩子（children） 女孩（girl）

析字：形声字。小篆写作"㤰"，楷书写作"孩"。左边的"子"表示字的意思，右边的"亥（hài）"表示字的读音。字的本义是"孩子笑"，后引申出"孩子""儿童"的意思。

Analysis of the character：It's a pictophonetic character. It had been written as "㤰" and "孩" in Seal Script(Xiaozhuan) and Regular Script(Kaishu) respectively. The left part "子" indicates the meaning of the character, and the right part "亥（hài）" indicates the pronunciation. The original meaning was "children laugh", and then the meaning extended to "children".

田字格书写 Writing in Tin Word Format：

书写提示：左侧的"孑"不能写成"子"。

Writing tips：The "孑" on the left should not be written as "子".

（四）教 jiào/jiāo

词语：教师（teacher） 教室（classroom）

析字:甲骨文写作"⿰𠂉攵",右边的"攵"表示教师手里拿着教学工具的样子,左边是表示字的读音。后来字形添加"𠂇"(子)变成"𢼂",以突出教育儿童的意思。小篆写作"𢼎",楷书写作"教"。

Analysis of the character: It had been written as "⿰𠂉攵" in Oracle Bone Script (Jiaguwen). On the right side "攵" meant the teacher holds the teaching tool in hand, on the left side was the pronunciation part. Later, the form added "𠂇" (子) and became "𢼂", in order to highlight the meaning of educating children. It had been written as "𢼎" and "教" in Seal Script (Xiaozhuan) and Regular Script (Kaishu) respectively.

田字格书写 Writing in Tin Word Format:

一 十 土 耂 耂 孝 孝 孝 教 教 教

书写提示:左侧下面"子"的横笔要写成提。

Writing tips: The stroke 横(héng) in the left of "子" should be written as 提(tí).

(五) 爷 yé

词语:爷爷(grandfather) 大爷(elder uncle)

析字:繁体汉字写作"爺",上面的"父(fù)"与字的意思有关,下面的"耶(yé)"表示字的读音。简化字省去下面"耶"的"耳",并把"阝"简写成"卩"。本义是"父亲"的意思,后来在汉语中主要用于表示"祖父"。

Analysis of the character: It had been written as "爺" in traditional Chinese, the "父(fù)" on the top showed its meaning while "耶(yé)" at the bottom suggested its pronunciation. In simplified character, the "耳" was simplified from "耶" at the bottom, and "阝" was simplified into "卩". The original meaning of this character was "father", later in the Chinese language it was mainly used to describe the grandfather.

田字格书写 Writing in Tin Word Format：

书写提示：下面的"刀"不能写成"阝"。

Writing tips：The lower part "刀" should not be written as "阝".

（六）睡 shuì

词语：睡觉（sleep）　睡着（asleep）

析字：形声字。左边的"目"与字的意思有关，右边的"垂"与字的读音有关。小篆写作"睡"，楷书写作"睡"。

Analysis of the character：It's a pictophonetic character. The "目" on the left is related to the meaning of the character，and the "垂" on the right is related to the pronunciation of the character. It had been written as "睡" and "睡" in Seal Script（Xiaozhuan）and Regular Script（Kaishu）respectively.

田字格书写 Writing in Tin Word Format：

书写提示：右边"垂"最后的横笔，比上面的横短一点。

Writing tips：The last stroke on the right side "垂" is a little shorter than the upper one.

汉字锦囊 Idea Box of Chinese Characters

常用偏旁——目字旁(目)
Commonly-used Components — Muzipang(目) Component

在合体字中,"目字旁"(目)是常用的表义偏旁,表示与眼睛有关的字义,经常出现在字的左侧。

In compound characters, the commonly-used character component "Muzipang"(目) indicates that the meaning of character related to the eye, and it often appears on the left side of the character.

(七) 看 kàn

词语:看书(read a book)　看电视(watch TV)

析字:小篆写作"䀡",楷书写作"看"。字形的上面是"手",下面是"目",表示"手放在眼睛上看"的意思。

Analysis of the character: It had been written as "䀡" and "看" in Seal Script(Xiaozhuan) and Regular Script(Kaishu) respectively. The upper part is "hands" and the lower part is "eyes", which means "put your hands on your eyes to look".

田字格书写 Writing in Tin Word Format:

一 二 三 手 丰 看 看 看 看

书写提示:第一笔是撇,不能写成横。

Writing tips: The first stroke is 撇(piě), not 横(héng).

（八）吃 chī

词语：吃饭（eat meal） 吃力（laborious）

析字：形声字。左边的"口"与字的意思有关，右边的"乞（qǐ）"表示字的读音，古代汉语中"乞"和"吃"的读音近似。

Analysis of the character：It's a pictophonetic character. The "口" on the left is related to the meaning of the character, the "乞（qǐ）" on the right is related to the character's pronunication. In ancient Chinese, the "乞（qǐ）" was similar to the pronunciation of "吃".

田字格书写 Writing in Tin Word Format：

书写提示：右边的"乞"不能写成"气"。

Writing tips：The "乞" on the right should not be written as "气".

（九）喝 hē/hè

词语：喝水（drink water） 喝茶（drink tea）

析字：形声字。左边的"口"与字的意义有关，右边的"曷"表示读音。字的本义是"口渴"的意思，后引申出动作"喝"的意思，后来又用来表示"大声喊叫"，如"喝彩""大喝一声"。

Analysis of the character：It's a pictophonetic character. The "口" on the left is related to the meaning of the character, and the "曷" on the right is related to the pronunciation of the character. The original meaning was "thirst", and then the meaning extended to "drink" and "shout out", such as "cheer" "yell".

田字格书写 Writing in Tin Word Format：

丨 丨' 丨" 丨"' 叮 叮 叮 叮 唱 唱 唱 喝

喝	喝	喝	喝	喝	喝	喝	喝	喝	喝	喝	喝	喝	喝

书写提示：左边的"口"略微窄一些，位置略微偏上。

Writing tips：The "口" on the left should be written slightly narrow and high.

(十) 叫 jiào

词语：叫喊(shout)　小狗叫(bark)

析字：形声字。左边的"口"与字的意思有关，右边的"丩(jiū)"表示字的读音。"丩"古代汉字写作"丩",表示两个东西纠缠在一起的意思。"叫"的本义是"大声叫喊",后引申出"称呼"(你叫什么名字?)、"让人做事"(老师叫你去办公室)等意思。

Analysis of the character：It's a pictophonetic character. The "口" on the left is related to the meaning of the character, and the "丩(jiū)" on the right is related to the pronunciation of the character. "丩" had been written as "丩" in ancient Chinese character to refer to two things tangled together. The original meaning of "叫" was "shout out", and then the meaning extended to "call" (what's your name), "let people do things" (a teacher calls you to the office) and so on.

田字格书写 Writing in Tin Word Format：

丨 丨' 口 叫 叫

叫	叫	叫	叫	叫	叫	叫	叫	叫	叫	叫	叫	叫	叫

书写提示：右边的"丩"不能写成"刂"。

Writing tips：The "丩" on the right should not be written as "刂".

（十一）和 hé/huò

词语：和平（peace） 温和（gentle）

析字：古代汉字写作"♉""♏"，楷书写作"和"，字的本义是"声音"或"音乐和谐"。后引申出"和谐""和平""温和""和睦"等意思，之后又进一步引申出作为介词的用法。

Analysis of the character: It had been written as "♉" "♏" in ancient Chinese character and "和" in Regular Script (Kaishu). The original meanings were "sound" or "music harmony", and then the meaning extended to "harmony" "peace" "moderation" "concord" and so on. Also, it can be used as a preposition.

田字格书写 Writing in Tin Word Format：

ノ 二 千 千 禾 禾 和 和

和	和	和	和	和	和	和	和	和	和	和	和

书写提示：右边"禾"的最后一笔是点，不能写成捺。

Writing tips: The last stroke on the right of "禾" is 点(diǎn), not 捺(nà).

（十二）号 hào/háo

词语：号码（number） 号令（order）

析字：战国时期写作"⚡"，小篆写作"号"，楷书写作"号"。上面是"口"，与字的意思有关，下面表示字的读音。字的本义是"大声哭"。后引申出"大声叫喊""命令""宣称""称号""记号"等意思。

Analysis of the character: It had been written as "⚡" "号" and "号" in the Warring States Period, Seal Script (Xiaozhuan) and Regular Script (Kaishu) respectively. The upper component "口" is related to the meaning of the character, and the lower part is related to the pronunciation of the character.

The original meaning was "cry loudly", and then the meaning extended to "scream" "command" "claim" "title" "mark" and so on.

田字格书写 Writing in Tin Word Format：

丶 丷 ㅁ 므 号

号	号	号	号	号	号	号	号	号	号	号	号	号	号

书写提示：最后一笔竖折折钩，不能写成竖钩。

Writing tips：The last stroke is 竖折折钩(shù zhé zhé gōu), not 竖钩(shù gōu).

(十三) 吗 ma/má

词语：是吗(yes or no) 好吗(okay or not)

析字："吗"在现代汉语中用作表示疑问的语气词,左边的"口"与字的意思有关（汉语中这类作为语气词的汉字,很多都有"口字旁",如"吧""呢""啊"等）,右边的"马"表示字的读音。

Analysis of the character："吗" is used as modal words expressing doubt in modern Chinese. The "口" on the left is related to the meaning of the character (in Chinese, this kind of Chinese characters as modal particles, many have the component "口", such as "吧" "呢" "啊" and so on), and the "马" on the right is related to the pronunciation of the character.

田字格书写 Writing in Tin Word Format：

丶 口 口 吋 吗 吗

吗	吗	吗	吗	吗	吗	吗	吗	吗	吗	吗	吗	吗	吗

书写提示：右边"马"的书写顺序是"フ、ㄅ、一"。

Writing tips：The writing order of the right part "马" is "フ、ㄅ、一".

(十四) 哪 nǎ

词语:哪里(where) 哪个(which)

析字:左边的"口"与字义有一定的关系("哪"多表示疑问的意思),右边的"那"表示字的读音。现代汉语中用作疑问代词,如"哪些""哪儿"等。

Analysis of the character: The "口" on the left is related to the meaning of the character("哪" usually expresses the meaning of doubt), and the "那" on the right is related to the pronunciation of the character. In modern Chinese, it is usually used as interrogative pronoun, such as "哪些""哪儿" and so on.

田字格书写 Writing in Tin Word Format:

丿 𠃍 口 叮 叨 叨 哪 哪 哪

哪 哪 哪 哪 哪 哪 哪 哪 哪 哪 哪 哪

书写提示:按照左、中、右的顺序书写,三部分大体均衡。

Writing tips: Write in the order of left, middle and right, and the three parts are generally balanced in size.

(十五) 吧 ba

词语:是吧(yes) 走吧(go)

析字:左边的"口"与字义有一定的关系("吧"用作语气词),右边的"巴"表示字的读音。现代汉语中用作语气词,如"好吧""我们走吧"等。

Analysis of the character: The "口" on the left is related to the meaning of the character("吧" is used as modal word), and the "巴" on the right is related to the pronunciation of the character. In modern Chinese, it is usually used as modal words, such as "好吧""我们走吧" and so on.

田字格书写 Writing in Tin Word Format：

书写提示：右边的"巴"不能写成"巳"。

Writing tips：The "巴" on the right should not be written as "巳".

（十六）呢 ne

词语：怎么办呢（what to do）　你呢（what about you）

析字：左边的"口"与字义有一定的关系（"呢"多表示说话的语气），右边的"尼（ní）"与字的读音近似。现代汉语中一般用作语气词，如"你干什么呢？""我们在上课呢。"

Analysis of the character：The "口" on the left is related to the meaning of the character（"呢" is usually used to express the tone of speech），and the "尼（ní）" on the right is similar to the pronunciation of the character. In modern Chinese, it is usually used as modal words, such as "What are you doing?" "We are in class." and so on.

田字格书写 Writing in Tin Word Format：

书写提示：右边的"尼"不能写成"尾"。

Writing tips：The "尼" on the right should not be written as "尾".

（十七）知 zhī

词语：知道（know）　知识（knowledge）

析字：小篆写作"𥎿"，楷书写作"知"。左边的"矢(shǐ)"表示字的读音（在古代汉语中"矢"与"知"的读音相近），右边的"口"与字的意思有关。"知"的本义是"知识"，后引申出"知道"的意思。

Analysis of the character: It had been written as "𥎿" and "知" in Seal Script(Xiaozhuan) and Regular Script(Kaishu) respectively. The "矢(shǐ)" on the left is related to the pronunciation of the character(the pronunciation of "矢" and "知" were similar in ancient Chinese), and the "口" on the right is related to the meaning of the character. The original meaning of "知" was "knowledge", and then the meaning extended to "know".

田字格书写 Writing in Tin Word Format：

书写提示：左边的"矢"最后一笔是点，不能写成捺。

Writing tips: The last stroke on the left of "矢" is 点(diǎn), not 捺(nà).

（十八）唱 chàng

词语：唱歌(sing)　唱戏(act in an opera)

析字：形声字。左边的"口"与字义相关，右边的"昌"表示字的读音。

Analysis of the character: It's a pictophonetic character. The "口" on the left is related to the meaning of the character, and the "昌" on the right is related to the pronunciation of the character.

田字格书写 Writing in Tin Word Format：

书写提示：右边偏旁"昌"上面的"曰"略窄。

Writing tips：The upper "曰" of "昌" on the right is slightly narrow.

（十九）问 wèn

词语：问题（question）　访问（visit）

析字：甲骨文写作"㕣"，小篆写作"問"，楷书写作"問"，简化字写作"问"。字形里面的"口"与字义有关，外面的"門（门）"表示读音。古代汉语中"門（门）"与"问"的读音近似。"问"的本义是"询问"，后引申出"问候""访问"等意思。

Analysis of the character：It had been written as "㕣" "問" and "問" in Oracle Bone Script（Jiaguwen）, Seal Script（Xiaozhuan）and Regular Script（Kaishu）respectively, and simplified as "问". The "口" in the form was related to the meaning of the character, and the "門（门）" outside the form was related to the pronunciation of the character. The pronunciation of "門（门）" and "问" were similar in ancient Chinese. The original meaning of "问" was "inquiry", and then the meaning extended to "regards" "visit" and so on.

田字格书写 Writing in Tin Word Format：

丶　丨　门　闩　问　问

书写提示：先写外面的"门"，后写里面的"口"。

Writing tips：Write the part "门" first, then wrote the part "口".

（二十）告 gào

词语：告诉（tell）　告别（say goodbye）

析字：甲骨文写作"𠙻"，字形像"牛"被放在祭祀的器皿中，秦代隶书写作"告"，楷书写作"告"。"告"的本义是"祭祀""祷告"，后引申出"报告""告诉"等意思。

Analysis of the character：It had been written as "𠙻" in Oracle Bone Script（Jiaguwen）, similar to the image of "cow" placed in a sacrificial vessel. It had been written as "吿" and "告" in Clerical Script (Lishu) and Regular Script (Kaishu) respectively. The original meanings of "告" were "sacrifice" "pray", and then the meanings extended to "report" "tell" and so on.

田字格书写 Writing in Tin Word Format：

丿 ㅗ 屮 生 牛 告 告

书写提示：上面的"⺧"不能误写成"生"或"牛"。

Writing tips：The upper part of the character should be written as "⺧", not "生" or "牛".

 汉字锦囊 Idea Box of Chinese Characters

常用偏旁——口字旁（口）

Commonly-used Components — Kouzipang（口）Component

"口字旁"（口）常表示与口的动作有关的意思，多数情况下出现在字的左侧。

The commonly-used character component "Kouzipang"（口）usually indicates the meaning related to the movement about mouth, and it often appears on the left side of the character.

三、词语练习 Phrase Practice

1. 找出方框B中由方框A中的每个汉字构成的词语，同学们互相检查正确与否。

Find out the phrase in Table B formed by each Chinese character in Table

A and check with your classmates.

A
学　好　孩　教　睡　眼　看　吃　喝　叫　和　号　知　唱　问　告

B
和平　记号　知足　唱歌　和谐　吃惊　喝茶　大叫　告辞　喝彩　看书 睡眠　眼镜　吃饭　问题　教学　爱好　男孩　午睡　公告　小孩　学习 美好　教室　知识

2. 看拼音写汉字。

Read the following pinyin to write Chinese characters.

① jiào(　　　)师　　② nǎ(　　　)里　　③ hào(　　　)码

④ hē(　　　)水　　⑤ hé(　　　)平　　⑥ wèn(　　　)句

3. 读出下面的句子。

Read out the following sentences.

① 我们在教室上课呢。

② 晚上不能睡那么晚。

③ 他去学校了吗？

④ 麻烦你告诉小王，有空就给我回个电话。

⑤ 你的电话号码是多少？

四、综合练习 Comprehensive Practice

1. 按照偏旁名称的拼音写出相应的偏旁。

Write out the corresponding components according to the pinyin of the components.

dān rén páng _____　　sì diǎn dǐ _____　　zhú zì tóu _____

cǎo zì tóu _____　　bǎo gài tóu _____　　yǔ zì tóu _____

2. 写出下列汉字的两个组成部件。

Write out the two components of the following characters.

① 它：_____ + _____　　② 点：_____ + _____

③ 会：_____ + _____　　④ 笑：_____ + _____

⑤ 资：_____ + _____　　⑥ 雷：_____ + _____

⑦ 告：_____ + _____　　⑧ 写：_____ + _____

3. 选字组词。

Choose characters to make out words.

① 爱(A. 奶　B. 好　C. 仔)

② (A. 和　B. 禾　C. 木)平

③ (A. 很　B. 恨　C. 眼)镜

④ (A. 告　B. 先　C. 牛)别

⑤ 合(A. 昌　B. 倡　C. 唱)

五、课外任务 After-class Task

1. 用拼音在电脑或手机上打出下面的词语。

Type out the following phrases on your computer or mobile phone with pinyin.

知识　吃饭　和谐　喝彩　看电视　告诉　喝咖啡　睡觉　问题　女孩

2. 把本课学习到的上下结构的汉字，制作成可上下拆分的卡片。打乱后，让同学们把汉字重新拼接回来。看谁拼得又快又好。

Make the Chinese characters of the upper-lower structure learned in this lesson into cards that can be split up and down. After scrambling, ask your classmates to put the Chinese characters back together again to see who can spell them more quickly and better.

第七课 汉字的意符
Lesson Seven Ideographic Symbols of Chinese Characters

一、汉字知识 Knowledge of Chinese Characters

(一) 偏旁的位置关系 The Position Relations of Chinese Character Components

这一课,我们来介绍包围结构。
In this lesson, let's introduce the enclosure structure.

如果汉字字形是由两边或两边以上包围起来构成的,这样的汉字属于包围结构。包围结构主要分为3种类型:

① 全包围结构。如"国""回""因""图"。

② 三面包围结构。其中有上方三面包围的,如"问""闹""风""冈"。有左方三面包围的,如"区""医""匠"。有下方三面包围的,如"凶""画""函"。

③ 两面包围结构。其中有右上两面包围的,如"句""可""岛"。有左上两面包围的,如"庆""居""压"。有左下两面包围结构的,如"边""建""超"。

If Chinese characters are surrounded by two or more sides, such Chinese characters belong to the enclosure structure. The enclosure structure is mainly divided into 3 types:

① Enclosed structure, such as "国""回""因""图".

② Three-sided enclosure structure. There are three sides above, such as "问""闹""风""冈". There are three sides surrounded by the left, such as "区"

"医""匠". There are three sides surrounded from below, such as "凶""画""函".

③ Two-sided enclosure structure. There are two sides on the right and upper, such as "句""可""岛". There are two sides on the left and upper, such as "庆""居""压". There are two sides on the left and lower, such as "边""建""超".

(二) 字符的功能 Symbol Function

这一课,我们来介绍意符。

In this lesson, let's introduce ideographic symbols.

按照结构功能,可以把汉字中的字符分为3种:意符、音符和记号。意符是汉字中与字的意义有关的字符。意符可以提示字的意义,是我们学习掌握汉字意义的重要线索,例如,"妈""姐""好"字中的"女";"唱""喝""吃"字中的"口";"河""汗""酒"字中的"氵"。

According to the structural function, we can divide the Chinese character symbols into 3 types: ideographic symbols, phonetic symbols and signs. The ideographic symbols are related to the meaning of the characters, and they can prompt the meaning of the characters, which are important clues for us to learn and grasp the meaning of Chinese characters. For example, "女" in "妈""姐""好"; "口" in "唱""喝""吃"; "氵" in "河""汗""酒".

二、汉字形音义 The Form, Pronunciation and Meaning of Chinese Characters

 目标汉字 Learning Objective

```
高  商  后  同  右  西  蛋  介  爸  打  拿  找  服  动  男  想
怎  忘  净  快
```

（一）高 gāo

词语：高兴（happy） 高山（high mountain）

析字：甲骨文写作""""，像高台上有建筑的样子。金文写作""，小篆写作"高"，楷书写作"高"。字的本义是"高处"，后引申出"高度""高级"等意思。

Analysis of the character：It had been written as """" in Oracle Bone Script(Jiaguwen), "" "高" and "高" in Bronze Script (Jinwen), Seal Script (Xiaozhuan) and Regular Script(Kaishu) respectively. The original meaning of the character was "high place", and then extended to "height" "senior" and so on.

田字格书写 Writing in Tin Word Format：

丶 一 亠 宀 古 亨 高 高 高 高

高	高	高	高	高	高	高	高	高	高	高	高	高	高

书写提示：下面的"冋"不能写成"回"。

Writing tips：The "冋" in the lower should not be written as "回".

（二）商 shāng

词语：商店（store） 商业（business）

析字：甲骨文写作""，金文写作""，小篆写作""，楷书写作"商"。"商"字本来用作国名，后表示"做生意"的意思，又引申出"商量""讨论"等意思。

Analysis of the character：It had been written as "" "" "" and "商" in Oracle Bone Script(Jiaguwen), Bronze Script(Jinwen), Seal Script(Xiaozhuan) and Regular Script(Kaishu) respectively. It was originally used as the name of the country. Later, it meant "business" and extended the meanings of "consult" "discuss" and so on.

田字格书写 Writing in Tin Word Format：

`丶 亠 ㄗ 广 产 产 产 商 商 商`

商	商	商	商	商	商	商	商	商	商	商	商	商	商

书写提示：字形里面的"ㄅ"不能写成"ㄣ"。

Writing tips：The inner "ㄅ" should not be written as "ㄣ".

（三）后 hòu

词语：后面（behind） 后天（the day after tomorrow）

析字："后"字主要有两个意思。第一个意思是表示方位或次序，意思与"前""先"相反。繁体字写作"後"，在古代，金文写作"𣥒""𢓈"，像人的足（𤴓）被丝线（𢆶）纠缠，所以有所延迟、退后，后来加上偏旁"彳"，以强化字义。汉字简化时，人们用同音字"后"代替了"後"字。第二个意思是"君主的妻子"。这个字古代写作"𤓞"，字形构造的意义不明，楷书写作"后"。

Analysis of the character：The character "后" has two main meanings. The first meaning is to indicate direction or order, as opposed to "before" or "first". The traditional Chinese character form of it was written as "後". In ancient times, it had been written as "𣥒" and "𢓈" in Bronze Script(Jinwen). It looked like a person's feet(𤴓) are entangled in silk threads(𢆶), so there was a delay and a retreat. Later it was added the Chinese character component "彳", in order to strengthen the meaning. When Chinese characters were simplified, the homophone "后" was used instead of "後". The second meaning is "the wife of the emperor". This character was written as "𤓞" in ancient times, and the meaning of the form structure was unclear. It had been written as "后" in Regular Script(Kaishu).

田字格书写 Writing in Tin Word Format：

`一厂厂斤后后`

书写提示：第一笔是平撇，第二笔是竖撇，不能连成一笔。

Writing tips：The first stroke 撇（piě）is flat and the second 撇（piě）is vertical. Don't write it in one stroke.

（四）同 tóng

词语：相同（the same） 同学（classmate）

析字：甲骨文写作"凨"，金文写作"𠔼"，小篆写作"同"，楷书写作"同"。"同"的本义是"共同做事"，后来引申出"相同"的意思。

Analysis of the character：It had been written as "凨" "𠔼" "同" and "同" in Oracle Bone Script(Jiaguwen)，Bronze Script(Jinwen)，Seal Script(Xiaozhuan) and Regular Script(Kaishu) respectively. The original meaning of the character "同" was "doing things together"，which later extended the meaning of "the same".

田字格书写 Writing in Tin Word Format：

`丨冂冂冋同同`

书写提示：笔顺应先外后内。

Writing tips：The stroke order should be outside first and then inside.

（五）右 yòu

词语：右手（right hand） 右边（right side）

析字：甲骨文写作"ᔑ"，像右手的形状。金文写作"ᔑ"，在字形下面加上起区别作用的"ᔱ"，以便把"左""右"两字区别开来。小篆写作"ᔱ"，楷书写作"右"。后来，"右手"字义引申出表示方位的"右边"。

Analysis of the character: It had been written as "ᔑ" in Oracle Bone Script (Jiaguwen). It's like a right hand. It had been written as "ᔑ" in Bronze Script (Jinwen). This part "ᔱ" served to distinguish between "左" and "右". It had been written as "ᔱ" and "右" in Seal Script (Xiaozhuan) and Regular Script (Kaishu) respectively. Later, the meaning of "right hand" extended to indicate the "right side" of the orientation.

田字格书写 Writing in Tin Word Format：

一ナ才右右

书写提示：注意"右"和"石"的区别。

Writing tips: Mind the difference between "右" and "石".

（六）西 xī

词语：西边（west）　东西（stuff, thing）

析字：甲骨文写作"ᔱ"，像鸟巢的形状，周代金文写作"ᔱ"，秦代隶书写作"ᔱ"，楷书写作"西"。自古至今，汉语借用像鸟巢形状的这个字来表示方向"西边"。

Analysis of the character: It had been written as "ᔱ" in Oracle Bone Script (Jiaguwen), like the shape of a bird's nest. It also had been written as "ᔱ" in Bronze Script (Jinwen) from Zhou Dynasty, "ᔱ" in Clerical Script (Lishu) from Qin Dynasty and "西" in Regular Script (Kaishu). Since ancient times, Chinese language has borrowed the character which has the shape of a bird's nest to represent the direction of the west.

田字格书写 Writing in Tin Word Format：

书写提示：注意"西"与"四"的区别。
Writing tips：Mind the difference between "西" and "四".

（七）蛋 dàn

词语：鸡蛋（egg） 脸蛋（face） 下蛋（lay eggs）

析字：这个字原来写作"蜑"。上面的"延（yán）"表示字的读音（由于古今音变，"延"和"蛋"现在的读音稍有差异），下面的"虫"与字的意思（指鸟、蛇等小动物）有关。字的本义是"鸟类、禽类、爬行类等动物生下的带有硬壳的卵"。后来为了便于书写，把上面的"延"简写成"疋"，"蜑"变成了"蛋"。

Analysis of the character：The character was originally written as "蜑". The upper part "延（yán）" represented this character's pronunciation（due to the phonetic changes since ancient times，the pronunciation of "延" and "蛋" has slight difference）. The below part "虫" was related to the meaning of the character（referring to some small animals，such as birds，snakes and so on）. The original meaning of the character was used to express "the eggs with hard shells laid by birds，poultries and reptiles". Later，for the sake of convenience in writing，the upper part "延" was simplified as "疋"，and the character "蜑" turned into "蛋".

田字格书写 Writing in Tin Word Format：

书写提示：第一笔横钩不能写成横。

Writing tips: The first stroke is 横钩(héng gōu), it should not be written as 横(héng).

(八) 介 jiè

词语:介绍(introduce)　介词(preposition)

析字:古代甲骨文写作"⺈",像人(亻)处于中间的状态,小篆写作"⺈",楷书写作"介"。本义是"在两者之间",后引申出"介绍"的意思。

Analysis of the character: The Oracle Bone Script(Jiaguwen) form "⺈" was like a man(亻) in the middle state. Then it had been written as "⺈" and "介" in Seal Script(Xiaozhuan) and Regular Script(Kaishu) respectively. The original meaning of the character was "between the two", later it was extended to mean "introduce".

田字格书写 Writing in Tin Word Format:

ノ 八 介 介

书写提示:下面的"丿丨"不能写成"川"。

Writing tips: The "丿丨" in the lower part should not be written as "川".

(九) 爸 bà

词语:爸爸(dad)

析字:上面的"父"是表示意思,下面的"巴"表示读音。

Analysis of the character: The "父" above indicates the meaning, and the "巴" below indicates the pronunciation.

田字格书写 Writing in Tin Word Format：

丶 ハ 乄 父 爷 谷 爸 爸

爸	爸	爸	爸	爸	爸	爸	爸	爸	爸	爸	爸	爸	爸

书写提示：上面的"父"第一笔是短撇，第二笔是点。

Writing tips：The first stroke of the upper "父" is a short 撇（piě），and the second stroke is 点（diǎn）.

（十）打 dǎ/dá

词语：打球（play a ball game） 打工（do work）

析字：左边的"扌"是形旁，右边的"丁"是声旁，表示读音（由于古今音变，现在"丁"与"打"的读音有差异）。本义是"敲打"，后引申出"攻打""殴打"的意思，再后来又引申出"做游戏""采取某种方式"的意思。

Analysis of the character：The "扌" on the left is the pictographic part, and the "丁" on the right is the phonetic part, which indicates the pronunciation (due to the phonetic changes since ancient times, the pronunciation of "丁" and "打" are different). The original meaning was "beating", and later extended to "attack" and "beat". Later on, the meanings of "play a game" "do it in a certain way" were extended.

田字格书写 Writing in Tin Word Format：

一 十 扌 扌 打

打	打	打	打	打	打	打	打	打	打	打	打	打	打

书写提示：右边的"丁"不能写成"丅"。

Writing tips：The "丁" on the right should not be written as "丅".

（十一）拿 ná

词语：拿出来（get out）　拿东西（get something）　拿手（be good at）

析字：会意字。上面的"合"和下面的"手"合在一起表示"手合起来，握住东西"的意思。后引申出"掌握""使用"等意思，如"拿手""拿笔写字"。

Analysis of the character：It is an associative character. This character is combined with "合" on the top and "手" under it, meaning to "hold things by one's hand". Then it has the extensive meanings of "master" or "use", like "be good at" and "get hold of the pen and write".

田字格书写 Writing in Tin Word Format：

书写提示：下面"手"的第一笔是撇，不能写成横。

Writing tips：The first stroke of "手" is 撇（piě）, which should not be written as 横（héng）.

（十二）找 zhǎo

词语：寻找（search）　找东西（look for something）

析字：本来写作"划"，表示"用刀割"或"划船前进"的意思。后来，"刂"变为"扌"，且"扌"的位置转移到左侧，写作"找"，引申出"寻找"的意思。

Analysis of the character：It was originally written as "划", meant "cut with a knife" or "row forward". Later, "刂" turned to "扌", and the position of the "扌" moved to the left, which was written as "找", extending as the meaning of "looking for".

田字格书写 Writing in Tin Word Format：

一 十 扌 扌 扎 找 找

书写提示："找"不能写成"我"。

Writing tips：The "找" should not be written as "我".

 汉字锦囊 Idea Box of Chinese Characters

常用偏旁——提手旁（扌）

Commonly-used Components — Tishoupang（扌）Component

"提手旁"（扌）常表示与人的手上动作有关的意思，一般都出现在字的左侧。

The "Tishoupang"（扌）usually means something associated with a human hand movement，and it usually appears on the left side of the character.

（十三）服 fú

词语：衣服（clothes）　服从（obey）　服务（service）

析字：早期汉字写作"𦥑""𦨶"，字形像从后面用手"又"强迫他人劳动、提供服务。后来楷书写作"服"——左边的劳动工具"片"变成"月"，右边的"𠬛"变为"𠬝"。字的本义是"提供服务""服从他人"，从这个意思引申出"提供穿衣之类的服务"的意思，后又引申出"衣服"的意思。

Analysis of the character：It had been written as "𦥑" and "𦨶" in early Chinese character，"又" was like a hand that forced others to work and provided service from back. Later the character was written as "服" in Regular Script (Kaishu) — the instrument of labor "片" in the left side was changed into "月"

and the “卩” in the right side was changed into “𠬝”. The original meanings of the character were “provide service” “be obedient to others”, then the meanings were extended to “provide the service of clothing”, and the meaning of “clothes” came out.

田字格书写 Writing in Tin Word Format:

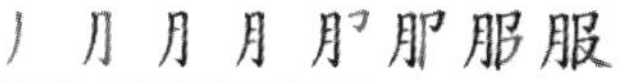

服	服	服	服	服	服	服	服	服	服	服	服	服	服	服

书写提示:右边不能写成“殳”。

Writing tips: The right side should not be written as “殳”.

(十四)动 dòng

词语:运动(exercise) 动作(action)

析字:繁体字写作“動”,左边的“重”表示读音,右边的“力”表示意思。本义是“活动”“行动”。简化字写成“动”,左边的“重”简化为“云”。

Analysis of the character: The traditional Chinese character form was written as “動”. The “重” on the left indicated the pronunciation, and the “力” on the right indicated the meaning. The original meanings were “activity” “action”. The simplified form was written as “动”, the “重” on the left was simplified as “云”.

田字格书写 Writing in Tin Word Format:

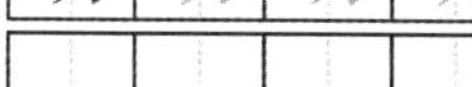

动	动	动	动	动	动	动	动	动	动	动	动	动	动	动

书写提示:左边的“云”位置略微偏上。

Writing tips: The “云” on the left should be slightly upper.

（十五）男 nán

词语：男人（man）　男同学（male students）

析字：甲骨文写作"🕱"，金文写作"🕱"，楷书写作"男"。上面是"田"，下面是"力"，"力"是古代用来耕田的一种农具。在古代，耕作是男人的一项主要职责，因此用"田""力"合在一起表示"男人"。

Analysis of the character：It had been written as "🕱" "🕱" and "男" in Oracle Bone Script(Jiaguwen), Bronze Script(Jinwen) and Regular Script (Kaishu) respectively. The upper part is written as "田", and the lower part is "力", a kind of agricultural tool used to plow the fields in ancient times. In ancient times, farming was a major duty for men, so the "田" and "力" were combined to mean "man".

田字格书写 Writing in Tin Word Format：

丨 冂 日 田 田 甲 男

书写提示：注意"力"和"刀"的区别。

Writing tips：Mind the difference between "力" and "刀".

（十六）想 xiǎng

词语：想法（thoughts）　梦想（dream）

析字：形声字。上面的"相"是声旁，表示读音，下面的"心"是形旁，表示字义。本义是"想象"，引申为"思索"的意思，后又引申为"希望""想要""思念"等意思。

Analysis of the character：It's a pictophonetic character. The upper "相" is the phonetic part that indicates the pronunciation. The lower "心" is the pictographic part that indicates the meaning. The original meaning was "imagination", then extended to the meaning of "thinking", and then extended to the meanings of "hope" "want" "miss" and so on.

第七课　汉字的意符

田字格书写 Writing in Tin Word Format：

一 十 才 木 机 机 相 相 相 想 想 想

想 想 想 想 想 想 想 想 想 想 想 想 想

书写提示：按照"木、目、心"的顺序书写。

Writing tips：Write as the order of "木、目、心".

（十七）怎 zěn

词语：怎么去（how to go）　怎样做（how to do）

析字：上面的"乍"表示读音（由于古今音变，在现代汉语中"乍"读"zhà"，与字的读音有差异），下面的"心"表示字义。用作疑问词，意思是"如何""怎么"。

Analysis of the character：The upper "乍" indicates the pronunciation（due to phonetic changes since ancient times，"乍" reads "zhà" in modern Chinese，which is different from this character）. The lower "心" indicates the meaning. The "怎" is used as a question word，meaning "how".

田字格书写 Writing in Tin Word Format：

丿 匚 仁 午 乍 乍 怎 怎 怎

怎 怎 怎 怎 怎 怎 怎 怎 怎 怎 怎 怎 怎

书写提示：上面的"乍"不能写成"生"。

Writing tips：The upper "乍" should not be written as "生".

（十八）忘 wàng

词语：忘记（forget）　忘我（oblivious of oneself）

析字：形声字。上面的"亡（wáng）"表示读音，下面的"心"表示字义。本义是"忘记""不记得"。

Analysis of the character: It is a pictophonetic character. The "亡(wáng)" on the top represents its pronunciation, "心" at the bottom represent its meaning. The original meanings of this character were "forget" "can't remember".

田字格书写 Writing in Tin Word Format：

丶 亠 亡 产 忘 忘 忘

忘	忘	忘	忘	忘	忘	忘	忘	忘	忘	忘	忘	忘	忘

书写提示：下面"心"的正确书写顺序是"亅、乚、丶、丶"。

Writing tips：The correct writing order of the "心" at the bottom is "亅、乚、丶、丶".

（十九）净 jìng

词语：干净(clean)　清净(peace and quiet)

析字：繁体字写作"淨"，左边的"氵"表示字义，右边的"争(zhēng)"表示读音（由于古今音变，"争"与"净"的读音有差异）。楷书字形变为"净"。字的意思是"清洁""干净"。

Analysis of the character: It was written as "淨" in traditional Chinese character. The left side "氵" was related to the character's meaning and the right side "争（zhēng）" represented its pronunciation (due to the phonetic changes since ancient times, the pronunciation of "争" and "净" is different now). Then the form was changed into "净" in Regular Script(Kaishu) with the meanings of "clean" "tidy".

田字格书写 Writing in Tin Word Format：

丶 冫 氵 氵 浄 净 净 净

净	净	净	净	净	净	净	净	净	净	净	净	净	净

书写提示：左边的"忄"不能写成"氵"。

Writing tips: The left side "忄" should not be written as "氵".

（二十）快 kuài

词语：快乐（happiness） 赶快（quickly）

析字：小篆写作"快"，楷书写作"快"。左侧的"忄"是声旁，右侧的"夬（guài）"是声旁，表示读音（因为古今音变，"夬"与"快"的读音略有差异）。本义是"高兴"，后来引申出"速度敏捷"的意思，后又表示"赶快""就要"的意思。

Analysis of the character: It had been written as "快" and "快" in Seal Script(Xiaozhuan) and Regular Script(Kaishu) respectively. The "忄" on the left is the pictographic part. The "夬(guài)" is the phonetic part that indicates the pronunciation(due to the phonetic changes since ancient times, the pronunciation of "夬" and "快" is slightly different now). The original meaning was "happy", and later came to mean "quick", and then to mean "hurry" and "be about to".

田字格书写 Writing in Tin Word Format：

丶 丶 忄 忄 忆 快 快

快	快	快	快	快	快	快	快	快	快	快	快	快	快

书写提示：右侧的"夬"不能写成"央"。

Writing tips: The "夬" on the right should not be written as "央".

汉字锦囊 Idea Box of Chinese Characters

意符"心"的3个变体
3 Variants of the Ideographic Symbol "心"

汉字中表示与"人的思想和情感"有关的意思，常用意符"心"。意符"心"有3个变体：一是出现在字的下面，叫作"心字底"，如"思""念""想"下面的"心"。

二是出现在字的左侧,叫作"竖心旁",如"怕""快""懂"等字的"忄"。还有一种比较少见,也出现在字的下面,如"慕""恭"的"小"。

The ideographic symbol "心" often denotes the meaning related to "human thoughts and emotions". The ideographic symbol "心" has 3 variants: One is to appear in the lower of the character, called "Xinzidi", such as the "心" in "思""念""想". The second is to appear on the left side of the character, called "Shuxinpang", such as the "忄" in "怕""快""懂". There is a relatively rare variant that also appears below the character, such as "小" in "慕""恭".

三、词语练习 Phrase Practice

1. 请填写包含指定汉字的词语。
Please fill in the words containing the given Chinese characters.
① 我晚上想去_____(商)买东西。
② 我爸爸在一家_____(司)工作。
③ 你能不能_____(助)我一下?
④ 你最近身体_____(怎)?

2. 读出下列汉字、词语、词组和句子。
Read the following Chinese characters, words, phrases and sentences.
① 高—很高—个子很高—他个子很高。
② 后—后面—学校后面—学校后面有一个邮局。
③ 同—不同—很不同—每个国家的文化都很不同。
④ 可—可是—虽然汉字很难,可是我很喜欢写汉字。

四、综合练习 Comprehensive Practice

1. 请将下列汉字分别放入相应的结构类型中。
Please put the following characters into the corresponding structure type.

后　同　司　可　爸　打　助　动　男　想　快　怎　国　回　问　风　医　句　边

结构类型 Structure types		包含汉字 Characters
左右结构 Left-right structure		例：打、
上下结构 Top-bottom structure		例：爸、
包围结构 Enclosure structures	全包围结构 Enclosed structure	例：国、
	三面包围结构 Three-sided enclosure structure	例：同、
	两面包围结构 Two-sided enclosure structure	例：后、

2. 选字填空，并猜一猜这些汉字的意思，然后查字典找出这些汉字的意思。
Fill in the blanks and guess the meaning of these characters. Then look up the meaning of these characters in the dictionary.

情　读　菜　挂

① 请大家一起_____课文。

② 请等一下，不要_____电话。

③ 他今天心_____很不错。

④ 她去超市买了很多_____，要请朋友们吃饭。

141

3. 请写出与下列汉字意思相反或相对的汉字。

Please write down the characters which are opposite or corresponding to the following characters.

例 Example：大—小

妈—   女—   买—   姐—

4. 请改正下列句子里的错别字。

Please correct the wrong characters in the following sentences.

① 我很喜欢体育运助。

② 她在一家公同工作。

③ 玛丽知安娜是好朋友。

④ 他爱唱咖啡。

五、课外任务 After-class Task

1. 用下列汉字写一个句子，比一比看谁写得对、写得长。

Please write a sentence using each given characters, and compare to see who can write better and longer.

① 想

② 能

③ 比

2. 找出已学过的所有包含下列意符的汉字，根据它们的意思填在该意符下的分类中，制成意符卡片。以后可不断扩充该意符包含的汉字。

Find all the Chinese characters that contain the following ideographic symbols and fill in the categories according to their meanings to make ideographic symbol cards. The characters contained under this classification can be continuously expanded later.

扌——手（hand）
使用手的动作（the act of using hands）：_____

不使用手的动作（the act of not using hands）：_____

抽象行为（abstract behavior）：_____

其他（other）：_____

口——嘴（mouth）
口部动作（the mouth movements）：_____

发出声响或言语的动作（the act of making a sound or speech）：_____

与口相近的部位（a part close to the mouth）：_____

语气助词（modal particles）：_____

其他（other）：_____

第八课 汉字的音符
Lesson Eight Phonetic Symbols of Chinese Characters

一、汉字知识 Knowledge of Chinese Characters

(一) 偏旁的位置关系 The Position Relations of Chinese Character Components

这一课,我们来介绍框架结构。

In this lesson, let's introduce the frame structure.

有些汉字既不是上下、左右结构,也不是包围结构,而是在一个大的框架之内填充、镶嵌了一些小的部件,这样的汉字结构属于框架结构,如"乘""爽""承""举""坐""噩"等。

Some Chinese characters are neither top-bottom structure, left-right structure, nor enclosure structure, but a large frame filled with some small components, such a Chinese character structure belongs to the frame structure, such as "乘""爽""承""举""坐""噩".

(二) 字符的功能 Symbol Function

这一课,我们来介绍音符。

In this lesson, let's introduce phonetic symbols.

音符是汉字中与整个字的读音有关的字符。音符可以提示字的读音,是我们学习掌握字音的重要线索,如"想"字中的"相","唱"字中的"昌","铜"字中的"同","芳"字中的"方",等等。

The phonetic symbols are related to the sound of the whole Chinese characters, which can suggest the pronunciation of the characters. They are important clues for us to master the pronunciation. Such as "相" in the character "想","昌" in the character "唱","同" in the character "铜","方" in the character "芳" and so on.

二、汉字形音义 The Form, Pronunciation and Meaning of Chinese Characters

 目标汉字 Learning Objective

慢 忙 您 息 读 请 认 识 说 语 谢 谁 记 试 诉 课 话 冷 准 明

(一) 慢 màn

词语:缓慢(slow) 傲慢(arrogant)

析字:左边的"忄"是形旁,右边的"曼"是声旁。本义是"懒惰",引申出"轻视""傲慢"的意思,后又引申出"速度不快""缓慢"的意思。

Analysis of the character: The "忄" on the left side is the pictographic part, "曼" on the right side is the phonetic part. The original meaning was "lazy", which extended to the meanings of "contempt" and "arrogance", which also extended to the meanings of "slow speed" and "slow" later.

田字格书写 Writing in Tin Word Format：

丶丶忄忄忄忄忄忄忄忄忄忄忄忄忄忄忄忄忄忄忄忄忄忄忄忄慢慢

书写提示：左边"忄"的笔顺：第一笔是左边的点，第二笔是右边的点，第三笔是中间的竖。

Writing tips：The stroke order of the "忄" on the left side：the first stroke is "diǎn" on the left, the second stroke is "diǎn" on the right, and the third stroke is "丨" in the middle.

(二) 忙 máng

词语：急忙(hurriedly) 忙碌(busy)

析字：左边的"忄"与字义有关，右边的"亡（wáng）"〔由于古今音变，声旁"亡（wáng）"的读音与"忙（máng）"的读音稍有差异〕与读音有关。本义是"心慌不安"，后引申出"行动急迫"的意思（如"赶忙""急忙""匆忙"），后又引申出"事情多""没有空闲"的意思（如"我最近很忙""忙碌"）。

Analysis of the character：The "忄" on the left side relates to the meaning of the character. The "亡（wáng）" on the right side〔due to the phonetic changes since ancient times, the pronunciation of the phonetic part "亡（wáng）" is slightly different from the "忙（máng）"〕relates to the pronunciation. The original meaning of "忙" was "anxious", which later came to mean "in a hurry" (such as "赶忙""急忙""匆忙"), and then came to mean "have a lot to do" "have no leisure"(such as "我最近很忙""忙碌").

田字格书写 Writing in Tin Word Format：

丶丶忄忄忙忙

书写提示：右边"亡"的书写顺序是"丶、一、乚"。

Writing tips：Write the "亡" on the right as the writing order of "丶、一、乚".

（三）您 nín

词语：您好（hello）

析字：上面的"你"与读音和字义都有关，下面的"心"与字义有关，字义是第二人称"你"的敬称。

Analysis of the character：The upper "你" relates to both the pronunciation and meaning, and the lower "心" relates to the meaning. "您" is a respectful address for the second person "你".

田字格书写 Writing in Tin Word Format：

丿 亻 伙 伙 伙 你 你 您 您 您

书写提示：按照"亻、尔、心"的顺序书写。

Writing tips：Write as the writing order of "亻、尔、心".

（四）息 xī

词语：休息（rest）　信息（information）

析字：古代汉字写作"𦣹"，上面是"自"（像人的鼻子的形状，表示"鼻子"的意思），下面是"心"（古人认为心脏参与了人的呼吸），"自"和"心"合在一起表示"呼吸"的意思，这是字的本义。后在本义的基础上引申出"休息""消息"等新的意思。

Analysis of the character：It had been written as "𦣹" in ancient Chinese character, the "自"（like the shape of man's nose, it means "nose"）on the top and "心"（the ancients believed that the heart is a part of our breathing system）at the bottom. "自" and "心" was combined together to represent the meaning of "breathing" which was the original meaning of this character. Later it was extended to some new contents as "rest" "news" and so on.

田字格书写 Writing in Tin Word Format：

书写提示：上面的"自"不能写成"白"。

Writing tips：The "自" on the top should not be written as "白".

(五) 读 dú

词语：阅读（read）　读书（read a book）

析字：繁体字写作"讀"，左边的"言"表示字义，右边的"賣"表示字的读音（由于古今音变，"賣"与"讀"的读音有差异）。简化字写作"读"。本义是"分析理解书上的内容"，后引申出"看（书）""研究""看着文字说出来"等意思。

Analysis of the character：The traditional Chinese character was written as "讀". The "言" on the left indicated the meaning, and the "賣" on the right indicated the pronunciation（due to the phonetic changes since ancient times，the pronunciation of the phonetic part "賣" was different from the "讀"）. The simplified form was written as "读". The original meaning was "to analyze and understand the content of the book"，and later extended to "read（books）" "study" "look at the text to speak out" and other meanings.

田字格书写 Writing in Tin Word Format：

书写提示：右边的"卖"按照"十、一、头"的顺序书写。

Writing tips：The "卖" on the right side should be written as the order of "十、一、头".

（六）请 qǐng

词语：请假（ask for leave）　请求（request）

析字：小篆写作"䚶"，楷书写作"請"。左边的"言"表示字义，右边的"青"表示字的读音。简化字写作"请"。字的本义是"拜见长者"，拜见的目的往往是有所请求，因而引申出"请求"的意思。

Analysis of the character: It had been written as "䚶" and "請" in Seal Script(Xiaozhuan) and Regular Script(Kaishu) respectively. The "言" on the left indicated the meaning, and the "青" on the right indicated the pronunciation. The simplified form was written as "请". The original meaning of the character was "pay a visit to the elderly". The purpose of an interview is often to make a request, which extended as the meaning of "request".

田字格书写 Writing in Tin Word Format：

丶 讠 讠 讠 请 请 请 请 请

请	请	请	请	请	请	请	请	请	请	请	请

书写提示：左边的"讠"不能写成"氵"。

Writing tips: The "讠" on the left side should not be written as "氵".

（七）认 rèn

词语：认识（know）　认真（careful）

析字：繁体字写作"認"，简化字写作"认"，左边的"讠"表示字义，是形旁，右边的"人"表示读音，是声旁。字的本义是"认识""识别"，后引申出"看作""认为"等意思。

Analysis of the character: The traditional Chinese character was written as "認". The simplified form was written as "认". The "讠" on the left is the pictographic part that indicates the meaning, and the "人" on the right is the phonetic part that indicates the pronunciation. The original meanings of "认"

were "know" and "identify", and then extended to "regard as" "think" and other meanings.

田字格书写 Writing in Tin Word Format：

`、 讠 认 认`

书写提示：左边的"讠"书写顺序是"、、乚"。

Writing tips：The "讠" should be written as the order of "、、乚".

(八) 识 shí

词语：认识（know） 知识（knowledge）

析字：小篆写作"𧬣"，楷书写作"識"，简化字用"只"代替"戠"，写作"识"。本义是"标记"，后引申出"认识"的意思，再引申出"知识"的意思。

Analysis of the character：It had been written as "𧬣" and "識" in Seal Script（Xiaozhuan） and Regular Script（Kaishu） respectively. The simplified form was written as "识". The original meaning was "mark", which later extended the meaning of "know", and then the meaning of "knowledge".

田字格书写 Writing in Tin Word Format：

`、 讠 讥 识 识 识`

书写提示：右边的"只"按照"口、丿、丶"的顺序书写。

Writing tips：The component "只" on the right should be written as the order of "口、丿、丶".

(九) 说 shuō

词语：说话（speak） 说明（explain）

析字：繁体字写作"說"，左边的"言"与字义有关，右边的"兑（duì）"本来与字的读音有关，但由于古今音变，现在"兑"与"说"的读音差异很大。字义是"解释""说明""说话"。

Analysis of the character: The traditional Chinese character was written as "說". The "言" on the left related to the meaning. The "兑（duì）" on the right originally related to the pronunciation of the character, but due to the phonetic changes since ancient times, the pronunciation of "兑" and "说" is very different now. The meanings of the character are "explain" "illustrate" "speak".

田字格书写 Writing in Tin Word Format：

丶 讠 讠 讠 讠 䛨 䛨 说

说	说	说	说	说	说	说	说	说	说	说	说	说	说

书写提示："兑"的上面是两点，不能写成三点。

Writing tips: The upper side of "兑" should be two strokes 点（diǎn）, not three.

(十) 语 yǔ

词语：汉语（Chinese） 口语（spoken language）

析字：繁体字写作"語"，左边的"言"是形旁，表示字义，右边的"吾（wú）"表示字音，但由于古今音变，"吾"与"语"的读音有了差异。本来用作动词，本义是"跟别人谈话"，后又用作名词，表示"语言""话语"。

Analysis of the character: The traditional Chinese character was written as "語". The "言" on the left was the pictographic part that indicated the meaning. The "吾（wú）" on the right indicated the pronunciation. But due to the phonetic changes since ancient times, the pronunciation of the phonetic part "吾" is different from the "语". The "语" originally used as a verb meaning "to talk to others", and it was later used as a noun meaning "language" "speech".

田字格书写 Writing in Tin Word Format:

丶 讠 讠 讠 讠 讠 讠 讠 讠
语 语 语 语 语 语 语 语 语 语 语 语 语 语

书写提示：按照"讠、五、口"的顺序书写。

Writing tips: Write as the order of "讠、五、口".

（十一）谢 xiè

词语：感谢(thank)　不用谢(you're welcome)

析字：左边的"讠"是形旁，表示字义；右边的"射(shè)"是声旁，表示字音（由于古今音变，"射"与"谢"的读音略有变化）。本义是"辞去""拒绝"，后来引申出"道歉"的意思，现代汉语常用的意思是"感谢"。

Analysis of the character: The "讠" on the left is the pictographic part that indicates the meaning, and the "射(shè)" on the right is the phonetic part that indicates the pronunciation(due to the phonetic changes since ancient times, the pronunciation of the phonetic part "射" is slightly different from the "谢"). The original meanings of "谢" were "resign" and "refuse", and later extended to mean "apologize", which is commonly used in modern Chinese to mean "thank".

田字格书写 Writing in Tin Word Format:

丶 讠 讠 讠 讠 讠 讠 讠 讠 讠 讠 讠
谢 谢 谢 谢 谢 谢 谢 谢 谢 谢 谢 谢 谢 谢

书写提示：右边的"寸"不能写成"才"。

Writing tips：The "寸" on the right side should not be written as "才".

（十二）谁 shéi/shuí

词语：谁（who）　谁在家（who is at home）

析字：左边的"讠"是形旁，表示字义；右边的"隹（zhuī）"是声旁，表示字的读音（由于古今音变，"隹"与"谁"的读音有一些变化）。用作疑问代词，表示"什么人"，如"你找谁?"也可以表示虚指，表示"不知道的人或无须说明的人"，如"我的词典不知道被谁拿走了"。也可以任指，表示"任何人"，如"这件事谁也不知道"。

Analysis of the character：The "讠" on the left is the pictographic part that indicates the meaning, and the "隹（zhuī）" on the right is the phonetic part that indicates the pronunciation(due to the phonetic changes since ancient times, the pronunciation of the phonetic part "隹" is slightly different from the "谁"). The "谁" is used as an interrogative pronoun to indicate "who", such as "Who are you looking for?" It can also be used as a phantom reference to indicate "a person who does not know or does not need to explain", such as "I don't know who has taken my dictionary". It can also be used as an arbitrary reference to indicate "anyone", such as "no one knows anything about it".

田字格书写 Writing in Tin Word Format：

丶 讠 讠 讠 讠 讠 诈 诈 谁 谁

书写提示：右边的"隹"不能写成"住"。

Writing tips：The "隹" on the right side should not be written as "住".

（十三）记 jì

词语：记录（record）　日记（diary）　记下（write down）

析字：形声字。左边的"讠"表示字义，右边的"己（jǐ）"表示字音。本义是"记录"，后来引申出"记忆"的意思。

Analysis of the character: It's a pictophonetic character. The left side "讠" is related to the character's meaning and the right side "己（jǐ）" represents its pronunciation. The original meaning of the character was "record", later the meaning of "memorize" was extended.

田字格书写 Writing in Tin Word Format：

`丶 讠 讠 记 记`

书写提示：右边的"己"不能写成"已"。
Writing tips：The "己" on the right should not be written as "已".

（十四）试 shì

词语：考试（examination） 实验（experiment）

析字：左边的"讠"是形旁，右边的"式（shì）"表示字音。本义是"考核""检验"，后来又引申出"考试""尝试"的意思。

Analysis of the character：The "讠" on the left is the pictographic part, and the "式（shì）" on the right indicates the pronunciation. The original meanings were "examination" "test", and later extended to the meanings of "examination" and "try".

田字格书写 Writing in Tin Word Format：

`丶 讠 讠 䜣 䜣 试 试`

书写提示：右边的"弋"不能写成"戈"。
Writing tips：The "弋" on the right should not be written as "戈".

汉字锦囊 Idea Box of Chinese Characters

> 常用偏旁——言字旁(讠)
>
> Commonly-used Components — Yanzipang(讠) Component
>
> "讠"是常用的汉字偏旁,也是常用的形旁,在汉字中表示与语言、说话有关的意思。出现在字的左边一般写成"讠",出现在字的下面时一般写作"言"。
>
> "讠" is a commonly-used character component, and also a commonly-used semantic component, means something related to language and speech in Chinese characters. It is usually written as "讠" when it appears on the left side in a Chinese character, and written as "言" when it appears in the lower.

(十五) 诉 sù

词语:告诉(tell) 诉说(recount)

析字:"讠"是形旁,与字义有关;"斥(chì)"是声旁,与字音有关(由于古今音变,"斥"与"诉"的读音有差异)。本义是"告诉""诉说"。后来引申出"控诉""告状"的意思。

Analysis of the character: The "讠" is the pictographic part that relates to the meaning, and the "斥(chì)" is the phonetic part that relates to the pronunciation(due to the phonetic changes since ancient times, the pronunciation of the phonetic part "斥" is different from the "诉"). The original meanings were "tell" and "recount". Later extended the meanings of "accusing" and "complaining".

田字格书写 Writing in Tin Word Format:

丶 讠 计 计 诉 诉 诉

诉	诉	诉	诉	诉	诉	诉	诉	诉	诉	诉	诉	诉	诉

书写提示：右边的"斥"不能写成"斤"。

Writing tips：The "斥" on the right should not be written as "斤".

（十六）课 kè

词语：上课（go to class）　课本（textbook）

析字："讠"是形旁，与字义有关；"果（guǒ）"是声旁，与字音有关（由于古今音变，"果"与"课"的读音有差异）。字的本义是"试验""考核"，后来引申出"功课""课程"的意思。

Analysis of the character：The "讠" is the pictographic part that relates to the meaning，and the "果（guǒ）" is the phonetic part that relates to the pronunciation（due to the phonetic changes since ancient times，the pronunciation of the phonetic part "果" is different from the "课"）. The original meanings were "experiment" and "examination"，and later extended to the meanings of "schoolwork" and "curriculum".

田字格书写 Writing in Tin Word Format：

丶 讠 讠 讠 讠 讠 课 课 课

书写提示："讠"略窄，"果"略宽。

Writing tips：The "讠" should be a little narrower，and the "果" should be a little wider.

（十七）话 huà

词语：说话（speak）　电话（telephone）

析字：古代这个字写作"話"，左边的"言"是形旁，表示字义，右边的"昏"是声旁，表示字音。汉代以后，右边的"昏"变成了"舌（shé）"，与字音有很大差异。本义是"谈话"，后来引申出"话语""语言"的意思。

Analysis of the character: In ancient times, this character was written as "話". The "言" on the left was the pictographic part that indicated the meaning. The "昏" on the right was the phonetic part that indicated the pronunciation. After the Han Dynasty, the "昏" on the right turned to "舌 (shé)", which was very different from the pronunciation of the character. The original meaning was "conversation", and later extended to "discourse" and "language".

田字格书写 Writing in Tin Word Format：

丶 讠 讠 讠 诋 诋 话 话

话	话	话	话	话	话	话	话	话	话	话	话	话

书写提示：右边"舌"的第一笔撇不能写成横。

Writing tips: The first stroke on the right of "舌" should not be written as 横 (héng).

(十八) 冷 lěng

词语：冷淡(coldly) 今天很冷(it's very cold today)

析字："冫"是形旁，与字义有关；"令(lìng)"是声旁，表示字音(由于古今音变，"令"与"冷"的读音稍有差异)。"冫"(两点水)是汉字常用意符之一，甲骨文写作"仌"，表示冰的意思，所以有"冫"的汉字都有"寒冷"的意思。

Analysis of the character: The "冫" is the pictographic part that relates to the meaning, and the "令 (lìng)" is the phonetic part that indicates the pronunciation(due to the phonetic changes since ancient times, the pronunciation of the phonetic part "令" is different from the "冷"). "冫"(Liangdianshui) is one of the commonly-used Chinese ideographic character. It had been written as "仌" in Oracle Bone Script(Jiaguwen), which meant ice. All the Chinese characters that include "冫" have the meaning of "cold".

田字格书写 Writing in Tin Word Format：

冷冷冷冷冷冷冷冷冷冷冷冷冷冷冷

书写提示："冫"不能写成"氵"，"令"不能写成"今"。

Writing tips：The "冫" should not be written as "氵", the "令" should not be written as "今".

(十九) 准 zhǔn

词语：准备（prepare）　标准（standard）

析字：古代汉字是形声字，小篆写作"𠅼"。左边是"氵"，与字义有关；右边是"隼（sǔn）"，表示字音（由于古今音变，"隼"与"准"的读音稍有差异）。最初的字义是"像水面一样平"。楷书写作"準"。简化字把"氵"简写为"冫"，并且省去了下面的"十"，变为现在的"准"。在"水平"这个意思的基础上，引申出"标准""准确""准许"等意思。

Analysis of the character：The ancient form of this character was a pictophonetic one，it had been written as "𠅼" in Seal Script(Xiaozhuan). "氵" on the left can be related to the meaning of this character while "隼(sǔn)" on the right stood for its pronunciation(due to the phonetic changes since ancient times，there is a difference when pronouncing the "隼" and "准"). The original meaning of this character was "as flat as the water surface". It also had been written as "準" in Regular Script(Kaishu). The modern Chinese has simplified the "氵" into "冫"，omitted the "十" at the bottom at the same time，so it turned into "准". Based on the original meaning "flat"，it generated the meanings of "standard" "accuracy" "permission"，etc.

田字格书写 Writing in Tin Word Format：

书写提示：左边不能写成"氵"。

Writing tips：The left side should not be written as "氵".

(二十) 明 míng

词语：明天(tomorrow)　明白(understand)

析字：金文写作"⊙刀"，左边是"⊙"（窗户），右边是"刀"，表示月亮照到窗户上，就是"光明"的意思。后来左边的"⊙"逐渐变成了"日"，战国时期写成"朙"，汉代隶书写成"明"，楷书写成"明"。本义是"光照""光明"，后来引申出"明亮""明白""明显"等意思。

Analysis of the character：It had been written as "⊙刀" in Bronze Script (Jinwen). The left side is "⊙"(window). The "刀" on the right side referred to the moon shines on the window, which meant "light". Later, "⊙" on the left was gradually changed into "日". Then it had been written as "朙" in the Warring States Period, "明" in Clerical Script (Lishu) of Han Dynasty, and "明" in Regular Script (Kaishu). The original meanings were "illumination" and "bright", and later extended to "shining" "clear" "obvious" and other meanings.

田字格书写 Writing in Tin Word Format：

书写提示：左边的"日"不能写成"目"。

Writing tips：The "日" on the left side should not be written as "目".

三、词语练习 Phrase Practice

1. 请填写包含指定汉字的词语。
Please fill in the words containing the given Chinese characters.
① 这个词是什么_____?（意）
② 你一共_____多少个汉字?（认）
③ 你生病了,最好_____去医院看看。（明）
④ 老师_____同学们,星期六晚上有一个留学生新年晚会。（诉）

2. 读出下列汉字、词语、词组和句子。
Read the following characters, words, phrases and sentences.
① 试—一试—试一试—你试一试这件衣服怎么样?
② 忙—有点儿忙—工作有点儿忙—我最近工作有点儿忙。
③ 冷—不太冷—天气不太冷—这几天天气不太冷。
④ 让—让我写汉字—老师让我写汉字—老师让我到黑板上写汉字。
⑤ 课—上课—开始上课—早上八点开始上课—我们每天早上八点开始上课。

四、综合练习 Comprehensive Practice

1. 请把汉字、拼音和意思连线。
Please match the Chinese character, pinyin and meaning.

| 请 | qíng | feeling, affection, sentiment |
| 情 | qǐng | ask, request, please |

| 吗 | ma | modal auxiliary usually after the a question |
| 妈 | mā | mother |

吧	ba	modal auxiliary after question or imperative sentence
爸	bà	father

眼	hěn	eye
很	yǎn	very

2. 找出下列汉字中包含的已学过的汉字。

Find out the characters you have learned in the following characters.

例 Example：慢：日、又

① 您：

② 意：

③ 读：

④ 语：

⑤ 息：

⑥ 明：

3. 选字填空。

Choose a character to fill in the blank.

谁　话　慢　请　课

① 老爷爷走得很_____。

② 我们每天有四节_____。

③ 这是_____的汉语字典？

④ 她不太喜欢说_____。

⑤ 我没听懂，_____您再说一遍。

4. 猜一猜，试着把下列汉字和拼音、意思连线。

Take a guess and try to match the following characters with pinyin and meaning.

跑	bǎ	hold
远	hèn	run
恨	yuǎn	hate
把	pǎo	far

五、课外任务 After-class Task

1. 请你写出由下列汉字联想到的字,并说一说它们与指定字之间的联系。比一比看谁想到的字多。

Please write down the characters that are associated with the following characters and say how they relate to the specified characters. Compare and see who can think of more characters.

① 读
② 课

2. 找出已学过的所有包含下列意符的汉字,根据它们的意思填在该意符下的分类中,制成意符卡片。以后可不断扩充该意符包含的汉字。

Find all the Chinese characters that contain the following ideographic symbols and fill in the categories according to their meanings to make ideographic symbol cards. The characters contained under this classification can be continuously expanded later.

亻——人（people）

人的品貌特征（the physical features of a person）：_____

_____

人做出的动作或行为（the act or movement of a person）：_____

_____

某一类人（a certain kind of person）：_____

_____

其他（other）：_____

_____

女——女人（woman）
女性亲属称谓（female kinship terms）：_____
_____

女性非亲属称谓（female non-kinship terms）：_____
_____

和女性相关的事物、行为、性质特征（things, behaviors, characteristics related to women）：_____
_____

其他（other）：_____
_____

第九课　汉字中的记号
Lesson Nine　Signs in Chinese Characters

一、汉字知识 Knowledge of Chinese Characters

（一）汉字学习方法——区分形近字 Learning Methods of Chinese Characters — Distinguishing the Characters with Similar Forms

汉字中有一些形体相近的字。例如：

There are some Chinese characters in similar forms, such as：

大—太　　天—夫　　田—由

人—入　　土—士　　字—宇

你还能写出哪些形近的字？

Can you write some more Chinese characters in similar forms?

学习掌握形近字和部件的方法：第一，注意区分其不同的来源和表示的意思。例如，"氵"的来源是"水",因此是三点水；"冫"的来源是"仌",因此是两点水。"衤"的来源是"衣",意思跟"衣服"有关；"礻"的来源是"示",意思跟"礼仪""祈祷"等有关。第二，注意进行对比，找出差异，多写多练。

There are some ways to master the Chinese characters in similar forms and their different parts: Firstly, pay attention to distinguish between different sources and meanings. For example, the source of the "氵" is "水", thus being three drops of water, while the source of the "冫" is "仌", so it is two drops of water. "衣" is the source of "衤", associating with "clothes", whereas the source of the "礻" is "示", relating to "etiquette" "prayer" and so on. Secondly, pay attention to the comparison, find out the differences and do more writing practice.

(二) 字符的功能 Symbol Function

这一课,我们来介绍记号。

In this lesson, let's introduce signs.

有一些字符(部件)跟字的读音和字的意思都无关,这样的字符(部件)是记号。现代汉字中的记号字符主要有3种:

Some characters(parts) have nothing to do with the character's pronunciation or meaning, such characters(parts) are signs. There are mainly 3 types of the signs in modern Chinese characters:

1. 古代汉字中的一些记号字符一直使用至今。例如,表示数字的汉字。

Some signs of ancient Chinese characters have been used up to now. For example, the digital characters.

2. 由于字形演变,一些原本不是记号的字符变成了记号。例如,"年"是形声字,小篆写作"秊",上面是"禾",下面是"千"。隶变之后,整个字变成了一个记号。

Because of the form evolution, some characters that were not signs in origin became signs later. For example, the character "年", which was a phonogram and written as "秊" in Seal Script(Xiaozhuan), the part "禾" was on the top and "千" was in the bottom. After transferred to Clerical Script (Lishu), the whole character changed into a sign.

3. 由于汉字简化,原来的字符失去了原有的构形功能而成为纯粹的记号。例如,"为""书""头"等草书、楷化字,整个字符就是一个记号。

Because of the simplification of Chinese characters, the original signs lost the function of character-formation and became a sign. For example, "为""书""头" and many other characters, after transferred into Cursive Script(Caoshu) and Regular Script(Kaishu), the whole character became a sign.

二、汉字形音义 The Form, Pronunciation and Meaning of Chinese Characters

 目标汉字 Learning Objective

跑 跟 路 这 过 还 进 送 边 道 远 楼 条 觉 视 很 得 行 先 起

（一）跑 pǎo

词语：跑步（running） 跑了（run away）

析字：左边的"𧾷"是形旁，与字义有关，右边的"包（bāo）"是声旁（由于古今音变，"包"与"跑"的读音稍有不同），表示字音。本义是"动物用脚刨地"，后来表示"奔跑"的意思，再引申出"逃走""消失"的意思。

Analysis of the character: The left side "𧾷" represents the character's meaning, the right side "包（bāo）" is related to its pronunciation (due to the **phonetic changes since ancient times**, there is a slight difference in **pronunciation between** "包" and "跑"). The original meaning of the character was "digging with feet by animals", then it could be referred as "running", later the meanings of the character were extended to "escape" and "disappear".

田字格书写 Writing in Tin Word Format：

书写提示:"⻊"最后的笔画是提。

Writing tips: The last stroke of "⻊" is 提(tí).

(二) 跟 gēn

词语:脚后跟(heel)　跟从(follow)

析字:形声字。左边的"⻊"表示字义,右边的"艮(gèn)"表示读音。本义是"脚后跟",后来引申出"跟从"的意思,又产生出作为介词的用法,如"小李跟小张都是大学生"。

Analysis of the character: It's a pictophonetic character. The "⻊" on the left side is related to the character's meaning and the "艮(gèn)" on the right side represents its pronunciation. The original meaning of the character was "heel", then the meaning was extended to "follow", besides, the character was added another usage as a preposition, for example, "both Xiao Li and Xiao Zhang are college students".

田字格书写 Writing in Tin Word Format:

书写提示:右边的"艮"不能写成"良"。

Writing tips: The "艮" on the right side should not be written as "良".

(三) 路 lù

词语:走路(walk)　马路(road)

析字:"⻊"是形旁,表示字义,右边的"各(gè)"表示字音(由于古今音变,"各"与"路"的读音有较大差异)。本义是"道路"。

Analysis of the character: The left side "⻊" represents the character's meaning, the right side "各(gè)" is related to its pronunciation (due to the phonetic changes since ancient times, there is a big difference in pronunciations between "各" and "路"). The original meaning was "road".

田字格书写 Writing in Tin Word Format:

丶 口 口 甲 甲 皀 足 趵 趵 路 路 路

书写提示:"各"上面的"夂"不能写成"攵"。

Writing tips: The upper part "夂" of "各" should not be written as "攵".

(四) 这 zhè

词语:这个(this) 这么(so)

析字:古代汉字写作"適","辶"与字义有关,"商"表示字音。隶变后楷书变成"這",后来又简化成"这"。字的本义是"前往""迎接",后来被借用表示"距离较近的人或事物"。

Analysis of the character: It had been written as "適" in ancient Chinese character, the part of "辶" was related to the character's meaning and the part of "商" represented its pronunciation. Then the character was changed into "這" in Regular Script(Kaishu) and finally it was simplified as "这". The original meanings of the character were "head for" and "greet". Later it was borrowed to express the meaning of "people or things nearby".

田字格书写 Writing in Tin Word Format:

丶 亠 寸 文 文 汶 这

书写提示:"文"先写,"辶"后写。

Writing tips: The part of "文" should be written as first, followed by the part of "辶".

汉字锦囊 Idea Box of Chinese Characters

常用偏旁——走之旁（辶）

Commonly-used Components — Zouzhipang(辶) Component

"辶"是常用的汉字偏旁,称为"走之旁"。在汉字中,"辶"经常用作意符,表示与行走有关的意思。甲骨文写作"𢓊",左边的"彳"（"行"的左半边）表示道路,右边的"止"是人的脚印,合在一起表示"人在路上行走"的意思。小篆写作"辵",楷书写作"辵",简化字写作"辶"。

"辶" is a commonly-used Chinese character component of Chinese characters, called "Zouzhipang". In Chinese characters, "辶" is often used as the ideogram, related to the meaning of walk. It was written as "𢓊" in Oracle Bone Script(Jiaguwen), the left "彳"(the left hemisphere of the "行") meant road, the "止" on the right was the footprints of a person, after putting the two parts together, it meant "walking on the road". Then it was written as "辵" and "辵" in Seal Script(Xiaozhuan) and Regular Script(Kaishu) respectively, and finally was simplified as "辶".

（五）过 guò

词语：过去(in the past)　经过(pass)

析字：繁体字写作"過","辶"表示字义,"咼"表示字音。简化字写作"过",本义是"经过",后来引申为"过去""超过""过错"的意思。现代汉语中可用在动词后,表示"曾经"或"已经",如"看过""吃过"。

Analysis of the character: It had been written as "過" in traditional Chinese character. The part of "辶" was related to the character's meaning and the part of "咼" represented its pronunciation. Then it was simplified as "过". The original meaning of the character was "pass", later it was extended to mean "past" "surpass" "fault". In modern Chinese, it can be used after a verb to express the meaning of "once" or "have done something", such as "have read" "have eaten".

田字格书写 Writing in Tin Word Format：

一 寸 寸 寸 过 过

书写提示："辶"的书写顺序是"丶、㇋、㇏"。

Writing tips：The stroke orders of "辶" is "丶、㇋、㇏".

（六）还 hái/huán

词语：归还（return） 还是（or）

析字：繁体字写作"還"，"辶"表示字义，"瞏"表示字音。简化字写作"还"，本义是"返回"，引申有"归还"的意思。现代汉语多用作副词，表示"仍然""程度增加或补充"等意思。

Analysis of the character：It had been written as "還" in traditional Chinese character, the part of "辶" was related to the character's meaning and the part of "瞏" represented its pronunciation. Then it was simplified as "还". The original meaning of the character was "go back", later it was extended to mean "return something". In modern Chinese, it can be used as an adverb to express the meanings of "still" "the degree of the increase or supplement" and so on.

田字格书写 Writing in Tin Word Format：

一 丆 不 不 不 还 还

书写提示："辶"是两笔，不能写成三笔。

Writing tips：There are only two strokes in the part of "辶", don't mistakenly write it into three strokes.

（七）进 jìn

词语：前进（forward）　进步（progress）

析字：西周金文写作"🐦"，由"隹（zhuī）"和"辵（chuò）"组成，合在一起表示小鸟飞翔前进的意思。楷书写作"進"，简化字用"井"代替"隹"，因此"进"变为形声字。本义是"前进"，后引申为"进步""进入"等意思。

Analysis of the character：It had been written as "🐦" in Bronze Script (Jinwen) in Western Zhou Dynasty, The character consists of "隹（zhuī）" and "辵（chuò）", referring that birds fly forward when the two parts were combined together. Then it had been written as "進" in Regular Script (Kaishu), when the character was simplified, "隹" was replaced by "井", so that the character "进" became a pictophonetic character. The original meaning of the character was "forward", then the meaning was extended to "progress" "into" and so on.

田字格书写 Writing in Tin Word Format：

一　二　テ　井　廾　讲　进

进	进	进	进	进	进	进	进	进	进	进	进	进

书写提示："井"不能写成"开"或"并"。

Writing tips：The part of "井" should not be written as "开" or "并".

（八）送 sòng

词语：送礼（give gifts）　送别（farewell）

析字：古代汉字写作"遂"，后来"弇"写成"关"，字形变成了"送"。"送"的本义是"送亲"，后来引申出"送行""赠送"等意思。

Analysis of the character：It had been written as "遂" in ancient Chinese character, then "弇" was taken placed by "关" and the form of the character became "送". The original meaning of "送" was "accompany bride to bridegroom's family on wedding day", then the meaning was extended to "see sb. off" "give as a present" and so on.

田字格书写 Writing in Tin Word Format：

书写提示："关"不能写成"夫"。

Writing tips：The part of "关" should not be written as "夫".

（九）边 biān

词语：外边（outside）　边境（border）

析字：原来写作"邊"，"辶"表示字义，"臱（mián）"表示读音。简化字用记号"力"代替"臱"，变成了"边"。本义是"边际""边境"，引申为"旁边""边远"等意思。

Analysis of the character：It had been written as "邊" in traditional Chinese writing, the part of "辶" was related to the character's meaning and the part of "臱（mián）" represented its pronunciation. Later it was simplified as "边", replacing the part of "臱" with "力". The original meanings of the character were "marginal" and "border", then the meanings were extended to "beside" "remote" and so on.

田字格书写 Writing in Tin Word Format：

书写提示："力"不能写成"刀"。

Writing tips：The part of "力" should not be written as "刀".

(十) 道 dào

词语：道理(reason)　道路(way)

析字："辶"表示字义，"首(shǒu)"表示字的读音(由于古今音变，"首"与"道"的读音差异较大)。本义是"行走的道路"，后来引申出抽象的"道理""方法""技艺""思想"等意思，也可作动词，意思是"说出来"，现代汉语还可以作为量词，如"一道闪电""三道题目"。

Analysis of the character：The part of "辶" is related to the character's meaning and the part of "首(shǒu)" represents its pronunciation (due to the phonetic changes since ancient times, there is a big difference in pronunciation between "首" and "道"). The original meaning of the character was the "path for walk". Later the abstract meanings as "truth" "method" "skill" "thought" and so on were extended. It can also be used as a verb, meaning "speak", besides, in modern Chinese, it can be used as a quantifier to express the quantity of the nouns, such as "一道闪电" "三道题目".

田字格书写 Writing in Tin Word Format：

丶　丶　丷　丷　䒑　䒑　首　首　首　道　道

书写提示："首"不能写成"百"。

Writing tips：The part of "首" should not be written as "百".

(十一) 远 yuǎn

词语：永远(forever)　遥远(far)

析字：繁体字写作"遠"，简化字写作"远"。"元"表示读音，"辶"标指字义。本义是"遥远""距离长"，后来也可以表示"时间久远""关系久远"等。

Analysis of the character：It had been written as "遠" in traditional Chinese character. Later it was simplified as "远". The part of "辶" is related to the character's meaning and the part of "元" represents its pronunciation. The original meanings of the character were "far away" and "long distance", then the character was extended to mean some abstract meanings, such as "long time" "long-established relationship" and so on.

田字格书写 Writing in Tin Word Format：

一 二 亍 元 元 沅 远

远	远	远	远	远	远	远	远	远	远	远	远	远	远

书写提示：先写"元"，后写"辶"。

Writing tips：The part "元" should be written first, followed by the part "辶".

（十二）楼 lóu

词语：楼房(building)　教学楼(teaching building)　三楼(the third floor)

析字：形声字。左边的"木"表示字义（古代楼房多用木材建造），右边的"娄(lóu)"表示字音。本义是"两层及两层以上的房子"。

Analysis of the character：It's a pictophonetic character. The left side "木" is related to the character's meaning（wood was always used in construction of building in ancient times）and the right side "娄(lóu)" represents its pronunciation. The original meaning of the character referred to "a house with two or more storeys".

田字格书写 Writing in Tin Word Format：

一 十 才 木 木 术 札 柈 栐 柊 楼 楼 楼

楼	楼	楼	楼	楼	楼	楼	楼	楼	楼	楼	楼	楼

书写提示：按照部件"木、米、女"的顺序书写。

Writing tips：The writing order of the character is "木、米、女".

(十三) 条 tiáo

词语：条件(condition)　面条(noodles)　一条河(a river)

析字：小篆写作"藨"，楷书写作"條"或"條"。上面是"攸(yōu)"，表示字的读音（由于古今音变，"攸"和"条"的读音有差异），下面是"木"，表示字的意义。"條"字后来省去左边的"亻"，再把"攵"写成"夂"，"木"写成"朩"，"條"字变成了"条"。字的本义是"树上细小的枝条"，后来也表示长条形的东西，如"面条""线条"。

Analysis of the character：It had been written as "藨" in Seal Script (Xiaozhuan), and "條" or "條" in the Regular Script(Kaishu). The "攸(yōu)" on the top represented its pronunciation(due to the phonetic changes since ancient times, there is a difference in pronunciation between "攸" and "条"), the "木" at the bottom represented its meaning. For the character "條", "亻" on the left was omitted afterwards, then "攵" was changed into "夂", "木" into "朩", so that "條" has been written into "条". The original meaning of this character was "tiny little branches on the tree", later it can be referred as strip-shaped objects, such as "noodles" "lines".

田字格书写 Writing in Tin Word Format：

丿　ク　夂　冬　冬　条　条

书写提示：下面的"朩"不能写成"小"。
Writing tips：The part "朩" at the bottom should not be written as "小".

(十四) 觉 jiào/jué

词语：睡觉(sleep)　感觉(feel)

析字：古代汉字写作"覺"，简化字写作"觉"。上面的"𦥯"是"學"（学）的上半部分，表示读音（由于古今音变，"学"与"觉"的读音稍有差异）。下面的"见"，与字义有关。本义是"睡醒"，后来引申出"发觉""觉悟""感觉"等意思。后来，从"睡醒"的意思引申出作为名词的用法，如"睡了一觉"。

Analysis of the character: It had been written as "覺" in traditional Chinese character. Later it was simplified as "觉". The "𦥯" on the top was the upper part of the "學"（学），representing the pronunciation（due to the phonetic changes since ancient times, there is a slight difference in pronunciations between "学" and "觉"). The bottom part "见" was related to its meaning. The original meaning of the character was "wake up", then it was extended to mean "find" "enlightenment" "feel" and so on. Later, it was used as a noun, for example, "have a sleep", which was produced from the meaning of "wake up".

田字格书写 Writing in Tin Word Format：

丶 丷 ⺌ ⺍ 兴 学 骨 觉 觉

觉	觉	觉	觉	觉	觉	觉	觉	觉	觉	觉	觉	觉	觉	觉

书写提示：上面的"⺌"不能写成"⺍"。

Writing tips: The "⺌" on the top should not be written as "⺍".

（十五）视 shì

词语：电视（TV） 重视（attach great importance to）

析字：甲骨文写作"𧢲"，像人站立着向远处观望，金文写作"𥄎"。小篆写作"視"，左边加上表示读音的"示（shì）"，变成了形声字。楷书写作"視"，简化字写作"视"，右边的"见"表示字义，"礻（shì）"表示读音。本义是"看"，汉语中由"视"构成的词语都与这个意思有关，如"视线""视野""视察"等。

Analysis of the character: In Oracle Bone Script(Jiaguwen), "𧢲" was like a man standing and looking away, Then the character had been written as "𥄎" and "視" in Bronze Script(Jinwen) and Seal Script(Xiaozhuan) respectively. The character turned into a phonogram with the part of "示(shì)" added to the left part. Later it was written as "視" in Regular Script(Kaishu) and simplified as "视", the right part "见" was related to its meaning and the left part "礻

(shi)" represented its pronunciation. The original meaning of the character was "see", all the expressions composed of "视" in Chinese are associated with this meaning, such as "视线""视野""视察" and so on.

田字格书写 Writing in Tin Word Format：

丶 亠 ァ 衤 衤 初 初 视 视

视	视	视	视	视	视	视	视	视	视	视	视	视	视

书写提示：左边的"衤"不能写成"衤"。

Writing tips：The left side "衤" should not be written as "衤".

 汉字锦囊 Idea Box of Chinese Characters

常用偏旁——见字旁（见）

Commonly-used Components — Jianzipang(见) Component

"见（jiàn）"也是常用的汉字偏旁。甲骨文是象形字，写作"🦴"，像跪着的人形，而突出其眼睛，表示"看见"的意思。现代汉字中有一些以"见"为偏旁的汉字，例如，"观""览""觉""规""视"等。这些汉字中的"见"都与字义有关系，因此这些汉字都含有"看"的意思。

"见（jiàn）" is also a commonly-used component of Chinese characters. Written as "🦴" in Oracle Bone Script(Jiaguwen), as a pictographic character, it was like a human shape and its eyes were highlighted to express the meaning of "see". In modern Chinese, some characters have the component of "见", for example, "观""览""觉""规""视", etc. The component "见" in these characters are all related to their meanings, so these characters all contain the meaning of "see".

（十六）很 hěn

词语：很大（very large） 好得很（very good）

析字："彳（chì）"本来与字义有关，"艮（gèn）"与字音有关（由于古今音变，"艮"与"很"的读音稍有差异）。字的本义是"行走艰难"或者"不听从"。后来由"不听从"引申出"凶狠"的意思（后来专门造出"狠"字来表示"凶狠"的意思）。在现代汉语中，这些意思都早已不使用了，现在用作程度副词，如"很好"。

Analysis of the character："彳（chì）" was originally associated with the character's meanings and "艮（gèn）" represented its pronunciation（due to the phonetic changes since ancient times，there is a slight difference in pronunciation between "艮" and "很"）. The original meanings were "walk hard" or "not obey". Later the meaning of "fierce" was extended from the meaning of "not obey"（later another character "狠" was especially created to mean "fierce"）. In modern Chinese, the meanings have already been abandoned, now it is used as an adverb of degree, such as "very good".

田字格书写 Writing in Tin Word Format：

丿 彳 彳 彳 彳 彳 彳 很 很 很

书写提示："彳"不能写成"亻"，"艮"不能写成"良"。

Writing tips："彳" should not be written as "亻", "艮" should not be written as "良".

汉字锦囊 Idea Box of Chinese Characters

常用偏旁——双人旁（彳）

Commonly-used Components — Shuangrenpang(彳) Component

"彳(chì)"是常用的构字能力很强的汉字偏旁。"彳"本来是"行"的左半边。"行(háng/xíng)"在古代汉字中本来写作"卝"，像十字路口，本义是"道路"。来源于"行"的"彳"在汉字中一般作为表义的偏旁使用，表示与道路或行走有关的意思。"彳"一般在字的左边，如"往""征""得""行""径"等。

As a commonly-used component, the part "彳(chì)" has great ability in forming Chinese characters. "彳" is the left side of "行" in original. "行（háng/xíng)" was written as "卝" in ancient Chinese character. It's just like a crossroad, and the original meaning of the character was "the way". So the component "彳" from "行" in Chinese characters is always related to the character's meaning, referring to road or walk. Generally it is written on the left side of the character, such as "往""征""得""行""径" and so on.

（十七）得 dé/de/děi

词语：得到(get)　看得见(visible)

析字：甲骨文写作"⿰彳⿱贝又""⿰彳⿱贝又"，左边的"彳"表示道路，右边的"⿱贝又"表示"得到贝（一种古代的钱）"，合在一起表示"获得"的意思。小篆写作"䙷"，楷书写作"得"。本义是"获得"，后来引申为"适合"（如"得当"）、"满意"（如"得意"）等意思。现代汉语中常用在动词或形容词后，连接表示情态或程度的补语，如"跑得快""好得很"。

Analysis of the character: In Oracle Bone Script(Jiaguwen), it was written as "⿰彳⿱贝又" "⿱贝又", "彳" on the left side referred to the road and the right part "⿱贝又" meant to "get a shell (a kind of ancient money)". The character had the meaning of "get" when the two parts were combined together. It had been written as "䙷" and "得" in Seal Script(Xiaozhuan) and Regular Script(Kaishu) respectively. The original meaning of the character was "get", then it was extended to mean "fit"(for example, "appropriate"), "satisfied"(for example, "complacent") and so on. In modern Chinese, the character is commonly used after a verb or an adjective to connect a modal or degree complement, such as "run fast" "good enough".

田字格书写 Writing in Tin Word Format:

丿 亍 彳 彳 彳 彳 彳 彳 得 得

书写提示:"䙴"上面不能写成"且"。
Writing tips: The upper part of "䙴" should not be written as "且".

(十八) 行 xíng/háng

词语:步行(walk)　行李(luggage)　银行(bank)

析字:古代汉字写作"井",像十字路口的形状,本义是"道路"。秦代隶书写作"行",楷书写作"行"。在本义的基础上,后来引申出"走路"的意思,后来又产生出"行列""行业"的意思。

Analysis of the character: It had been written as "井" in ancient Chinese character, the shape of it is like a crossroad, the original meaning of this character was "road". It also had been written as "行" in Clerical Script(Lishu) from Qin Dynasty, and "行" in Regular Script(Kaishu). The meaning was extended later as "walk", later it generated the meanings of "line/queue" "industry/business".

田字格书写 Writing in Tin Word Format:

丿 亍 彳 彳 行 行

书写提示:右边的"亍"不能写成"于"。
Writing tips: The "亍" on the right should not be written as "于".

(十九) 先 xiān

词语：先进(advanced)　原先(original)

析字：甲骨文写作"𦥑"，上面的"止"像脚印的形状，表示"往前走"的意思，下面是人形，合在一起表示"走在前面"。小篆写作"兂"，楷书写作"先"。本义是"时间或次序在前"，与"后"相反。

Analysis of the character：It had been written as "𦥑" in Oracle Bone Script (Jiaguwen), the part "止" on the top was like a footprint, meaning to "go forward", and the bottom was a human shape, the character meant "go ahead" when putting the two parts together. Later it was written as "兂" and "先" in Seal Script(Xiaozhuan) and Regular Script(Kaishu) respectively. The original meaning of the character was "in the first place in time sequence", and was opposite to "after".

田字格书写 Writing in Tin Word Format：

丿 𠂉 牛 生 先 先

先	先	先	先	先	先	先	先	先	先	先	先	先	先	先

书写提示：注意"先"与"失(shī)"的区别。

Writing tips：Pay attention to the difference between "先" and "失(shī)".

(二十) 起 qǐ

词语：站起来(stand up)　起床(get up)

析字：左边的"走"表示字义，右边的"己(jǐ)"与读音有关。本义是"起身"或"站起来"，引申为"起床""开始""发生"等意思。现代汉语中，也用在动词后，表示动作的趋向，如"想起""说起"。

Analysis of the character：The left side "走" represents the character's meaning, the right side "己(jǐ)" is related to its pronunciation. The original meanings of the character were "up" or "stand up", then the character was extended to mean "get up" "beginning" "happen" and so on. In modern Chinese, it can also be used after a verb to express the trend of the action, such as "remember" "talk about".

田字格书写 Writing in Tin Word Format：

一 十 土 丰 丰 走 走 起 起

书写提示：先写"走"，后写"己"。

Writing tips: The part of "走" should be written first, followed by the part of "己".

三、词语练习 Phrase Practice

1. 请填写包含指定汉字的词语。

Please fill in the words containing the given Chinese characters.

① 他每天晚上都_____锻炼身体。（跑）

② 她_____跳得非常好。（跳）

③ 过_____的时候要小心。（路）

④ 麦克每天早上七点_____。（起）

2. 用下列汉字组词。

Make out the words with the following characters.

跑 来 进 动 得 电 觉 起 去 路 这 运 视 话 步 马 边 那

四、综合练习 Comprehensive Practice

1. 选字填空。

Choose a character to fill in the blank.

A.

① 我家离学校不太_____。（远、运）

② 他_____到一个好工作。（找、我）

③ 我_____得汉语很有意思。（觉、学）

④ 你_____道玛丽的手机号码吗？（知、和）

B.

还　送　边　得　先

① 我们一起吃了饭，_____看了电影。

② 请大家_____听老师读一遍课文。

③ 学校后_____有一个小超市。

④ 爸爸_____给我一台电脑。

⑤ 孩子们玩_____很高兴。

2. 请写出与下列汉字意思相反或相对的汉字。

Please write down the characters which are opposite or corresponding to the following characters.

例 Example：大—小

出—　　　　远—　　　　前—　　　　快—

3. 把下列汉字拆分成部件。

Please split the following characters into parts.

例 Example：路 < 𧾷 < 夂
　　　　　　　　各 < 口

① 跑

② 这
③ 得
④ 谁
⑤ 请
⑥ 您
⑦ 想
⑧ 哪

五、课外任务 After-class Task

1. 用下列汉字写一个句子，比一比看谁写得对、写得长。

Please write a sentence using each given character, and compare to see who can write better and longer.

① 跑
② 送
④ 谢
⑤ 让

2. 找出已学过的所有包含下列意符的汉字，根据它们的意思填在该意符下的分类中，制成意符卡片。以后可不断扩充该意符包含的汉字。

Find all the Chinese characters that contain the following ideographic symbols and fill in the categories according to their meanings to make ideographic symbol cards. The characters contained under this classification can be continuously expanded later.

辶——行走(walk)；路程(journey)
行走类动作(action of walking)：_____
_____
与路程相关的性质和状态(properties related to journey)：_____
_____

与路程相关的事物(things related to journey)：_____

_____

其他(other)：_____

_____

讠——语言(language)；说话(speak)

话语类(utterance)：_____

_____

使用语言进行的动作或行为(action or movement related to speech)：_____

_____

与语言相关的性质特征(characteristics related to speech)：_____

_____

其他(other)：_____

_____

第十课 字的本义和引申义
Lesson Ten Original Meaing and Extended Meaning of Chinese Characters

一、汉字知识 Knowledge of Chinese Characters

(一) 区分形近的偏旁 Distinguishing the Different Components in Similar Forms

汉字中有些偏旁的形体比较近似,例如:
Some component forms of Chinese characters are similar to each other, such as:

氵(河)—冫(冷)　　衤(初)—礻(礼)
禾(和)—木(村)　　广(庆)—疒(病)
户(房)—尸(展)　　日(晴)—目(睛)

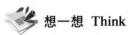 想一想 Think

> 你还能写出哪些形近的偏旁?
> Can you write any other components similar to each other?

在学习这些形近的偏旁时,要注意:
Learning those similar components of Chinese characters, we should notice:

1. 书写汉字时,仔细观察偏旁形体的细微差别。例如,衤—礻;日—目。

Observing carefully the slight difference between two similar components of Chinese characters when you are writing them. For example, 衤—礻;日—目.

2. 这些偏旁一般都有比较清楚的来源,以及所表示的意义或读音,注意学习掌握这些偏旁不同的来源以及它们不同的功能,是学习汉字的重要方法。

Generally, there are clear sources, indicated meanings and pronunciations of those components. It is an important way to learn Chinese characters through learning the different sources and different functions of those components in Chinese characters.

(二) 字的本义与引申义 The Original Meaning and Extended Meaning of Chinese Characters

很多汉字来源较早,在数千年前的甲骨文、金文中就已经出现并使用了。这些汉字在最早使用时的意义就是字的本义。例如,"水"在甲骨文中写作"𣱱",本义是"河流"或"水流"。本义一般可以在早期的字形中看出来。汉字在使用过程中,不断产生出新的字义,这些后来产生的新的字义就是后起义。例如,"日"的本义是"太阳",后来衍生出"白天""时间""每天"等意思。

Many Chinese characters have very early origins, which appeared and were used in Oracle Bone Script(Jiaguwen) and Bronze Script(Jinwen), dating back to thousands of years ago. The original meanings of those Chinese characters were the meaning it was firstly used. For example, "water" had been written as "𣱱" in Oracle Bone Script(Jiaguwen) with original meanings as "a river" or "a stream". Generally, original meanings of Chinese characters can be seen in their early forms. In the process of using these Chinese characters, many new meanings were produced which were called later meanings. For example, the original meaning of "日" was "the sun", then it was extended to mean "day" "time" "every day" and so on.

学习了解字的本义,可以帮助我们掌握现在所用字义的来源,更好地记忆、理解词语的意思。

Learning the original meaning of Chinese characters can help us grasp their sources in order to better memorize and understand their meanings.

二、汉字形音义 The Form, Pronunciation and Meaning of Chinese Characters

 目标汉字 Learning Objective

爱 有 友 开 事 站 欢 歌 次 半 出 正 对 病 地 坏
鸡 菜 茶 花

（一）爱 ài

词语：爱情（love）　友爱（friendship）

析字：金文写作"♥"，上面是"旡（jì）"，表示读音（由于古今音变，"旡"与"爱"的读音差距很大），下面是"心"，表示字义。小篆在下面添加"夂"写作"爱"，楷书变成"愛"，简化字把"心"和"夂"合在一起写成"友"，简写作"爱"。本义是"对人或事有很深的感情"。后来引申为"喜好""重视并加以保护"的意思，如"爱唱歌""爱护"。

Analysis of the character: It had been written as "♥" in Bronze Script (Jinwen), the "旡（jì）" on the top represented its pronunciation (due to the phonetic changes since ancient times, there is a big difference in pronunciations between "旡" and "爱") and "心" at the bottom was related to the character's meaning. Then it was written as "夂" in Seal Script (Xiaozhuan) by adding "爱" at the bottom and "愛" in Regular Script (Kaishu), later it was simplified as "爱" by combining the character "心" and "夂" together. The original meaning of the character was "having a lot of affection to someone or something". Later the meaning was extended to "love something" "attaching importance to and protection", such as "love singing" "cherish".

田字格书写 Writing in Tin Word Format：

一 爫 爫 爫 爫 哂 哂 哑 孚 旁 爱

爱	爱	爱	爱	爱	爱	爱	爱	爱	爱	爱	爱	爱	爱

书写提示：上面的"爫"不能写成"⺌"。

Writing tips："爫" on the top should not be written as "⺌".

（二）有 yǒu

词语：拥有（possess）　有关（relevant）

析字：金文写作"🖐"，上面的"🖐"是"又"（"手"的象形），既表意思也表读音，下面的"夕"（"肉"的象形）标指字义，合在一起表示"用手拿着肉"，就是"拥有""持有"的意思。楷书字形将"🖐"变成"ナ"，写作"有"。本义是"拥有"，后来引申为"具有""存在"等意思。

Analysis of the character：It had been written as "🖐" in Bronze Script (Jinwen), the "🖐" on the top is "又"(pictograph of "手"), referring to both the meaning and its pronunciation, the "夕" at the bottom (pictograph of "肉") was related to the character's meaning. When the two parts were put together to mean "carry the meat with a hand", the meanings of "own" and "possess" were produced. Then the character was written as "有" in Regular Script (Kaishu) by changing the upper part from "🖐" to "ナ". The original meaning of the character was "own" and later the meaning was extended to "have" "existence" and so on.

田字格书写 Writing in Tin Word Format：

一 ナ 𠂇 冇 有 有

有	有	有	有	有	有	有	有	有	有	有	有	有	有

书写提示：下面的"月"不能写成"目"。

Writing tips：The "月" at the bottom should not be written as "目".

（三）友 yǒu

词语：朋友(friend)　友谊(friendship)

析字：甲骨文写作"🖐"，金文写作"ɔɔ"，小篆写作"🖐"，隶书写作"友"，楷书写作"友"。早期的字形像两只手并列，表示"以手相助"，也就是"朋友"的意思，这是字的本义。后来引申出"有亲近关系""伙伴"等意思，如"友邦""友好""队友""校友"。

Analysis of the character：It had been written as "🖐" "ɔɔ" "🖐" "友" and "友" in Oracle Bone Script（Jiaguwen），Bronze Script（Jinwen），Seal Script（Xiaozhuan），Clerical Script（Lishu）and Regular Script（Kaishu）respectively. The early form was like the shape of two hands tied to mean "give sb. a hand", namely the meaning of "friends", which was the original meaning of the character. Later the meaning was extended to "having a close relationship" "partners" and so on, such as "friendly nation" "friendly" "teammate" "alumni".

田字格书写　Writing in Tin Word Format：

一ナ方友

友	友	友	友	友	友	友	友	友	友	友	友	友	友

书写提示：先写"ナ"，后写"又"。

Writing tips：The part of "ナ" should be written first, followed by the part of "又".

汉字锦囊 Idea Box of Chinese Characters

常用偏旁——又字旁

Commonly-used Components — Youzipang(又) Component

"又"是汉字很常见的偏旁。现代汉字中的"又",大多是从甲骨文、金文的"ㄟ"(即"手"的象形)变来的。其变化过程是:ㄟ 甲骨文 → ㄋ 金文 → ㄋ 小篆 → 又、ナ 楷书。

"又" is a very common component of Chinese characters. "又" in the modern Chinese characters is mostly derived from "ㄟ"(that is the pictograph of "手") in Oracle Bone Script(Jiaguwen) and Bronze Script(Jinwen). The changing process is:ㄟ Jiaguwen → ㄋ Jinwen → ㄋ Xiaozhuan → 又、ナ Kaishu.

以"又"或者"ナ"作为意符的汉字,字义一般与"手的部位"或"手的动作"有关。例如,"发""友""反""受""取""有""右"等。

Chinese characters, with "又" or "ナ" as the ideogram, have the meaning associated with "hand" or "hand movements". For example, the "发""友""受""取""有""右" and so on.

(四) 开 kāi

词语:开会(have a meeting) 开车(drive a car)

析字:战国时期写作"閛",两边是两扇门,相互对应,中间一横是门闩,下面是一双手,表示两手打开门闩,本义是"开门"。楷书写作"開",两只手和门闩合在一起写成了"开",简化字去掉外边的"門",直接简写成"开"。后来字义引申为"打开""开展""开始""开会"等意思。

Analysis of the character: During the Warring States Period, the character was written as "閛". In the character form, there are two doors at both sides, opposite to each other, the stroke 横(héng) in the middle of two doors was a latch. The hands below the stroke 横(héng) symbolized to open the latch, the original meaning of the character was "opening the door". Then it was written as "開" in Regular Script(Kaishu), two hands and the latch was combined together into the character "开". Later in simplified Chinese character, the outer part "門" was omitted and it was finally abbreviated as "开". The meaning was extended to "open" "conduct" "beginning" "having a meeting" and so on.

田字格书写 Writing in Tin Word Format：

书写提示：第三笔是"丿"，不能写成"｜"。
Writing tips：The third stroke of the character is "丿", not "｜".

（五）事 shì

词语：事情（thing） 故事（story）

析字：甲骨文写作"𠁧"，金文写作"𠁨"，像手（⺕）上拿着捕猎工具（丨、屮）的样子，意思是"做事"。小篆写作"事"，楷书写作"事"。本义是"从事""做事"，引申为名词时表示"事业""事情"。

Analysis of the character：It had been written as "𠁧" and "𠁨" in Oracle Bone script（Jiaguwen）and Bronze Script（Jinwen）respectively, liking holding a hunting tools（⺕、屮）on hand（屮）with the meaning of "working or doing things". Then it was written as "𠁨" and "事" in Seal Script（Xiaozhuan）and Regular Script（Kaishu）respectively. Instead of the original meanings as "do things" and "to do", it was used as a noun to mean "career" and "things".

田字格书写 Writing in Tin Word Format：

书写提示：第一笔横稍长，最后一笔是中间的竖钩。

Writing tips: The first stroke 横(héng) should be a bit longer, and the last stroke is 竖钩(shù gōu) in the middle.

(六) 站 zhàn

词语:站起来(stand up) 车站(station)

析字:左边的"立"表示字义,右边的"占(zhàn)"表示字音。本义是"站立""直立",后来引申出"停止不前"的意思,如"站住"。又引申为名词,表示"交通线上停车的地方",如"火车站""站台"。

Analysis of the character: The left side of the character "立" is related to its meaning and the right side "占(zhàn)" represents its pronunciation. The original meaning was "stand" and "up-right". Then it was extended to mean "stop forward", such as "stop". Later it was used as a noun with the meaning of "a place to park on the line of traffic", such as "the railway station" "platform".

田字格书写 Writing in Tin Word Format:

书写提示:右边的"占"不能写成"古"。

Writing tips: The "占" on the right side should not be written as "古".

(七) 欢 huān

词语:喜欢(like) 欢乐(joy)

析字:繁体字写作"歡",左边的"雚"表示字音,右边的"欠"表示字义。古代汉字中,"欠"字写作"𣥺",像人张口的样子。以"欠"为偏旁的汉字,一般都与张口的动作有关。"欢"表示欢乐,所以"张口"。简化字把左边的偏旁简化成"又","歡"变成了"欢"。字的本义是"喜悦""高兴",后来引申出"活跃""喜欢""欢迎"等意思。

Analysis of the character: It was written as "歡" in traditional Chinese character. The "雚" on the left side represented the pronunciation and the "欠" on the right side represented its meanings. In ancient Chinese character, the character "欠" was written as "🧍", just like a person opening mouth. The Chinese characters, with "欠" as the component, are generally associated with the action of opening the mouth. "欢" indicates joy, so people will "open the mouth". Then "歡" was simplified as "欢" by changing its component into "又". The original meanings of the character were "happy" and "joy", later the meanings were extended to "active" "like" "welcome" and so on.

田字格书写 Writing in Tin Word Format:

丁 又 ㄨ ㄨ′ 欢′ 欢

书写提示：右边的"欠"不能写成"夂"。

Writing tips: The "欠" on the right side should not be written as "夂".

(八) 歌 gē

词语：唱歌（sing） 歌曲（song）

析字：左边的"哥"表示读音，右边的"欠"表示字义。古代汉字中，"歌"最早写作"訶"（訶），秦汉时期变为"歌"（歌）。本义是"歌曲""唱歌"，后来又表示"可以唱的文词"，如"诗歌""民歌"。

Analysis of the character: The "哥" on the left side represents pronunciation and "欠" on the right side represents its meaning. In ancient Chinese character, the earliest writing of "歌" was "訶"（訶），then it was changed into "歌"（歌）in Qin and Han dynasties. The original meanings of the character were "songs" and "sing", and then it could be used to expressing "words that can be sung", such as "poetry" "folk songs".

田字格书写 Writing in Tin Word Format:

书写提示:"哥"上面的"可"与下面的"可"写法略有区别。(看一看区别在哪儿?)

Writing tips: There is a slight different in writing between the upper part "可" and the below part "可". (Take a look and find out what the difference is?)

(九) 次 cì

词语:一次(once)   多次(many times)

析字:金文写作"弓",小篆写作"弓",楷书写作"次",字的左边是"二",右边是"欠"("欠"有"缺少"的意思)。"二"和"欠"合在一起表示"次等""质量稍差""有欠缺"的意思。现代汉字把左边的"二"写为"冫",字形也就变为了"次"。字义后来引申出"第二""顺序"的意思,如"次要""次序",还可以作动量词,如"去过两次"。

Analysis of the character: It had been written as "弓" and "弓" in Bronze Script(Jinwen) and Seal Script(Xiaozhuan) respectively. Then it was written as "次" in Regular Script(Kaishu), the left part was the character "二" and the right part was the character "欠"("欠" has the meaning of "missing"). "二" and "欠" were put together to mean "inferior" "poorer quality" and "lacking". In modern Chinese character, the left part "二" is written as "冫", so the form of the character becomes "次". The meanings are extended to "the second" and "order", such as "secondary" "order". It can also be used as a momentum term, such as "have been to somewhere twice".

田字格书写 Writing in Tin Word Format：

丶 冫 冫 次 次 次

书写提示：左边的"冫"不能写成"氵",右边的"欠"不能写成"夂"。

Writing tips：The left part "冫" should not be written as "氵", the right part "欠" should not be written as "夂".

(十) 半 bàn

词语：一半(half) 半天(half day)

析字：古代汉字写作"半",上面的"八"表示分开的意思,下面是"牛"字,合在一起表示"把一个事物从中间分开"。小篆写作"半",楷书写作"半"。

Analysis of the character：It had been written as "半" in ancient Chinese character, the upper part "八" meant "to separate", the below part was "牛", the two parts compounded represented the meaning of "to separate a thing from the middle". It had been written as "半" and "半" in Seal Script(Xiaozhuan) and Regular Script(Kaishu) respectively.

田字格书写 Writing in Tin Word Format：

丶 丷 兰 半

书写提示：下面的横是两笔,不能写成三笔。

Writing tips：There are two strokes 横(héng) in the below part, don't wrongly write it into three strokes 横(héng).

（十一）出 chū

词语：出发（go）　出来（go out）

析字：甲骨文写作"𣥂"，像人的一只脚（𣥂）从住所（凵）走出去。小篆写作"出"，隶书写作"出"，楷书写作"出"，脚印变成了"屮"。"出"的本义是"从里面到外面"，后来引申出很多新的意思：① 表示"离开"，如"出发"；② 表示"发生"，如"出问题"；③ 表示"显现"，如"出面""出现""出席"等。

Analysis of the character: It had been written as "𣥂" in Oracle Bone Script (Jiaguwen), liking a man going out from his residence(凵) on foot(𣥂). Then it was written as "出" and "出" in Seal Script(Xiaozhuan) and Clerical Script (Lishu) respectively. Later the form was changed into "出" in Regular Script (Kaishu) with the part "屮" referring to the footprint. The original meaning of the character was "from inside to outside". Then a lot of new meanings were extended: ① "depart", such as "start off"; ② "happen", such as "have a problem"; ③ "show", such as "appear personally" "present" "attend" and so on.

田字格书写 Writing in Tin Word Format:

乚 凵 屮 出 出

书写提示：中间的"丨"是第三笔，不是最后一笔。

Writing tips: The "丨" in the middle is the third stroke, not the last.

（十二）正 zhèng

词语：正好（just）　正确（right）

析字：甲骨文写作"𤴓"，上面的"囗"表示城市，下面的"𣥂"表示脚步，合在一起表示"出发去征讨一个城市"，就是"出征"的意思。在金文中，表示城市的"囗"

变成了一个黑点"■",后来变成"——",小篆写成"𤴒",楷书写作"正"。"正"的字义从最早的"出征",后来演变出"正义""纠正""正确"等意思("出征打仗"的目的是为了"纠正"错误或祸乱,也为了突出显示"正义"或"正确")。

Analysis of the character: It had been written as "𤴒" in Oracle Bone Script (Jiaguwen), the upper part "囗" represented a city and the "止" in the below referred to steps. The two parts were put together to mean "to set out to conquer a city", namely "going out to battle". In Bronze Script (Jinwen), the "囗" that used to symbolize a city became a black spot "■" and a "——" later. Then the character was written as "𤴒" and "正" in Seal Script (Xiaozhuan) and Regular Script (Kaishu) respectively. Derived from the earliest meaning of "going out to battle", the meaning of the character developed into "justice" "correct" "right" and so on (the purpose of "going out to battle" was to "correct" the mistakes or troubles and to highlight the "justice" or "right" as well).

田字格书写 Writing in Tin Word Format:

一 丁 下 正 正

正	正	正	正	正	正	正	正	正	正	正	正	正	正	正

书写提示:上面的横稍短,下面的横稍长。

Writing tips: The stroke 横(héng) on the top is a bit shorter while the stroke 横(héng) at the bottom is a bit longer.

(十三) 对 duì

词语:对话(dialogue)　不对(false)

析字:金文写作"對",小篆写作"對",楷书写作"對"。简化字用"又"代替左边笔画很多的"丵"。字的本义是"对答""回答",在这个意思的基础上,引申出一系列新的意思:① 处于相反方向,如"对立""对面";② 正确,如"对错";③ 用作介词,如"他对我说";④ 用作量词,如"一对情侣"。

Analysis of the character: It had been written as "對" "對" and "對" in Bronze Script(Jinwen), Seal Script(Xiaozhuan) and Regular Script(Kaishu) respectively. Then the left part "丵" which contained a lot of strokes was simplified as "又". The original meanings of the character were "answer back" and "answer". On the basis of the meanings, a series of new meanings were extended: ① in the opposite direction to each other, such as "be opposite to" "the opposite side"; ② correct, such as "right and wrong"; ③ used as a preposition, such as "he said to me"; ④ used as a quantifier, such as "a couple of lovers".

田字格书写 Writing in Tin Word Format:

フ 又 又 对 对

对	对	对	对	对	对	对	对	对	对	对	对	对

书写提示:注意左边"又"的写法与"又"稍有不同。(想一想区别在哪儿？为什么？)

Writing tips: Pay attention to the slight difference between "又" and "又". (Think about where is the difference? Why?)

(十四) 病 bìng

词语:生病(sick)　看病(see a doctor)

析字:"疒"是形旁,标指字义,"丙(bǐng)"表示字的读音。在甲骨文中,"疒"写成"𤕫",像生病的人躺在床上,小篆写作"病",楷书写作"病"。本义是"生病",后来引申出"疾病""毛病"的意思。

Analysis of the character: The part "疒" refers to the character's meaning and the part "丙(bǐng)" represents its pronunciation. It had been written as "𤕫" in Oracle Bone Script(Jiaguwen), liking a sick man lay on the bed. Then it was written as "病" and "病" in Seal Script(Xiaozhuan) and Regular Script(Kaishu) respectively. The original meaning of the character was "sick", and later it was extended to mean "disease" and "fault".

田字格书写 Writing in Tin Word Format：

` 亠 广 广 疒 疒 疒 病 病 病 `

书写提示："疒"不能写成"广"。

Writing tips：The part "疒" should not be written as "广".

（十五）地 dì/de

词语：地方（place）　土地（land）

析字：左边的"土"表示字义，右边的"也"与字的读音有关〔由于古今音变，"也（yě）"与"地"的读音有差别〕。字的本义是"大地""土地"，后来汉语借用这个字作为状语和中心语之间的结构助词，如"慢慢地走过来"。

Analysis of the character：The left side "土" represents the character's meaning. The right side "也" is related to the character's pronunciation（due to the phonetic changes since ancient times, the pronunciation of "也（yě）" and "地" is different〕. The original meanings of the character were "earth" "land". Later it was borrowed to express as a structural particle between the adverbial and central language, for example "walk here slowly".

田字格书写 Writing in Tin Word Format：

` 一 十 土 圠 圳 地 `

书写提示：左边"土"的第三笔写作提，不能写成横。

Writing tips：The third stroke of the left side "土" is 提（tí）. It should not be written as 横（héng）.

（十六）坏 huài

词语：坏人（a bad person） 破坏（destroy）

析字：古代汉字写作"壞"，左边的"土"表示字义，右边的"裹（huái）"表示字音。本义是"用土制作的建筑物倒塌、毁坏"，后来引申出"不好""有害"的意思。简化字用笔画简单的"不"代替复杂难写的"𰀁"，写成"坏"。

Analysis of the character: It had been written as "壞" in ancient Chinese character, the left side "土" was related to the character's meaning and the right side "裹（huái）" represented its pronunciation. The original meaning of the character referred to "the collapsing and destroying of building made of soil", later the meaning was extended to "bad" and "harmful". In simplified character, the easily-writing form "不" replaces the hard-writing "𰀁" and the character turned into "坏".

田字格书写 Writing in Tin Word Format：

一 十 土 土 圡 坏 坏

坏	坏	坏	坏	坏	坏	坏	坏	坏	坏	坏	坏	坏

书写提示：左边"𰀁"的最后一笔是提，注意与横的区别。

Writing tips: The last stroke of the left side "𰀁" is 提（tí）, and pay attention to the difference with the stroke 横（héng）.

（十七）鸡 jī

词语：鸡蛋（egg） 母鸡（hen）

析字：甲骨文写作"𤿥"，像鸡的样子。小篆写作"鷄"，左边的"奚（xī）"表示字音，右边的"鳥"（鸟）标指字义（古代人们认为鸡和鸟一样属于禽类）。楷书写作"鷄"，简化字写作"鸡"。古今字义没有变化。

Analysis of the character: Firstly appeared in Oracle Bone Script (Jiaguwen), "𤿥" was liking a chicken. Then it was written as "鷄" in Seal Script (Xiaozhuan), the left part "奚（xī）" was related to its pronunciation and the right part "鳥"(鸟) referred to its meaning(the ancients thought that the chicken belonged to poultry as well as the birds). Later it was written as "鷄" in Regular Script(Kaishu) and simplified as "鸡". The meaning of the character has never changed since the ancient times.

田字格书写 Writing in Tin Word Format：

丿 又 又′ 又⁄ 又⁄ 鸡 鸡

鸡	鸡	鸡	鸡	鸡	鸡	鸡	鸡	鸡	鸡	鸡	鸡	鸡	鸡

书写提示：右边的"鸟"不能写成"乌"。

Writing tips：The "鸟" on the right should not be written as "乌".

(十八) 菜 cài

词语：白菜(Chinese cabbage)　菜单(menu)

析字：上面的"艹"标指字义，下面的"采(cǎi)"表示字音。本义是"蔬菜这样的植物"，后来也泛指"主食以外的食品"。

Analysis of the character：The upper part "艹", is associated with the character's meaning and the below part "采(cǎi)" represents its pronunciation. The original meaning of the character referred to "vegetables", later it also referred to "food other than the staple food" in general.

田字格书写 Writing in Tin Word Format：

一 ナ 艹 艹 艹 艾 芯 苎 苹 菜

菜	菜	菜	菜	菜	菜	菜	菜	菜	菜	菜	菜	菜	菜

书写提示：下面的"采"不能写成"朶"。

Writing tips：The below part "采" should not be written as "朶".

(十九) 茶 chá

词语：茶叶(tea) 喝茶(drink tea)

析字：本来写作"荼"，"艹"表示字义，"余(yú)"表示字音(由于古今音变，现在"余"与"荼"的读音不同)。后来，人们把"余"下面的"禾"写成"朩"，于是"荼"字变成了"茶"。从古至今，字义没有变化。

Analysis of the character：It was originally written as "荼", the part "艹" on the top was related to the character's meaning and the part "余(yú)" was associated with its pronunciation(due to the phonetic changes since ancient times, there is a difference between "余" and "荼"). Later, people changed the part "禾" under the "余" to be "朩", thus "荼" became "茶". The meaning of the character has never changed since the ancient times.

田字格书写 Writing in Tin Word Format：

一 十 艹 艹 犮 苁 苓 茶 茶

书写提示：下面的"朩"不能写成"小"。

Writing tips：The lower part "朩" should not be written as "小".

 汉字锦囊 Idea Box of Chinese Characters

常用偏旁——草字头(艹)

Commonly-used Components — Caozitou(艹) Component

"艹"称为"草字头"，是常用的汉字偏旁，出现在字的上面。以"艹"为偏旁的汉字，字义一般都与植物有关。"艹"来源于古代汉字"艸"，像小草的形状，楷书变成"艹"，现在简写为"艹"。

> Known as the "Caozitou", "艹" is a commonly-used Chinese character component, appearing on the top of the character. The Chinese characters, with "艹" as the component, are usually associated with plants. "艹" derives from the ancient Chinese character "屮", the form of which was liking a blade of grass, then it became "艹" in Regular Script(Kaishu) and now it is known as the "艹".

(二十) 花 huā

词语:红花(red flower)　花钱(spend money)

析字:形声字。上面的"艹"表示字义("艹"一般表示与花草、植物相关的意思),下面的"化(huà)"表示字音。本义是植物的"花朵",后来也借用来表示"用掉时间、金钱",如"花时间""花钱"。

Analysis of the character: It's a pictophonetic character. The upper part "艹" refers to the character's meaning("艹" is usually related to the meaning of flowers, grasses and some plants), the lower part "化(huà)" represents its pronunciation. The original meaning of the character was the "flower" of plants, later it has been borrowed to express the meaning of "spending time and money", such as "spend time" "spend money".

田字格书写 Writing in Tin Word Format:

一 十 艹 艹 艿 芢 花 花

花	花	花	花	花	花	花	花	花	花	花	花	花	花	花

书写提示:按照"艹、亻、匕"的顺序书写。

Writing tips: The writing order is "艹、亻、匕".

三、词语练习 Phrase Practice

1. 请读出下列汉字、词语、词组和句子。
Read the following characters, words, phrases and sentences.
① 事—什么事—有什么事—你来找我有什么事吗?
② 歌—唱歌—唱歌唱得很好听—她唱歌唱得很好听。
③ 次—一次—去过一次—去过一次北京—我去过一次北京。
④ 对—对留学生—对留学生很热情—中国同学对留学生很热情。

2. 用下列汉字组词。
Make out the words with the following characters.
朋　车　唱　友　开　欢　站　生　门　跑　事　喜　歌　步　情　对　面　爱　病

_____

_____

3. 辨字组词。
Please distinguish the following each group of characters and make words for each of them.

得_____　茶_____　还_____　读_____
很_____　菜_____　这_____　卖_____

四、综合练习 Comprehensive Practice

1. 选字填空。
Choose a character to fill in the blank.

A.

① 我想下午去_____行换钱。(很、银)

② 出门以后_____右走,大概五十米,就可以看到药店。(住、往)

③ _____问,去人民医院怎么走?(情、请)

④ 现在很多人喜欢上网,不喜欢看_____纸。(报、服)

B.

爱　站　病　正　药

① 你生_____了,要吃_____。

② 这件衣服不大不小_____好。

③ 他很_____他的女朋友。

④ 请你_____起来。

2. 为下列词语中指定汉字的意思选择合适的解释。

Please choose the appropriate explanation for specific characters in the following words.

① 开:开门;开始;开会;开车

(A. to hold;　B. to start;　C. to drive;　D. to open)

② 出:出来;出发;出生

(A. to be born;　B. to go out;　C. to set out)

③ 对:对不对;对面;对他说

(A. correct;　B. to, towards;　C. opposite)

五、课外任务 After-class Task

1. 请写出由下列汉字联想到的字,并说一说它们与指定字之间的联系。比一比看谁想到的字多。

Please write the associative characters with the following characters, and find out the links between the written characters and the following characters. Compare and see who can think of more characters.

① 菜

② 药

2. 请用下列每组给出的字写一个句子。

Please write sentences containing the following characters.

① 友　爱　茶
② 知　号　话
③ 每　睡　起

3. 请写出包含部件"口"的汉字,比一比看谁写得多。

Please write the characters with component "口", and compare and see who can write more.

第十一课 偏旁的变体
Lesson Eleven Variant of Character Components

一、汉字知识 Knowledge of Chinese Characters

(一) 简化字、繁体字与传承字 Simplified Chinese Characters, Traditional Chinese Characters and Inherited Chinese Characters

从商代甲骨文开始一直到楷书阶段,汉字的字形在不断发展变化。进入楷书阶段以后,汉字的形体就没有大的改变了,但是仍然还有很多汉字的笔画很多,不利于书写和学习。从古代开始,人们就开始有意识地对一些汉字进行简化,并在民间使用。1949年政府对一部分汉字进行了系统的整理和简化,1964年公布的《简化字总表》收录了2235个简化字。人们把这些字形笔画经过省简、有对应繁体、官方正式公布的汉字称为简化字,与简化字相对应的汉字叫作繁体字,在中国这些繁体字已经不再通行使用。

From the Oracle Bone Script(Jiaguwen) in Shang Dynasty to the stage of Regular Script(Kaishu), the form of Chinese characters has been developing and changing constantly. After entering the Regular Script(Kaishu) stage, the form of Chinese characters has not changed greatly, but there are still many Chinese characters with many strokes, which is not conducive to writing and learning. Since ancient times, people have consciously simplified some Chinese characters for folk use. In 1949, the government systematically sorted out and simplified some Chinese characters. The *General List of Simplified Chinese Characters* published in 1964 included 2235 simplified Chinese characters. People refer to the officially announced characters with reduced strokes and corresponding traditional Chinese characters as simplified characters, while the characters opposite simplified characters are called traditional Chinese characters. Of course, in China these traditional Chinese characters are no longer in common use.

实际上,在现代通行使用的汉字中,并不是所有的汉字都是简化字。大部分汉字从古至今字形都没有发生大的变化,如"山""石""土""火""人""牛""虫"等。这样的汉字叫作传承字。2013年公布的《通用规范汉字表》中共有8105个字,其中简化字2546个,传承字5559个,简化字占总数的31.4%,传承字占68.6%。

In fact, not all of the Chinese characters used in modern times are simplified characters. Most Chinese characters have not changed much since ancient times, such as "山""石""土""火""人""牛""虫" and so on. Such characters are called inherited Chinese characters. *The List of General Standard Chinese Characters* published in 2013 contains 8105 characters, of which 2546 are simplified and 5559 are inherited, accounting for 31.4 percent of the total and 68.6 percent of the inherited characters.

(二) 汉字的学习方法 The Learning Methods of Chinese Characters

这一课,我们来介绍如何区分同音字。

In this lesson, let's introduce how to distinguishing homophones.

读音相同,但形体、意义不同的一组字叫作同音字。例如,"感""赶""敢"都读"gǎn",是一组同音字。汉语普通话有1200多个音节,平均每个音节有5个多汉字。实际上有的音节没有同音字,有的音节有少量同音字,有的音节有大量同音字。同音字读起来读音一样,但是字形不同、所表示的语义不同,学习时应注意区分字形和意义。

A group of words that have the same pronunciation but different shape and meaning are called homophones. For example, "感""赶""敢" all read "gǎn", which is a group of homophones. Mandarin Chinese has more than 1200 syllables, with an average of more than 5 Chinese characters per syllable. In fact, some syllables have no homophones, some have a small number of homophones, and some have a large number of homophones. Homophone sounds the same, but forms and meanings are different, so we should pay attention to distinguishing forms and meanings when learning.

此外,同音字虽然不少,但是构成词语时,同音的词语不多,因此一般不会造成使用混淆。例如,"感""赶""敢"是同音字,但是"感"构成"感动""感谢"等词语,"赶"构成"赶快""赶上"等词语,"敢"构成"勇敢""敢于"等词语,这些词语并不同音。这说明学习汉字时,字和词语结合起来学习十分重要。

In addition, although many homophones, but the formation of words, homophone words are not many, so generally will not cause confusion in use. For example, "感" "赶" "敢" are homophones, but "感" constitutes words such as "感动" and "感谢", "赶" constitutes words such as "赶快" and "赶上", and "敢" constitutes words such as "勇敢" and "敢于", which are not homophones. This shows that the combination of words and characters is very important when learning Chinese characters.

(三) 偏旁的变体 Variant of the Chinese Character Components

汉字中有些偏旁出现在不同部位时,可能有不同的变化形式。例如,"王""土""工""立"等,出现在字的左边时,最下面的横都要写成提,变成"𤣩""𠂉""工""立"。

Some partial parts of Chinese characters may have different forms when they appear in different parts. For example, "王" "土" "工" "立" and so on, appear in the left side of the word, the bottom 横(héng) should be written as 提 (tí), become "𤣩" "𠂉" "工" "立".

此外,"人"在左边写成"亻","手"在左边写成"扌","心"在左边写成"忄","木"在左边写作"木"。这些也属于偏旁的变体。变体一般都是比较微小的字形改变,不会改变原偏旁的构形功能。偏旁产生细微改变的原因,一般都是为了书写方便或者使字形更加均衡美观。

In addition, the "人" is written on the left as "亻", "手" is written on the left as "扌", "心" is written on the left as "忄", the "木" is written on the left as

"木". These are also partial variants. Variants are generally relatively small glyph changes, do not change the original parts of the structure function. The reasons for the slight change of the parts are generally for the convenience of writing or to make the form more balanced and beautiful.

二、汉字形音义 The Form, Pronunciation and Meaning of Chinese Characters

 目标汉字 Learning Objective

果 桌 树 机 校 样 床 杯 答 笑 等 票 影 常 旁 假
考 习 哥 北

（一）果 guǒ

词语：水果（fruit）　苹果（apple）

析字：金文写作"🌳"，像树上长有果实。楷书写作"果"。本义是"果实"，引申可以表示抽象意义的"成果""结果"，后来也表示事情与原来预想的一样，"果然""如果"的意思由此而来。

Analysis of the character：It had been written as "🌳" in Bronze Script (Jinwen), like fruit growing on a tree. It had been written as "果" in Regular Script (Kaishu). The original meaning of the character was "fruit". It can be extended to express the abstract meanings of "achievement" "result", and then also means that things are as expected, which "as expected" and "if" meaning from.

田字格书写 Writing in Tin Word Format：

丨 冂 冂 曰 旦 早 果 果

果	果	果	果	果	果	果	果	果	果	果	果	果	果

书写提示：注意不能写成"呆"或"杲"。

Writing tips：Be careful not to write "呆" or "杲".

 汉字锦囊 Idea Box of Chinese Characters

> 常用偏旁——木字旁（木）
> Commonly-used Character Component — Muzipang（木）Component
>
> "木"是常用的汉字表义偏旁，在汉字中表示与树木、木头有关的意思。出现在字的左边比较多，写作"木"。
>
> The "木" is commonly used in Chinese characters to indicate the meaning of the characters, in Chinese characters, it means something to do with trees, wood. It appears more frequently on the left side of the word. It is written as "木".

（二）桌 zhuō

词语：课桌（desk） 桌子（table）

析字："桌"字结构很特别。下面的"木"表示字义（桌子由木头制成），字形中的"卓（zhuó）"（借用了"木"的一部分）表示字音。另外，"卓"也标指字义（"卓"字有"高"的意思，指桌面比地面高）。

Analysis of the character：The structure of the word "桌" is very special. The "木" below indicates the meaning of the character（the table is made of wood），and the "卓（zhuó）"（borrows some parts of the "木"）in the character indicates the pronunciation. In addition，"卓" also refers to the meaning of the word（"卓" has the meaning of "high"，which means the table is higher than the ground).

田字格书写 Writing in Tin Word Format：

丨 卜 广 卢 占 占 <u>点 卓 卓 桌</u>

桌	桌	桌	桌	桌	桌	桌	桌	桌	桌	桌	桌	桌	桌

书写提示：上面的"卢"不能写成"占"。

Writing tips：The "卢" above should not be written as "占".

（三）树 shù

词语：树林（forest） 一棵树（a tree）

析字：繁体字写作"樹"，左边的"木"表示字义，右边的"尌（shù）"表示读音。简化字把"尌"的左边简写成"又"，"樹"变成了"树"。字的本义是动词"栽树"，后来主要用来表示名词"树木"。

Analysis of the character：The traditional Chinese character form was "樹", "木" on the left represented its meaning, "尌（shù）" on the right represented its pronunciation. The modern Chinese has simplified the left part of "尌" into "又", so the character "樹" turned into "树". The original meaning of this character was a verb meant "planting trees", later it was mainly used as a noun to describe "trees".

田字格书写 Writing in Tin Word Format：

一 十 才 木 <u>杧 权 权 树 树</u>

树	树	树	树	树	树	树	树	树	树	树	树	树	树

书写提示：按照"木、又、寸"的顺序书写。

Writing tips：The writing order of the character is "木、又、寸".

（四）机 jī

词语：飞机（plane） 司机（driver）

析字：形声字。左边的"木"表示字义，右边的"几"表示读音。本义是"机器"（古代用木头制成，所以有"木"）。后来字义引申，用来表示"事物发生和变化的关键"，这就是"机会""时机"意思的来源。

Analysis of the character：It's a pictophonetic character. The left part "木" indicates the meaning of the character, and the right part "几" indicates the pronunciation. The original meaning was "machine"（ancient machines were made of wood, so there is "木"）. Later the meaning of the word extended, used to express "the key to the occurrence and change of things", this is the origin of the meaning of "chance" and "opportunity".

田字格书写 Writing in Tin Word Format：

一 十 才 木 朾 机

机 机 机 机 机 机 机 机 机 机 机 机 机 机 机 机

书写提示："几"不能写成"九"。

Writing tips：The "几" should not be written as "九".

（五）校 xiào/jiào

词语：学校（school） 校园（campus）

析字："木"表示字义，"交（jiāo）"标指字音（由于古今音变，"交"与"校"的读音稍有差异）。本义是"学校"。

Analysis of the character："木" indicates the meaning of the character, "交（jiāo）" indicates the pronunciation（due to the phonetic changes since ancient times, the pronunciation is slightly different between "交" and "校"）. The original meaning was "school".

田字格书写 Writing in Tin Word Format：

一 十 才 木 术 杧 栌 栌 柠 校

书写提示：右边的"交"不能写成"文"。

Writing tips：The "交" on the right side should not be written as "文".

(六) 样 yàng

词语：怎么样(how)　同样(same)

析字："木"表示字义，"羊"表示字音。繁体字写作"樣"。本义是"树上的一种果实"，后来被人们借用来作为"式样"的意思。

Analysis of the character：The "木" indicates the meaning of the character，"羊" indicates the pronunciation. It was written as "樣" in traditional Chinese character. The original meaning was "a kind of fruit on a tree"，later borrowed by people as the meaning of "pattern".

田字格书写 Writing in Tin Word Format：

一 十 才 木 术 杧 栏 栏 样

书写提示：右边的"羊"不能写成"羊"。

Writing tips：The "羊" on the right side should not be written as "羊".

(七) 床 chuáng

词语：起床(get up)　机床(machine tool)

析字：甲骨文写作"𠙴"，像竖起来的床。后来右边加上"木"，写成"牀"，楷书写作"牀"，再后来人们用"广"代替"爿"，字形简写作"床"。本义是"可以坐或躺的器具",后来也用作表示像床一样的东西或可以放置物品的架子,如"车床""河床""机床"等。

Analysis of the character: It had been written as "丬" in Oracle Bone Script (Jiaguwen), like an upturned bed. Later, it was written as "牀" with "木" added to the right, and it was written as "牀" in Regular Script (Kaishu). And then people used "广" instead of "丬", so it was written as "床" in simple form. The original meaning was a "sitting or lying instrument", later also used to refer to something like a bed or a frame on which things can be placed, such as a "lathe bed" "riverbed" "machine tool", etc.

田字格书写 Writing in Tin Word Format:

丶 一 广 广 庁 庄 床 床

书写提示:"广"不能写成"厂"。

Writing tips: The "广" should not be written as "厂".

(八) 杯 bēi

词语:茶杯(tea cup)　一杯水(a glass of water)

析字:"木"表示字义,"不(bù)"表示字音(由于古今音变,"不"与"杯"的读音有差异)。本义是"盛酒、水、茶等的器皿",后来也可以表示像杯子一样的东西,如"奖杯",现代汉语也用作量词,如"一杯茶"。

Analysis of the character: The "木" indicates the meaning of the character, "不(bù)" indicates the pronunciation(due to the phonetic changes since ancient times, the pronunciation is different between "不" and "杯"). The original meaning was "a vessel for holding wine, water, tea and so on". Then it can also express something like a cup, such as "a trophy". It is also used as a quantifier in modern Chinese, for example, "a cup of tea".

田字格书写 Writing in Tin Word Format:

一 十 才 木 木 术 杯 杯

书写提示:右边的"不"不能写成"木"。

Writing tips: The "不" on the right side should not be written as "木".

(九) 答 dá/dā

词语:回答(answer) 问答(questions and answers)

析字:上面的"⺮"和下面的"合"都表示字义,两个部分合在一起表示"用竹子补篱笆"。汉语中后来借用这个字来表示"回答"的意思。

Analysis of the character: Both the upper part "⺮" and the below part "合" are related to the meaning of the character, the two parts compounded represented the meaning of "patch the fence with bamboo". Later the character was often borrowed to express the meaning of "answer".

田字格书写 Writing in Tin Word Format:

丿 𠂉 𠂉 𠂉 ⺮ 竺 竺 竺 笌 笞 答 答

书写提示:上面的"⺮"不能写成"kk"。

Writing tips: The "⺮" on the top should not be written as "kk".

(十) 笑 xiào

词语:笑脸(smile) 欢笑(laugh)

析字:古代汉字写作"𥬇",上面是"艹",下面是"犬",构形义不明确。后来小篆写作"𥬇",上面是"⺮",下面是"夭(yāo)"。有人说,风吹使得竹子舞动起来,就像人笑起来的样子,所以写成"笑"。

Analysis of the character: It was written as "𥫗" in ancient Chinese character. The upper part is "艹", the lower part is "犬", and the configurational meaning is not clear. It was written as "笑" in Seal Script (Xiaozhuan). The upper part is "⺮", the lower part is "夭(yāo)". Some people say that when the wind blows, it makes the bamboos dance just like when people laugh, so it was written as "笑".

田字格书写 Writing in Tin Word Format:

丿 𠂉 𠂉 𠂉 𥫗 𥫗 竺 竺 笑 笑

笑	笑	笑	笑	笑	笑	笑	笑	笑	笑	笑	笑	笑	笑	笑

书写提示:下面的"夭"不能写成"天"。

Writing tips: The lower part "夭" should not be written as "天".

(十一) 等 děng

词语:等待(wait)　等级(rank)

析字:"⺮"表示字义,下面的"寺(sì)"表示字音(由于古今音变,"寺"与"等"的读音差别很大)。字的本义是"竹简(中国古代用竹子书写的书)长度相同"。后来引申为"同样"的意思,如"同等",又引申为"等级"的意思,后来也借用来表示"等候"的意思。

Analysis of the character: The "⺮" indicates the meaning of the character, the lower part "寺(sì)" indicates the pronunciation(due to the phonetic changes since ancient times, the pronunciation of the "寺" and "等" is very different). The original meaning of the character was that "bamboo slips(ancient Chinese books written in bamboo) are of the same length". Then it had been extended to "the same", for example, "of the same class". It also extended to the meaning of "rank". Then it was also borrowed to mean "wait".

田字格书写 Writing in Tin Word Format：

丿 ㇒ ⺁ ⺮ ⺮ 竺 笃 笃 笋 等 等

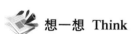

书写提示：按照"⺮、土、寸"的顺序书写。

Writing tips：The writing order is "⺮、土、寸".

 汉字锦囊 Idea Box of Chinese Characters

常用偏旁——竹字头（⺮）

Commonly-used Component — Zhuzitou（⺮）Component

"竹字头"（⺮）是常用偏旁，可以构成很多字，如"笔""等""笑""策""第""筐"等。"⺮"的特点很明显：① 作为意符，一般都与字义有某种联系；② 它的位置都出现在字的上面。

"Zhuzitou"（⺮）is commonly used and can form a lot of characters, such as "笔""等""笑""策""第""筐" and so on. The characteristics of "⺮" are very obvious：① As ideographic symbols, they are generally related to the meaning of the characters；② It always appears above the characters.

想一想 Think

汉字中还有什么偏旁与"⺮"的特点类似？

What other components of Chinese characters have similar characteristics with "⺮"?

（十二）票 piào

词语：车票（ticket） 机票（air ticket）

析字：小篆写作"䙆"，下面的"火"是"火"，上面的"𰼜"表示用双手抬起东西。楷书写作"票"。本义是"火焰飘升起来"，后来意思发生了一系列引申变化：火焰飞升→迅速→迅速下达的政府文书→作为凭证的纸片，如"车票""电影票"。

Analysis of the character：It had been written as "䙆" in Seal Script (Xiaozhuan)，the underneath "火" is "火"，the upside "𰼜" means to lift something with both hands. And it has been written as "票" in Regular Script (Kaishu). The original meaning was "flames floating up". Later，its meaning has undergone a series of extended changes：flames fly→quickly→government documents sent swiftly→scraps of paper as a voucher，for example，"train tickets""movie tickets".

田字格书写 Writing in Tin Word Format：

一 厂 冖 丙 西 西 要 栗 票 票

书写提示：上面的"覀"不可写成"西"。

Writing tips：The upper "覀" should not be written as "西".

（十三）影 yǐng

词语：电影（movie） 影响（influence）

析字：左边的"景（jǐng）"表示字音（由于古今音变，"景"与"影"的读音稍有差异），右边的"彡（shān）"表示字义。本义是"影子"，后来引申出"照片""画像"等意思，如"摄影""合影""电影"。

Analysis of the character：The left part "景（jǐng）" indicates the pronunciation (due to the phonetic changes since ancient times，the pronunciation is slightly different between "景" and "影")，the right part "彡（shān）" indicates the meaning of the character. The original meaning was the "shadow"，and then extended to the meanings of "photos" and "portraits"，such as "photography" "group photos" and "movies".

田字格书写 Writing in Tin Word Format：

书写提示：右边的"彡"不能写成"氵"。

Writing tips：The "彡" on the right side should not be written as "氵".

（十四）常 cháng

词语：经常（regular） 日常（daily）

析字：上面的"尚（shàng）"表示读音（由于古今音变，"尚"与"常"的读音稍有差异），下面的"巾（jīn）"表示字义。本义是指"裙子"。因为"裙子"是日常所用物品，所以引申出"平常""日常"的意思，又引申为"一般""经常"的意思。现代汉语早已不再使用原来"裙子"的本义。

Analysis of the character：The upper "尚（shàng）" indicates the pronunciation (due to the phonetic changes since ancient times，the pronunciation is slightly different between "尚" and "常")，the lower part "巾（jīn）" indicates the meaning of the character. The original meaning referred to the "skirt" and because the "skirt" is the daily use of goods，so it extended the meanings as "ordinary" "daily"，and then extended the meanings as "general" and "regular". The original meaning as "skirt" is no longer used in modern Chinese.

田字格书写 Writing in Tin Word Format：

书写提示：上面的"⺌"不可写成"⺍"。

Writing tips：The upper "⺌" should not be written as "⺍".

(十五) 旁 páng

词语：旁边(side)　旁听(audit)

析字：甲骨文写作"𠂇"，上面是"凡"，下面是"方"（表示读音）。小篆写作"𣂺"，后来楷书写成"旁"。现代汉语中，字义是"左右两边"或"其他"的意思。

Analysis of the character: It had been written as "𠂇" in Oracle Bone Script (Jiaguwen), the top is "凡", the bottom is "方"(indicating the pronunciation). It was written as "𣂺" "旁" in Seal Script(Xiaozhuan) and Regular Script (Kaishu). In modern Chinese, it means "side" or "something else".

田字格书写 Writing in Tin Word Format：

丶 亠 亡 冇 冇 产 产 旁 旁

旁	旁	旁	旁	旁	旁	旁	旁	旁	旁	旁	旁	旁	旁	旁

书写提示：上面的"产"不能写成"立"。

Writing tips: The upper "产" should not be written as "立".

(十六) 假 jiǎ/jià

词语：假如(if)　请假(ask for leave)

析字：形声字。左边的"亻"表示字义，右边的"叚(jiǎ)"表示字音。本义是"不真实"，后来引申出"借用""利用"的意思，再后来引申出"假日""假期"的意思。

Analysis of the character: It is a pictophonetic character. The left side "亻" is related to the character's meaning and the right side "叚(jiǎ)" represents its pronunciation. The original meaning of the character was "not real", later it was extended to mean "borrow" "make use of", and then the meanings of "vacation" and "holiday" were extended.

田字格书写 Writing in Tin Word Format：

书写提示：右边的"叚"不能写成"段"。

Writing tips：The right side "叚" should not be written as "段".

（十七）考 kǎo

词语：考试（test）　考验（ordeal）

析字：甲骨文写作"𦥑"（像拄着拐杖的老人）。后来小篆写作"𦒽"，楷书写作"考"。本义是"岁数大"，"考试"的意思是后来引申出来的。

Analysis of the character：It had been written as "𦥑"(like an old man with a cane)，"𦒽" and "考" in Oracle Bone Script(Jiaguwen)，Seal Script (Xiaozhuan) and Regular Script(Kaishu) respectively. The original meaning was "old age"，then extended to the meaning of "test".

田字格书写 Writing in Tin Word Format：

书写提示：下面的"丂"不能写成"万"。

Writing tips：The "丂" in the lower should not be written as "万".

（十八）习 xí

词语：学习（study）　练习（practice）　习惯（habit）

析字：古代汉字写作"習"，上面的"羽[羽（yǔ）]"是鸟的羽毛，下面的"日"是"日"，合在一起本义是"小鸟在阳光下学习飞翔"。小篆写作"習"，楷书写作"習"，简化字只保留上面"羽"的一半,简写为"习"。后来在"小鸟在阳光下学习飞翔"这个本义的基础上,引申出"练习""习惯"等意思。

Analysis of the character: It had been written as "🦅" in ancient Chinese character. The "🦅[羽(yǔ)]" on the top meant the bird's feather, "☉" at the bottom was "日(sun)". The two components were combined together to express the meaning of "a bird flying beneath the sun". It also had been written as "習" in Seal Script(Xiaozhuan), "習" in Regular Script(Kaishu), "羽" on the top was abbreviated by the simplified character to "习". Later, the original meaning of "a bird flying beneath the sun" had generated meanings like "practice" "habit".

田字格书写 Writing in Tin Word Format:

书写提示:里面是点、提,不能写成"二"。

Writing tips: The strokes inside are 点(diǎn)、提(tí), and cannot be written as "二".

(十九) 哥 gē

词语:哥哥(elder brother) 大哥(eldest brother)

析字:下面是"可","可"表示字的读音(古代的"可"与"哥"的读音相同)。本义是"唱歌",从唐朝开始被借用来表示"哥哥"的意思。

Analysis of the character: The bottom is "可". The "可" indicates the pronunciation (the pronunciation of "可" is the same as "哥" in ancient times). The original meaning was "singing". From Tang Dynasty, it had been borrowed to indicate "elder brother".

田字格书写 Writing in Tin Word Format：

一一一一一一一一一一
哥哥哥哥哥哥哥哥哥哥哥哥哥哥哥

书写提示：上面的"可"与下面的"可"稍有不同。

Writing tips：The upper "可" is slightly different from "可".

(二十) 北 běi

词语：北京（Beijing）　北方（north）

析字：古代汉字写作"㇇㇇"，像两个人背对背站立，本义是"违反""违背"，假借来表示北方的意思。小篆写作"北"，楷书写作"北"。

Analysis of the character：The ancient Chinese character "㇇㇇" was like two people standing back-to-back, the original meaning was "violate" "disobey", it was often borrowed to express the meaning of north direction. It had been written as "北" and "北" in Seal Script(Xiaozhuan) and Regular Script(Kaishu) respectively.

田字格书写 Writing in Tin Word Format：

丨 ㇇ 丨 北 北
北北北北北北北北北北北北北北北

书写提示：右边的"匕"不能写成"七"。

Writing tips：The "匕" in the right side should not be written as "七".

三、词语练习 Phrase Practice

1. 请填写包含指定汉字的词语。

Please fill in the words containing the given Chinese characters.

① 超市的_____又好吃又便宜。（果）

② 我买了一个新_____。（机）

③ 我喜欢看中国_____。（影）

④ 这件衣服很好看，_____有点儿贵。（但）

2. 读出下列汉字、词语、词组和句子。

Read the following Chinese characters, words, phrases and sentences.

① 样——一样——一样高—弟弟和哥哥一样高。

② 笑—笑得很开心—她笑得很开心。

③ 旁—旁边—学校旁边—学校旁边有个超市。

④ 票—车票—我已经买了今晚的车票。

3. 辨字组词。

Please distinguish the following each group of characters and make words for each of them.

常_____　　工_____　　歌_____

长_____　　公_____　　哥_____

四、综合练习 Comprehensive Practice

1. 选字填空。

Choose a character to fill in the blank.

票　等　笔　考

① 我＿＿＿＿＿了他很长时间。

② 这次我＿＿＿＿＿得不太好。

③ 上车前请买＿＿＿＿＿。

④ 我要买一支＿＿＿＿＿和一个本子。

2. 请改正下列句子里的错别字。

Please correct the wrong characters in the following sentences.

① 我爱中国文化。

② 她请朋友去家里喝茶。

③ 外面有点儿泠。

④ 这此词语要常常练匀。

⑤ 下个星期就要老试了。

五、课外任务 After-class Task

1. 根据给出的拼音,请写出每个拼音包含的汉字,比一比看谁写得多(声调可以不同)。

Please write out the characters with the following pinyin and see who can write the most(the tone can be different).

① shi　② xi　③ yi　④ ji　⑤ ge

2. 用每组给定的三个汉字写一个句子。

Please write a sentence using the three given Chinese characters in each group.

① 桌　椅　床

② 公　校　离

③ 哥　考　明

④ 果　店　校

⑤ 树　北　房

第十二课 常用的意符
Lesson Twelve Commonly-used Ideographic Symbols

一、汉字知识 Knowledge of Chinese Characters

汉字系统中使用的意符总数并不算很多。在现代汉字中共含有意符200多个。汉字中最常用的、构字数最多的10个意符分别是"氵""艹""口""扌""木""钅""亻""虫""讠""土"。常用意符的特点是：第一，常用意符都有很早的来源，一般都是由独体字变来的。第二，常用意符基本上都与自然界、动物、人体及人的行为有关系。例如，"氵""艹""木""钅""土"与自然界有关；"口""亻"与人体有关；"虫"与动物有关；"讠""扌"与人的行为有关。

The total number of ideographic symbols used in the Chinese character system is not very large. There are more than 200 ideographic symbols in modern Chinese characters. The 10 most commonly-used and most constructed ideographic symbols in Chinese characters are respectively "氵""艹""口""扌""木""钅""亻""虫""讠""土". The characteristics of the commonly-used ideographic symbols are: Firstly, they have a very early source, which is generally changed from a single character. Secondly, they are basically related to nature, animals, human body and human behavior. For example, "氵""艹""木""钅""土" are related to nature; "口""亻" are related to the human body; "虫" is related to animals; "讠""扌" are related to human behavior.

了解常用意符的意思、意符与字义的联系，掌握意符构字的规律，对于学习汉字很有帮助。

It is very helpful for learning Chinese characters to understand the meaning of commonly-used ideographic symbols, the relationship between ideographic symbols and the meaning of characters, and to master the rules of constructing the characters of ideographic symbols.

二、汉字形音义 The Form, Pronunciation and Meaning of Chinese Characters

 目标汉字 Learning Objective

```
坐 块 在 场 钱 差 错 汉 没 洗 星 渴 汽 点 热 重
喜 岁 外 名
```

(一) 坐 zuò

词语：坐下(sit down)　坐车(by car)

析字：字形本来像两个人坐在土上，后来，又引申出搭乘交通工具的意思，如"坐飞机""坐汽车"。

Analysis of the character: It was like two people sitting on the earth. Later, the meaning of taking a vehicle was extended, for example, "take a plane" "by car".

田字格书写 Writing in Tin Word Format：

丿 人 凢 从 쓰 坐 坐

坐	坐	坐	坐	坐	坐	坐	坐	坐	坐	坐	坐	坐	坐

书写提示：上面的"人"，最后一笔不能写成捺。

Writing tips: The last stroke of "人" should not be written as 捺(nù).

(二) 块 kuài

词语:一块钱(one dollar)　两块糖(two lumps of sugar)

析字:繁体字写作"塊",左边的"土"表示意思,右边的"鬼"表示读音(由于古今音变,"鬼"与"块"的读音有了差别),本义是"土块"。用作量词是后来引申出来的用法。

Analysis of the character: The traditional Chinese character form of this character is written as "塊". The "土" on the left indicates the meaning, and the "鬼" on the right indicates the pronunciation (due to the phonetic changes since ancient times, the pronunciation of the phonetic part "鬼" is different from the "块"). The original meaning was "soil block", and later extended to be used as a quantifier.

田字格书写 Writing in Tin Word Format:

一 十 土 扫 扫 护 块 块

书写提示:右边是"夬",不能写成"尺"。

Writing tips: The "夬" on the right side should not be written as "尺".

(三) 在 zài

词语:在家(at home)　在看书(reading a book)

析字:古代汉字写作"扗",楷书写作"在"。左边的"才"表示读音,右边的"土"表示意思。本义是"存在"。

Analysis of the character: It had been written as "扗" and "在" in ancient Chinese character and the Regular Script(Kaishu) respectively. The "土" on the right indicates the meaning, and the "才" on the left indicates the pronunciation. The original meaning was "existence".

田字格书写 Writing in Tin Word Format：

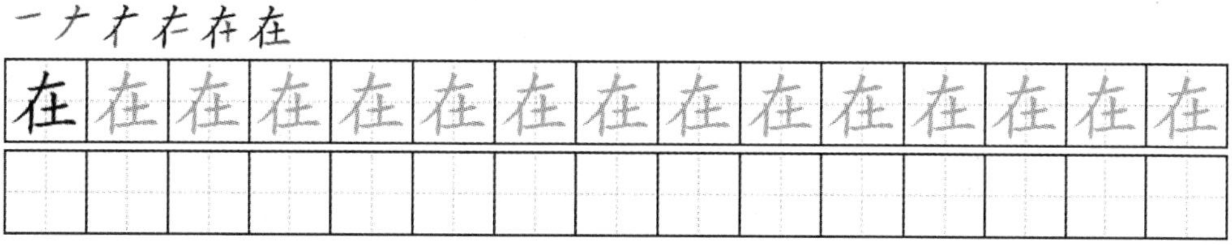

书写提示："才"不能写成"ナ"。

Writing tips：The "才" should not be written as "ナ".

（四）场 chǎng

词语：体育场(stadium)　剧场(theater)

析字：左边的"土"与字义有关，右边的"𠃓"表示读音。本义是"古代祭神的平地"，后来引申指"活动的场地"。

Analysis of the character：The "土" on the left indicates the meaning. The "𠃓" on the right indicates the pronunciation. The original meaning was "the flat for the ancient worship of the gods", later extended to refer to "the place for activity".

田字格书写 Writing in Tin Word Format：

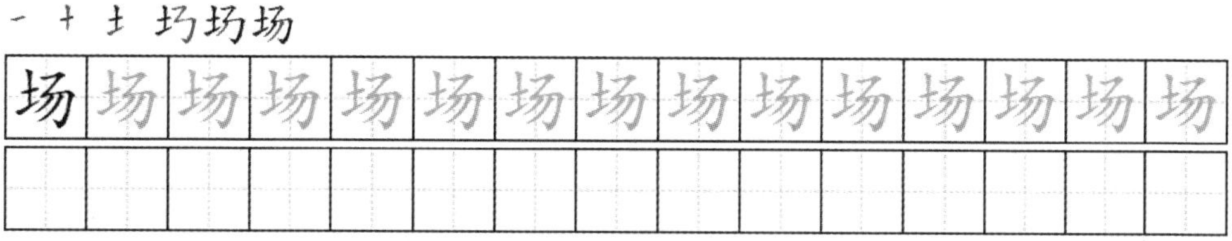

书写提示：右边的"𠃓"不能写成"勿"或"易"。

Writing tips：The "𠃓" on the right side should not be written as "勿" or "易".

汉字锦囊 Idea Box of Chinese Characters

常用偏旁——土字旁(土)

Commonly-used Component — Tuzipang(土) Component

"土"是常用的汉字表义偏旁，常表示与泥土、土地有关的字义。出现在字的左边时,要写成"土"。

"土" is a commonly-used character component which indicates the meaning, means something related to soil and land in Chinese characters. It should be written as "土" when it appears on the left side in a Chinese character.

(五) 钱 qián

词语:多少钱(how much)　金钱(money)

析字:左边的"钅"表示字义,右边的"戋"表示字音。古代的字义是"一种金属做的农具",后来用来指"货币""费用",如"坐车的钱""吃饭的钱"。

Analysis of the character: The "钅" on the left indicates the meaning. The "戋" on the right indicates the pronunciation. The ancient meaning of the word is "a kind of metal farm tool", later used to refer to "money" "expenses", such as "expenses of travel" "expenses of food".

田字格书写　Writing in Tin Word Format:

丿 𠂉 𠂉 钅 钅 钅 钅 钱 钱 钱

钱	钱	钱	钱	钱	钱	钱	钱	钱	钱	钱	钱	钱	钱

书写提示:右边的"戋"不能写成"戈"。

Writing tips: The "戋" on the right side should not be written as "戈".

(六) 差 chā/chà/chāi

词语:差别(distinction)　差不多(almost)　出差(on business trip)

析字:小篆写作"䇎",上面的部分表示读音,下面的"𠂇"[左(zuǒ)]表示用手帮助别人做事。楷书写作"差"。字的本义是"帮助""辅助",后来引申出"出差""差遣"的意思,再后来引申出"差别"的意思。

Analysis of the character: It had been written as "䍮" in Seal Script (Xiaozhuan), the upper part was related to this character's pronunciation, the below part "𠂇"[左(zuǒ)] expressed the meaning of helping others do things with hands. It had been written as "差" in Regular Script (Kaishu) with its original meanings of "help" "assist", later the meanings were extended to "go on business trip" "send sb. on an errand", and then the meaning of "distinction" was extended.

田字格书写 Writing in Tin Word Format:

丶 ⺍ ⺌ 䒑 兰 䒑 羊 差 差 差

差	差	差	差	差	差	差	差	差	差	差	差	差

书写提示：下面的"工"不能写成"土"。

Writing tips: The "工" in the lower part should not be written as "土".

（七）错 cuò

词语：错误(mistake)　不错(not bad)

析字：左边的"钅"表示字义，右边的"昔"表示字音。本义是"用金属填涂在文字或花纹的凹槽中"，后来引申出"交错""错开""不正确"的意思。

Analysis of the character: The "钅" on the left indicates the meaning. The "昔" on the right indicates the pronunciation. The original meaning was "to fill with metal in the text or pattern of the groove". Later extended to the meanings as "staggered" "stagger" "incorrect".

田字格书写 Writing in Tin Word Format:

丿 𠂉 𠂋 钅 钅 钅 钅 铅 锆 错 错 错

错	错	错	错	错	错	错	错	错	错	错	错	错

书写提示：右边的"昔"不能写成"昔"。

Writing tips：The "昔" on the right side should not be written as "昔".

（八）汉 hàn

词语：汉语（Chinese language） 汉字（Chinese characters）

析字：繁体字写作"漢"，左边的"氵"表示字义，右边的"堇"表示字音。汉字简化写作"汉"。本义是"河流的名字——汉水"，汉朝也由此得名。后来，由朝代名又引申出"汉族"的意思。

Analysis of the character：The traditional Chinese character form of this character was written as "漢". The "氵" on the left indicated the meaning. The "堇" on the right indicated the pronunciation. It had been simplified and written as "汉". The original meaning was "the name of the river — the Han River", and that's why the Han Dynasty got its name. Later，the meaning of the "Han nationality" was derived from the name of the dynasty.

田字格书写 Writing in Tin Word Format：

丶 ㇇ 氵 汋 汉

汉	汉	汉	汉	汉	汉	汉	汉	汉	汉	汉	汉	汉	汉

书写提示：右边的"又"不能写成"文"。

Writing tips：The "又" on the right side should not be written as "文".

（九）没 méi/mò

词语：没有（no） 没关系（never mind）

析字：古代汉字写作"𣴬"，右上的"@"像水的漩涡，本义是"沉没在水中"，所以左边有"氵"，后来楷书字形变为"没"，由此引申出作为否定副词的用法。

Analysis of the character：It had been written as "𣴬" in ancient Chinese character，the "@" on the right like the whirlpool of water. The original meaning was "sunk in the water"，so the left side had "氵"，and then it had been written as "殳" in Regular Script(Kaishu). This extended out as the use of the negative adverb.

田字格书写 Writing in Tin Word Format：

丶 丶 氵 氵 氻 没 没

书写提示："殳"不能写成"凸"。

Writing tips：The "殳" should not be written as "凸".

(十) 洗 xǐ

词语：洗脸(wash the face)　洗衣服(wash the clothes)

析字："氵"与字义有关，"先"与字音有关(由于古今音变，"先"与"洗"的读音稍有差异)。

Analysis of the character："氵" indicates the meaning of the character, "先" indicates the pronunciation(due to the phonetic changes since ancient times, the pronunciation is slightly different between "先" and "洗").

田字格书写 Writing in Tin Word Format：

丶 丶 氵 氵 汫 泎 洴 涉 洗

书写提示："先"不能写成"失"。

Writing tips：The "先" should not be written as "失".

汉字锦囊 Idea Box of Chinese Characters

常用偏旁——三点水(氵)

Commonly-used Component — Sandianshui(氵) Component

"氵"是常见的汉字表义偏旁,一般出现在字的左侧,表示水流、液体等有关的意思。

The "氵" is a common character component to represent the meaning of character, and it usually appears on the left side of the character. It refers to water flow, liquid, etc.

(十一) 星 xīng

词语:星期(weak)　星星(star)　歌星(singer)

析字:古代汉字是形声字,写作"曐",上面3个"日"表示天上的很多星星,下面的"生(shēng)"表示字音(由于古今音变,现在"生"和"星"的读音有差异)。秦代小篆写作"曐",后来楷书简写成"星"(省去两个"日")。字的本义是"天上的星星"。古人用7个最重要的天体名称(太阳、月亮、金星、木星、水星、火星、土星)来记录连续的7天时间,即星期日到星期六,所以叫作"星期"。

Analysis of the character: In ancient Chinese character, this character was a pictophonetic one, and was written as "曐". The 3 "日" on the top meant the countless stars in the sky, "生(shēng)" at the bottom represented its pronunciation(due to the phonetic changes since ancient times, there are some differences in pronunciation between "生" and "星"). It also had been written as "曐" in Seal Script(Xiaozhuan) from Qin Dynasty, then it was simplified as "星"(two "日" were omitted) in Regular Script(Kaishu). The original meaning of this character was "the stars in the sky". Ancient Chinese counted the consecutive seven days with the most important 7 planets(Sun, Moon, Venus, Jupiter, Mercury, Mars, Saturn), from Sunday to Saturday, so that the consecutive 7 days were named as "week".

田字格书写 Writing in Tian Word Format：

丶 丨 冂 曰 日 尸 甲 毘 星 星

星	星	星	星	星	星	星	星	星	星	星	星	星	星

书写提示：下面的"生"不能写成"主"。

Writing tips：The "生" at the bottom should not be written as "主".

(十二) 渴 kě

词语：口渴（thirsty）　渴望（yearn for）

析字：形声字。左边的"氵"表示字义，右边的"曷（hé）"表示读音。本义是"水干""没有水"，后来引申出"口干""想喝水"的意思。

Analysis of the character：It's a pictophonetic character. The left side "氵" is related to the meaning of the character and the right side "曷（hé）" represents its pronunciation. The original meaning of the character was "water-drying", later it was extended to mean "thirsty" "want to drink water".

田字格书写 Writing in Tian Word Format：

丶 冫 氵 沪 沪 沪 沪 渴 渴 渴 渴

渴	渴	渴	渴	渴	渴	渴	渴	渴	渴	渴	渴	渴

书写提示：右边的"曷"按照"日、勹、人、乚"的顺序书写。

Writing tips：The writing order of the right "曷" is "日、勹、人、乚".

(十三) 汽 qì

词语：汽车（car）　水汽（water vapor）

析字："氵"与字义有关（"汽"特指水或其他液体受热变成的气体），"气"既与字音有关，也与字义有关。

Analysis of the character: "氵" indicates the meaning of the character("汽" especially refers to the gas of other liquid which is heated), "气" indicates the pronunciation and meaning.

田字格书写 Writing in Tin Word Format:

书写提示:右边的"气"不能写成"乞"。
Writing tips: The "气" on the right side should not be written as "乞".

(十四) 点 diǎn

词语:地点(place)　十点(ten o'clock)

析字:繁体字写作"點",左边的"黑"表示字义,右边的"占"表示字音。简化字省去了"黑"的上半部分,简写成"点"。本义是"人脸上的黑色斑点",后来引申出"细小的东西""地方""部分""时间"等意思,可以用作动词、名词、量词。

Analysis of the character: The traditional Chinese character was written as "點". The "黑" on the left indicated the meaning, the "占" on the right indicated the pronunciation. The simplified Chinese characters omitted the upper part of "黑" and was abbreviated as "点". The original meaning was "a black spot on a person's face", later extended to "little thing" "place" "part" "time" and other meanings, and it can be used as a verb, noun, quantifier.

田字格书写 Writing in Tin Word Format:

书写提示:上面的"占"不能写成"古"。

Writing tips：The upper "占" should not be written as "古".

（十五）热 rè

词语：热水（hot water）　热情（enthusiasm）

析字：繁体字写作"熱"，上面的部分表示读音，下面的"灬"（火）表示字义，本义是"温度高"。小篆写作"爇"，楷书写作"熱"，简化字写作"热"。

Analysis of the character：The traditional Chinese character was written as "熱". The upper part indicated the pronunciation，the under "灬"（火）indicated the meaning. The original meaning was "high temperature". It had been written as "爇" "熱" and "热" in Seal Script（Xiaozhuan），Regular Script（Kaishu）and simplified Chinese characters respectively.

田字格书写 Writing in Tin Word Format：

一 十 扌 扌 执 执 执 热 热 热

书写提示：右上的"丸"不能写成"九"。

Writing tips：The upper "丸" on the right side should not be written as "九".

（十六）重 zhòng/chóng

词语：重要（important）　重量（weight）　重复（repeat）

析字：古代汉字写作"𡔷"，像人背着沉重的口袋，表示"沉重"的意思。秦代隶书写成"重"，人形与口袋的形状合并到一起，楷书变成"重"。本义是"东西很重"的意思，后来引申出"重要""重量"等抽象的意思，之后又引申出"重复""重叠"的意思。

Analysis of the character：It had been written as "𡔷" in ancient Chinese character，like a man carrying a heavy package，meaning "heavy". It also had been written in "重" in Clerical Script（Lishu）in Qin Dynasty，the shape of man and the package had intermingled, and "重" in Regular Script(Kaishu). The original meaning of this character was "something very heavy", later it extended into some abstract concepts like "important" "weight". Then it generated the meanings of "repeat" and "overlap".

田字格书写 Writing in Tin Word Format：

书写提示：第一笔是撇，不能写成横。

Writing tips：The first stroke is 撇(piě), not 横(héng).

（十七）喜 xǐ

词语：喜欢(enjoy)　喜悦(joyful)　恭喜(congratulation)

析字：古代汉字写作"𠷂"，上面的"𠷂"是乐器鼓的形状（表示音乐的声音），下面是"口"（表示人的欢笑声）。音乐的声音和人的欢笑声合在一起表示"欢乐""喜悦""喜庆"的意思。小篆写作"𠷂"，楷书写作"喜"。后来引申出"喜欢""喜爱"的意思。

Analysis of the character：It had been written as "𠷂" in ancient Chinese character, "𠷂" on the top showed the shape of the drum(meant the sound of music), "口" at the bottom(meant the laughter). The sound of music and the laughter mixed together to show the meanings of "happy" "joyful" "celebration". It also had been written as "𠷂" in Seal Script(Xiaozhuan), "喜" in Regular Script (Kaishu). Later the meanings were extended to "like" "enjoy".

田字格书写 Writing in Tin Word Format：

书写提示：上面的"士"不能写成"土"，"壴"不能写成"豆"。

Writing tips：The "士" on the top should not be written as "土", the "壴" should not be written as "豆".

（十八）岁 suì

词语：年岁（age） 二十岁（twenty years old）

析字：金文写作"󰎯"，隶书写作"歲"，楷书写作"歲"，汉字简化后写作"岁"。字的本义是"天空运行的岁星"，后来引申出"岁月""年龄"的意思。

Analysis of the character：It had been written as "󰎯" "歲" and "歲" in Bronze Script（Jinwen），Clerical Script（Lishu）and Regular Script（Kaishu）respectively. It was written as "岁" in simplified Chinese character. The original meaning of the word was "the lucky star running in the sky", and later extended to "years" and "age".

田字格书写 Writing in Tin Word Format：

书写提示：下面的"夕"不能写成"夕"。

Writing tips：The "夕" in the lower part should not be written as "夕".

（十九）外 wài

词语：外边（outside） 外国（other countries）

析字：古代汉字写作"󰎯"，小篆写作"󰎯"，楷书写作"外"。左边的"夕"和右边的"卜"合在一起表示"事外占卜"，后来引申出"外边"的意思。

Analysis of the character：It had been written as "󰎯" "󰎯" and "外" in ancient Chinese character，Seal Script（Xiaozhuan）and Regular Script（Kaishu）respectively. "夕" on the left and "卜" on the right together to indicate "outside divination", later extended to indicate "outside".

田字格书写 Writing in Tin Word Format：

丿ㄅㄆ夕卜外

书写提示：右边的"卜"不能写成"丨"。

Writing tips：The "卜" on the right side should not be written as "丨".

（二十）名 míng

词语：名字（name） 姓名（full name）

析字：古代汉字写作"名"，隶书写作"名"，楷书写作"名"，"夕"和"口"合在一起表示"晚上天黑，自己报出名字"。从古到今，字的意思没有很大的变化。

Analysis of the character：It had been written as "名" "名" and "名" in ancient Chinese character，Clerical Script（Lishu）and Regular Script（Kaishu）respectively. "夕" and "口" together means "it's dark at night，say your name". From ancient times to modern times，the meaning has not changed much.

田字格书写 Writing in Tin Word Format：

丿ㄅㄆ夕名名

书写提示：不能写成"各"。

Writing tips：It should not be written as "各".

三、词语练习 Phrase Practice

1. 请填写包含指定汉字的词语。

Please fill in the words containing the given Chinese characters.

① 你会说_____吗?（汉）

② 他喝了一瓶_____。（汽）

③ 我们先吃饭，_____去看电影。（然）

④ 我请老师给我起了一个中文_____。（名）

2. 读出下列汉字、词语、词组和句子。

Read the following Chinese characters, words, phrases and sentences.

① 外—外边—教室外边—教室外边有几盆（pén, basin）花。

② 点——一点儿——一点儿水——杯子里只有一点儿水。

③ 块——一块——一块蛋糕——一块生日蛋糕——她请我吃了一块生日蛋糕。

④ 洗—洗衣服—洗了很多衣服—昨天晚上我洗了很多衣服。

3. 连线。

Link the Phrase.

A. 机

飞机　　　　　　　　television

手机　　　　　　　　washing machine

洗衣机　　　　　　　plane

电视机　　　　　　　cellphone

B. 场

市场　　　　　　　　airport

机场　　　　　　　　basketball court

篮球场　　　　　　　market

操场　　　　　　　　playground

C. 票

机票　　　　　　　　plane ticket

车票　　　　　　　　train or bus ticket

门票　　　　　　　　entrance ticket

电影票　　　　　　　movie ticket

四、综合练习 Comprehensive Practice

1. 选字填空。

Choose a character to fill in the blank.

A. 坐　钱　钟　没　岁

① 我们学校每天早上八点_____上课。

② 请进！请_____！

③ 我妹妹今年二十_____。

④ 这些水果一共多少_____？

⑤ 学校里_____有邮局。

B. 坡　场　汁　煮

① 她走在山_____上。

② 他喝了一瓶果_____。

③ 饺子已经_____好了，快来吃吧。

④ 他们在球_____上踢球呢。

2. 请写出与下列汉字意思相反或相对的汉字。

Please write down the characters which are opposite or corresponding to the following characters.

冷—　　里—　　错—　　哥—　　白—

五、课外任务 After-class Task

1. 用下列汉字写一个句子，比一比看谁写得对、写得长。

Please write a sentence using each given character, and compare to see who can write better and longer.

① 汉

② 在
③ 喜
④ 星

2. 找出已学过的所有包含下列意符的汉字，根据它们的意思填在该意符下的分类中，制成意符卡片。以后可不断扩充该意符包含的汉字。

Find all the Chinese characters that contain the following ideographic symbols and fill in the categories according to their meanings to make ideographic symbols cards. The characters contained under this classification can be continuously expanded later.

木——树（tree）

树的名称(the name of the tree)：_____

树的部分(part of a tree)：_____

木制品(woodwork)：_____

其他(other)：_____

氵——水（water）

水的某种形态(some form of water)：_____

液体的一种(one of the liquids)：_____

和水有关的地点(water related places)：_____

和水有关的动作、行为(the act and behavior in relation to water)：_____

和水有关的性质、状态(the nature and state in relation to water)：_____
_____

其他(other)：_____
_____

第十三课　常用的音符
Lesson Thirteen　Commonly-used Phonetic Symbols

一、汉字知识 Knowledge of Chinese Characters

　　在汉字中，音符的数量比意符多得多。据统计，在现代汉语通用字中，音符有1300多个，音符的数量几乎是意符的5倍。从构字能力看，音符比意符弱很多。不仅如此，音符与意符之间存在着较为明显的角色分工：构字能力强的意符很少充当音符使用，构字能力强的音符很少作为意符使用。现代汉字中最为常用的10个音符是："者""工""艮""古""分""丁""肖""隹""且""羊"。学习了解这些常用音符，对于掌握汉字读音很有帮助。

　　In Chinese characters, the number of phonetic symbols is much more than that of ideographic symbols. According to statistics, there are more than 1300 phonetic symbols in modern Chinese common characters, and the number of phonetic symbols is 5 times that of the ideographic symbols. From the perspective of character formation ability, phonetic symbols are much weaker than ideographic symbols. Not only that, there is a relatively obvious division of roles between phonetic symbols and ideographic symbols: Ideographic symbols with strong character formation ability are rarely used as phonetic symbols, and phonetic symbols with strong character formation ability are rarely used as ideographic symbols. The 10 most commonly-used phonetic symbols in modern Chinese characters are: "者""工""艮""古""分""丁""肖""隹""且""羊". Learning to understand these commonly-used phonetic symbols is very helpful for mastering the pronunciation of Chinese characters.

二、汉字形音义 The Form, Pronunciation and Meaning of Chinese Characters

 目标汉字 Learning Objective

时 昨 东 晚 间 早 最 是 家 客 字 脑 难 穿 房 店 期 院 都 那

（一）时 shí

词语：时间（time） 当时（at that time）

析字：繁体字写作"時"，左边的"日"与字义有关，右边的"寺（sì）"与读音有关（由于古今音变，"寺""時"的读音已有差异）。简化字省简右边，写成"时"。本义是"时间"。

Analysis of the character: The traditional Chinese characters are written as "時", the "日" on the left is related to the meaning of the word, and the "寺 (sì)" on the right was related to the pronunciation (due to the phonetic changes since ancient times, the pronunciation of "寺" is different from "時"). The simplified character simplified the right side and turned into "时". The original meaning of this character was "time".

田字格书写 Writing in Tin Word Format：

丨 冂 冃 日 日⁻ 时 时

书写提示：右边的"寸"不能写成"才"。

Writing tips：The "寸" on the right side should not be written as "才".

(二) 昨 zuó

词语：昨天(yesterday)　昨晚(last night)

析字：左边的"日"与字义有关，右边的"乍(zhà)"表示字音(由于古今音变，"乍""昨"的读音有差异)。

Analysis of the character：The "日" on the left is related to the meaning of the character，and the "乍(zhà)" on the right represents the pronunciation of the character(due to the phonetic changes since ancient times，the pronunciation of "乍" is different from "昨" now).

田字格书写 Writing in Tin Word Format：

丨 冂 日 日 日' 旷 昨 昨 昨

昨	昨	昨	昨	昨	昨	昨	昨	昨	昨	昨	昨	昨	昨

书写提示：左边的"乍"不能写成"午"。

Writing tips：The "乍" on the left side should not be written as "午".

 汉字锦囊 Idea Box of Chinese Characters

常用偏旁——日字旁(日)

Commonly-used Component — Rizipang(日) Component

"日"是常见的汉字表义偏旁，表示与"太阳""时间"等有关的意思，称为"日字旁"。"日字旁"用在字的左边比较多。

The component "日" is a common Chinese character with meanings and its meanings related to "sun" and "time", and it is called "Rizipang" in Chinese. It is often used on the left side of the character.

(三) 东 dōng

词语：东方(east)　东西(stuff)

析字：古代汉字写作"🈳"，像是两头用绳子扎住的口袋。小篆写作"🈳"，繁体字写作"東"，现在简化字写成"东"。汉语中，自古就借用这个原本表示"口袋"意思的字来表示"东方"。

Analysis of the character：In ancient Chinese character "🈳" was like a pocket tied with a string at both ends. Then it turned into "🈳" and "東" in Seal Script (Xiaozhuan) and traditional Chinese character respectively, now the character is simplified as "东". In Chinese, the meaning of "pocket" has been borrowed to express the meaning of "the Orient" since ancient times.

田字格书写　Writing in Tin Word Format：

一 七 乍 午 东

东	东	东	东	东	东	东	东	东	东	东	东

书写提示：按照"一、乙、小"的顺序书写。

Writing tips：The writing order of the character is "一、乙、小".

(四) 晚 wǎn

词语：晚上(night)　晚会(evening party)

析字：左边的"日"与字义有关，右边的"免(miǎn)"表示字音(由于古今音变，"免""晚"的读音稍有差异)。

Analysis of the character：The "日" on the left is related to the meaning of the word, and the "免(miǎn)" on the right represents the pronunication of the character(due to the phonetic changes since ancient times, the pronunciation of "免" is slightly different from "晚").

田字格书写 Writing in Tin Word Format：

丨 冂 月 日 旷 旷 旷 晚 晚 晚

书写提示：右边的"免"不能写成"兔"。

Writing tips：The right part "免" should not be written as "兔".

（五）间 jiān

词语：时间(time)　房间(room)

析字：金文写作"🀆"，像月光从门外照进屋内，本义是"缝隙"。楷书写作"閒"，后来字形简化写作"间"（"月"变成了"日"）。由本义引申出"时间""空间"等意思。

Analysis of the character：It had been written as "🀆" in Bronze Script (Jinwen)，like moonlight shining into the house from outside the door，the original meaning was "a gap". The Regular Script(Kaishu) was written as "閒"，and later the form was simplified as "间"（"月" became "日"）. The meanings of "time" and "space" were derived from the original meaning.

田字格书写 Writing in Tin Word Format：

丶 冂 门 门 问 问 间

书写提示：不能写成"问"。

Writing tips：It should not be written as "问".

（六）早 zǎo

词语：早晨(morning)　早上好(good morning)

析字：小篆写作"🀆"，后来简写成"早"。本义是"早晨"，后来引申出"早先"等意思。

Analysis of the character: It had been written as "𠭂" in Seal Script (Xiaozhuan), which was later simplified as "early". The original meaning was "morning", and later it was extended to mean "earlier".

田字格书写 Writing in Tin Word Format：

丨 冂 日 旦 早

早	早	早	早	早	早	早	早	早	早	早	早	早	早

书写提示：下面的"十"不能写成"土"。
Writing tips：The lower "十" should not be written as "土".

(七) 最 zuì

词语：最后（last） 最好（best）

析字：小篆写作"𠷎"，楷书写作"最"，上面的"冃"是"帽子"的意思，表示字义，下面的"取"表示读音（由于古今音变，读音已有变化）。由于帽子戴在人的头上，所以用"冃"来表示"最高"或"最突出"的意思。后来汉字简化，上面的"冃"变成了形近的"日"。

Analysis of the character: It had been written as "𠷎" and "最" in Seal Script(Xiaozhuan) and Regular Script(Kaishu). The upper "冃" meant "hat", which meant the meaning of the character, and the lower "取" meant the pronunciation(due to the phonetic changes since ancient times, the pronunciation has changed). Since the hat is worn on a person's head, "冃" was used to mean "the highest" or "most prominent". Later, the Chinese characters were simplified, and the "冃" above became a similar form of "日".

田字格书写 Writing in Tin Word Format：

丨 冂 日 旦 早 旱 甼 𣅳 冣 最 最

最	最	最	最	最	最	最	最	最	最	最	最	最	最

书写提示：注意"取"和"取"的微小区别。

Writing tips：Mind the slight difference between "取" and "取".

(八) 是 shì

词语：他是学生(he is a student)　是非(right or wrong)

析字：金文写作"𠆢"，小篆写作"是"，楷书写作"是"。字的本义是"端正"，后来引申出"正确""表示判断"等意思。

Analysis of the character：It had been written as "𠆢" "是" and "是" in Bronze Script(Jinwen)，Seal Script(Xiaozhuan) and Regular Script(Kaishu). The original meaning of the word was "correct", and later extended the meaning and usage to "upright" "expressing judgment" and so on.

田字格书写 Writing in Tin Word Format：

丨 冂 日 日 旦 早 早 昰 是

书写提示：下面的"疋"不能写成"走"。

Writing tips：The lower part "疋" should not be written as "走".

(九) 家 jiā

词语：家庭(family)　家乡(hometown)

析字：金文写作"家"，小篆写作"家"，外面的是"宀(房子)"，里面的是"豕(猪)"，合在一起表示"居家""家庭"的意思。楷书写作"家"。

Analysis of the character：It had been written as "家" in Bronze Script(Jinwen), and "家" was written in Seal Script(Xiaozhuan). The outside is "宀(house)", and the inside is "豕(pig)", which together mean home and family. It had been written as "家" in Regular Script(Kaishu).

田字格书写 Writing in Tin Word Format：

丶丶宀宁宇穷家家家

家	家	家	家	家	家	家	家	家	家	家	家	家	家

书写提示："豕"不能写成"豖"。

Writing tips：The part "豕" should not be written as "豖".

（十）客 kè

词语：客人（guest）　不客气（you're welcome）

析字：上面的"宀"与字义有关，下面的"各"与读音有关。本义是"客人"，后来引申出"顾客""乘客"等意思。

Analysis of the character：The "宀" above is related to the meaning of the character, and the "各" below is related to the pronunciation. The original meaning was "a guest", and later it was extended to mean "customer" "passenger" and so on.

田字格书写 Writing in Tin Word Format：

丶丶宀宁宇灾灾客客

客	客	客	客	客	客	客	客	客	客	客	客	客	客

书写提示："各"不能写成"名"。

Writing tips：The part "各" should not be written as "名".

（十一）字 zì

词语：汉字（Chinese characters）　名字（name）

析字：金文写作"㊉"，小篆写作"㊉"，楷书写作"字"。"宀（房子）"和"子"在一起表示在家里养育孩子的意思。本义是"生育"，后来引申出"文字""名字"等意思。

Analysis of the character: It had been written as "⺤" in Bronze Script (Jinwen), "⺤" in Seal Script(Xiaozhuan), "字" in Regular Script(Kaishu). "宀 (house)" and "子" together meant raising children at home. The original meaning was "birth", and later it was extended to mean "character" "name" and so on.

田字格书写 Writing in Tin Word Format:

、丶宀㝉宁字

字	字	字	字	字	字	字	字	字	字	字	字	字	字

书写提示:注意"子"和"于"的微小区别。

Writing tips: Mind the slight difference between "子" and "于".

 汉字锦囊 Idea Box of Chinese Characters

常用偏旁——宝盖头(宀)

Commonly-used Component — Baogaitou(宀) Component

"宀"是常用的汉字表义偏旁,常表示与"家庭""房屋"等有关的字义,只用在字的上部。

The "宀" is a commonly-used Chinese component to represent the meaning of the component. It often indicates the meaning of the character related to "family" "house", etc. It is only used in the upper part of the character.

(十二)脑 nǎo

词语:电脑(computer) 头脑(brain)

析字:形声字。左边的"月(肉)"表示字义(与人的身体组织有关),右边的"𡿺"表示读音。本义是"头脑",如"大脑""脑袋",后来也用来表示类似脑袋的事物,如"电脑""首脑"。

Analysis of the character: It is a pictophonetic character. The "月(肉)" on the left represents its meaning (related to people's body) and the "囟" on the right represents its pronunciation. The original meaning of this character was brain, like "brain" "head", later it was used to represent things that have the function of the brain, like "computer" "leader".

田字格书写 Writing in Tin Word Format:

丿 几 几 月 月` 𦓇 肵 胶 脑 脑

脑	脑	脑	脑	脑	脑	脑	脑	脑	脑	脑	脑	脑

书写提示:右边的"囟"不能写成"卤"。
Writing tips: The "囟" on the right side should not be written as "卤".

(十三) 难 nán/nàn

词语:难过(sad)　困难(difficulty)　灾难(disaster)

析字:繁体字写作"難",左边的"堇"表示读音(由于古今音变,"堇"与"難"的读音已经差异很大),右边的"隹(zhuī)"(像禽鸟的样子)表示字义与鸟类有关,"難"字的本义是一种鸟。古代借用这个字来表示"困难""不容易"的意思,至今没有改变。简化字写作"难",左边的"堇"简写成"又"。

Analysis of the character: The traditional Chinese character form was "難", "堇" on the left originally represented its pronunciation (due to the phonetics changes since ancient times, the pronunciation of "堇" is different from what "難" pronounces nowadays). "隹(zhuī)" on the right (this part was like the shape as a bird) showed its meaning is related with birds. The original meaning of "難" was a bird, which was used to refer to "being difficult" in ancient times, the same as what it means nowadays. The simplified character was "难", and the original left "堇" was simplified as "又".

田字格书写 Writing in Tin Word Format：

书写提示：右边的"隹"不能写成"住"。

Writing tips：The "隹" on the right side should not be written as "住".

（十四）穿 chuān

词语：穿衣服（wear clothes） 穿鞋（wear shoes）

析字：小篆写作"穿"，楷书写作"穿"，"穴"和"牙"合在一起表示小动物用牙齿咬穿洞穴的意思。本义是"打通""穿透"，后来引申出"从……通过"（如"穿过马路"），又引申出"把（衣服、鞋子）套在身体上"等意思。

Analysis of the character：It had been written as "穿" in Seal Script (Xiaozhuan)，and Regular Script(Kaishu) was written as "穿". The combination of "穴" and "牙" means that small animals bite through the cave with their teeth. The original meaning was "get through" and "penetrate". Later，it was extended to "pass through"（such as "cross the road"），and then extended to "put（clothes，shoes）on the body" and other meanings.

田字格书写 Writing in Tin Word Format：

书写提示：上面的"穴"不能写成"宀"。

Writing tips：The upper part "穴" should not be written as the "宀".

(十五) 房 fáng

词语:房间(room)　厨房(kitchen)

析字:上面的"户(hù)"与字义有关,下面的"方"与读音有关,本义是"古代正室东西两旁的房子",后来指"各种房屋"。

Analysis of the character: The upper "户(hù)" is related to the meaning of the character, and the lower "方" is related to the pronunciation. The original meaning was related to "the houses on the east and west sides of the ancient main room", and later referred to "various houses".

田字格书写 Writing in Tin Word Format:

丶 冫 冖 户 户 户 房 房

书写提示:"户"不能写成"广"。

Writing tips: The part "户" should not be written as "广".

(十六) 店 diàn

词语:商店(store)　书店(bookstore)

析字:外面的"广"与字义有关,里面的"占(zhàn)"与字音有关(由于古今音变,"占""店"的读音有差异)。古代指商家卖东西的台子,后来引申指各类商业店铺,如"酒店""饭店""书店"等。

Analysis of the character: The "广" on the outside is related to the meaning of the character, and the "占(zhàn)" on the inside is related to the pronunciation of the character(due to the phonetic changes since ancient times, the pronunciation of "占" and "店" is different). In ancient times, it referred to the desk where merchants sold things, and later extended to refer to various commercial shops, such as "hotel" "restaurant" "bookstore" and so on.

第十三课　常用的音符

田字格书写 Writing in Tin Word Format:

`、 一 广 广 广 庐 庐 店 店`

店 店 店 店 店 店 店 店 店 店 店 店 店

书写提示:"占"不能写成"古"。

Writing tips: The part "占" should not be written as "古".

(十七) 期 qī

词语:日期(date)　星期(week)　学期(term)

析字:形声字。左边的"其(qí)"表示读音,右边的"月"与字的意思(时间)有关,本义是"时期"。后来也表示与时间有关的意思,如"假期""学期";也用作与时间有关的动词,如"期望""期待"。

Analysis of the character: It is a pictophonetic character. "其(qí)" on the left represents its pronunciation, and the "月" on the right represents its meaning (time). The original meaning of this character was "time", and later was used to represent meanings related with time, such as "holiday" "term". It was also used in words to show actions related with time, like "hope" and "expect".

田字格书写 Writing in Tin Word Format:

`一 十 # # # 甘 其 其 期 期 期 期`

期 期 期 期 期 期 期 期 期 期 期 期 期

书写提示:左边"其"的最后一笔"点"要稍短一点。

Writing tips: The last stroke of "其" on the left side is a short 点(diǎn).

(十八) 院 yuàn

词语:医院(hospital)　院子(courtyard)　学院(college)

析字:"阝"与字义有关,"完(wán)"表示字音(由于古今音变,"完""院"的读音稍有差异)。本义是"围墙里的空地",后来引申出"一些机构或公共场所"的意思,如"法院""医院""学院"。

Analysis of the character: "阝" is related to the meaning of the character, and "完(wán)" means the pronunciation of the character(due to the phonetic changes since ancient times, the pronunciation of "完" and "院" is slightly different). The original meaning was "open space in the wall", and later extended the meaning of "some institutions or public places", such as "court" "hospital" and "college".

田字格书写 Writing in Tin Word Format:

㇇ 阝 阝' 阝` 阝宀 阝宁 阝宇 阝完 院

书写提示:左边的"阝"不能写成"卩"。
Writing tips: The part "阝" on the left side should not be written as "卩".

(十九) 都 dōu/dū

词语:他们都是学生(all of them are students)　首都(capital)

析字:左边的"者(zhě)"表示读音(由于古今音变,"者"和"都"的读音差别很大),右边的"阝"表示字义。本义是"大的城市",由"城市"引申出"聚集"的意思,再引申出"总体""全部"的意思。

Analysis of the character: The left part "者(zhě)" represents the pronunciation (due to the phonetic changes since ancient times, the pronunciation of "者" and "都" is very different), and the "阝" on the right represents the meaning of the character. The original meaning was "big city", and the meaning of "gathering" was derived from "city", and then the meanings of "total" "all" were extended.

田字格书写 Writing in Tin Word Format：

一 十 土 耂 耂 者 者 者 者 都 都

书写提示：右边的"阝"不能写成"卩"。

Writing tips：The part "阝" on the right side should not be written as "卩".

 汉字锦囊 Idea Box of Chinese Characters

> 两个不同的"阝"
> Two Different Components "阝"
>
> 汉字中常用偏旁"阝"比较特殊：同一个形体，但是出现在字的左边和右边表示不同的字义。出现在左边的"阝"来源于"阝（阜）"，一般表示"高处"；出现在右边的"阝"来源于"邑"，一般表示"地域""地方"。
>
> The common component "阝" in Chinese characters is special：The same form，but appears on the left and right sides of the character to indicate different meanings. The "阝" that appears on the left is derived from "阝（阜）"，which generally means "high place"；The "阝" that appears on the right is derived from "邑"，which generally means "region" and "place".

（二十）那 nà

词语：那里(there)　那些(those)

析字：小篆写作"𨙻"，字的本义是"地名"，楷书简写作"那"。现代汉语借用这个字作为指示代词，指较远的人、事物等。

Analysis of the character：It had been written as "𨙻" in Seal Script (Xiaozhuan)，the original meaning of the character was "a place name"，and the Regular Script(Kaishu) was written as "那". Modern Chinese borrows this word as a demonstrative pronoun, referring to distant people, things, etc.

田字格书写 Writing in Tin Word Format:

丁 ヲ 寻 月 那阝 那

那	那	那	那	那	那	那	那	那	那	那	那	那

书写提示：左边的"阝"不能写成"月"或"刀"。

Writing tips: The part "阝" on the left side should not be written as "月" or "刀".

三、词语练习 Phrase Practice

1. 请填写包含指定汉字的词语。

Please fill in the words containing the given Chinese characters.

① 你生病了，要去_____。（院）

② 家里来了很多_____。（客）

③ 我想去_____买一些日用品。（店）

④ 我们班_____在二楼。（室）

2. 读出下列汉字、词语、词组和句子。

Read the following Chinese characters, words, phrases and sentences.

① 完—学完—学完第十三课—我们已经学完第十三课了。

② 早—很早—起得很早—他每天都起得很早。

③ 间—中间—教学楼和图书馆中间—操场在教学楼和图书馆中间。

3. 辨字组词。

Please distinguish the following each group of characters and make words for each of them.

字_____ 那_____ 快_____ 气_____

子＿＿＿＿　　哪＿＿＿＿　　块＿＿＿＿　　汽＿＿＿＿

四、综合练习 Comprehensive Practice

1. 选字填空。

Choose a character and fill in the blank.

家　穿　都　最

① 我们班玛丽学习＿＿＿＿认真。

② 她喜欢＿＿＿＿深色的衣服。

③ 我＿＿＿＿爱吃中国菜。

④ 我＿＿＿＿离学校不太远。

2. 请写出与下列汉字意思相反或相对的汉字。

Please write down the characters which are opposite or corresponding to the following characters.

晴—　　　早—　　　那—

3. 请把汉字、拼音和意思连线。

Please match the Chinese character, pinyin and meaning.

坦	kuài	loyal, devoted
忠	tǎn	to float (on the water)
漂	piāo	chopsticks
筷	zhōng	broad and level

五、课外任务 After-class Task

1. 想一想学过的哪些汉字含有下列音符？它们和音符的关系属于哪种类型？（完全相同；声母、韵母相同，声调不同；韵母相同，声母不同；声母、韵母都不同）

Which Chinese characters you have learned contain the following phonograms? What kind of relationship do they have with phonograms? (Exactly the same; The initials and finals are the same, but the tones are different; The finals are the same, but the initials are different; The initials and finals are both different.)

① 青 qīng

② 元 yuán

③ 巴 bā

④ 艮 gèn

⑤ 同 tóng

⑥ 方 fāng

2. 请你写出由下列汉字联想到的字,并说一说它们与指定字之间的联系。比一比看谁想到的字多。

Please write out the characters associated with the following Chinese characters, and talk about the connection between them and the specified characters. Compete with your classmate to see who thinks of more words.

① 校:

② 时:

③ 穿:

第十四课 假借字
Lesson Fourteen　Phonetic Loan Characters

一、汉字知识 Knowledge of Chinese Characters

汉语中有不少假借字。假借字主要有两种：

There are many phonetic loan characters in Chinese. There are two main types of phonetic loan characters:

1. 有一些字本来没有特定的符号来记录，而是借用其他读音相同的字来表示。如"来"这个字借用了表示"小麦"的字来记录，"我"这个字借用了表示"兵器"的字。

In Chinese, some characters were not recorded by specific symbols, but expressed by other characters with the same pronunciation. For example, the character "来" borrowed the character recording the word "wheat", and the character "我" borrowed the character recording the word "weapon".

2. 有一些词语本来有专门的字记录，但是后来专门造的字不用了，而借用一个音同或音近的其他的字来代替。如"足球"的"球"，汉语本来写作"毬"。"球"字本来表示一种美玉，后来人们借用"球"字来表示"毬"，"毬"字逐渐不使用了。

Some words were originally recorded with special characters, but later they were replaced by other characters with the same or similar pronunciation. For example, "ball" of "football" was originally written in Chinese as "毬". The character "球" originally meant a kind of beautiful jade, but later people used it to mean "毬", and the character "毬" was gradually not used.

二、汉字形音义 The Form, Pronunciation and Meaning of Chinese Characters

 目标汉字 Learning Objective

```
分 前 到 别 班 绍 给 馆 饿 累 玩 球 现 贵 南 回
放 听 新 写
```

（一）分 fēn/fèn

词语：分开(separate)　分别(leave each other)

析字：甲骨文写作"⺍"，上面是"八"，下面是"刀"，合在一起表示用刀把东西分开，楷书写作"分"。由"分开"引申出"区分""分配""分数"等意思。

Analysis of the character：It had been written as "⺍" in Oracle Bone Script (Jiaguwen). Above is "八", below is "刀", together means to separate things with a knife. It had been written as "分" in Regular Script(Kaishu). "Separation" was extended to mean "differentiation" "distribution" "score" and so on.

田字格书写 Writing in Tin Word Format：

丿 八 分 分

分	分	分	分	分	分	分	分	分	分	分	分	分

书写提示：上面的"八"不能写成"人"或"入"。

Writing tips：The above part should be written as "八", not "人" or "入".

（二）前 qián

词语：以前（before）　前面（front）

析字：小篆写作"𦦪"，上面是"止"（脚趾向前，表示前进的意思），下面是"舟"（小船），合在一起表示"小船前进"。后来字形写作"歬"，楷书写作"前"。

Analysis of the character：It had been written as "𦦪" in Seal Script (Xiaozhuan). Above is "止"(toe forward，meaning forward)，below is "舟"(boat)，together meant "boat forward". Then it had been written as "歬"，and been written as "前" in Regular Script(Kaishu) respectively.

田字格书写 Writing in Tin Word Format：

丶　丷　䒑　产　方　肯　肯　前　前

前	前	前	前	前	前	前	前	前	前	前	前

书写提示：上面的"䒑"不能写成"艹"。

Writing tips：The above part should be written as "䒑"，not "艹".

汉字锦囊 Idea Box of Chinese Characters

"刀"与"刂"

The Component "刀" and "刂"

"刀"和"刂"都是常用的汉字偏旁，"刀"称为"刀字旁"，一般出现在字的下面，"刂"称为"立刀边"，一般出现在字的右边。

The "刀" and "刂" are both common Chinese character components. "刀" is called "Daozipang" and generally appears below the character. "刂" is called "Lidaobian" and generally appears on the right side of the character.

(三) 到 dào

词语：到达(arrive)　迟到(be late)

析字：小篆写作"到",楷书写作"到",左边的"至(zhì)"表示字义,右边的"刂(刀)"表示读音。本义是"到达",后来引申为"动作有结果、达到目的"的意思,如"看到""回到家里"等。

Analysis of the character：It had been written as "到" and "到" in Seal Script(Xiaozhuan) and Regular Script(Kaishu) respectively. The "至(zhì)" on the left represents the meaning of the character, and the "刂(刀)" on the right represents the pronunciation. The original meaning of this character was "arriving", later extended to mean "action has a result, to achieve the purpose", such as "see" "back home" and so on.

田字格书写 Writing in Tin Word Format：

一 エ 工 至 至 至 到 到

到	到	到	到	到	到	到	到	到	到	到	到	到	到

书写提示：左边的"至"不能写成"至"。

Writing tips：The left part "至" should not be written as "至".

(四) 别 bié

词语：分别(leave each other)　告别(farewell)

析字：小篆写作"别",楷书写作"刚",左边的"冎"是"骨",右边的"刂"是"刀",合在一起表示用刀剔骨头,本义是"分离"。后来字形简写成"别",由分开的意思引申出"区别""其他"等意思。

Analysis of the character：It had been written as "别" and "刚" in Seal Script(Xiaozhuan) and Regular Script(Kaishu) respectively. "冎" on the left is "bone" and "刂" on the right is "knife". It means to pick the bone with a knife. The original meaning was "separation". Later, it was abbreviated as "别". The meaning had been extended to mean "difference" "other" and so on.

田字格书写 Writing in Tin Word Format：

丶 冂 口 弓 另 别 别

别 别 别 别 别 别 别 别 别 别 别 别 别

书写提示：左边的"另"不能写成"吊"。

Writing tips：The left part "另" should not be written as "吊".

（五）班 bān

词语：上班（go to work） 班级（class）

析字：金文写作"班"，小篆写作"班"，楷书写作"班"。本义是"分开"，"根据学习、工作的需要而分出来的组织（如学校的班级、工作的班组）"，是从本义引申出来的意思。

Analysis of the character：It had been written as "班" "班" and "班" in Bronze Script（Jinwen），Seal Script（Xiaozhuan）and Regular Script（Kaishu）respectively. The original meaning was "separation", and "the divided organization according to the needs of study and work（such as the class of the school and the working group）" is the meaning extended from the original meaning.

田字格书写 Writing in Tin Word Format：

一 二 干 王 王 刬 玎 班 班 班

班 班 班 班 班 班 班 班 班 班 班 班

书写提示：中间的"丿"不能写成"刂"。

Writing tips：The middle part "丿" should not be written as "刂".

(六) 绍 shào

词语：介绍(introduce)

析字：形声字。左边的"纟"与字义有关，右边的"召（zhāo）"表示字的读音（由于古今音变，"召"和"绍"的读音稍有差异）。本义是"两件丝织品的线纠缠、连接在一起"，后来引申出"连接""连续"的意思，再后来引申出"介绍"的意思——把人或事情告诉其他人。

Analysis of the character: It is a pictophonetic character. The "纟" on the left represents its meaning, and "召（zhāo）" on the right represents its pronunciation(due to the phonetic changes since ancient times, "召" has a slight different pronunciation from "绍"). The original meaning was "the two pieces of silk thread are entwined together", and later extended its meaning to "continue" and "connect", and at last it had the meaning of "introduce", that is, to introduce somebody or something to others.

田字格书写 Writing in Tin Word Format：

乙 纟 纟 纠 纫 织 绍 绍

绍	绍	绍	绍	绍	绍	绍	绍	绍	绍	绍	绍	绍

书写提示："纟"的最后一笔是提，不能写成横。

Writing tips: The last stroke of the "纟" is 提(tí), and it should not be written as 横(héng).

(七) 给 gěi/jǐ

词语：送给(send)　给同学帮忙(help students)

析字：左边的"纟"与字义有关，右边的"合"（由于古今音变，"合"与"给"的读音差别很大）与读音有关。本义是"生活富裕"，后来引申出"提供""给予"等意思。

Analysis of the character: The left side "纟" is related to the meaning of the character, and on the right side, the "合"(due to the phonetic changes since ancient times, the pronunciation of "合" and "给" is different) is related to the pronunciation. The original meaning was "rich life", and later extended to "provide" "give" and so on.

田字格书写 Writing in Tin Word Format:

乙 纟 纟 纟 纮 纮 纮 给 给

给	给	给	给	给	给	给	给	给	给	给	给	给	给

书写提示:右边的"合"不能写成"合"。

Writing tips: The "合" on the right should not be written as "合".

 汉字锦囊 Idea Box of Chinese Characters

常用偏旁——绞丝旁(纟)

Commonly-used Component — Jiaosipang(纟) Component

"纟"是常用的汉字表义偏旁,经常出现在汉字左侧,表示"纺织""丝织品"之类的意思。

The "纟" is a commonly-used component of Chinese characters, which often appears on the left side of Chinese characters and means "textile" "silk" and so on.

(八) 馆 guǎn

词语:图书馆(library) 茶馆(tea house) 大使馆(embassy)

析字:形声字。左边的"饣"表示字义["饣"是从"食(shí)"简化来的,用作汉字偏旁时,表示饮食之类的意思],右边的"官(guān)"表示字音。本义是"接待宾客的房子",如"宾馆""茶馆""饭馆",后来也表示公众活动的场所,如"图书馆""科技馆""文化馆"等。

Analysis of the character: It is a pictophonetic character. The "饣" on the left side is related to the character's meaning["饣" is simplified from the character "食（shí）", as a commonly-used character component，it is always used to express the meaning of diet]. The right side "官（guān）" represents the pronunciation. The original meaning of the character referred to "the house that receives guests", such as "hotel" "tea house" and "restaurant", later the meaning was extended to public places，such as "library" "science and technology museum" "cultural center" and so on.

田字格书写 Writing in Tin Word Format：

ノ 夕 亇 亇 忾 忾 馆 馆 馆 馆

书写提示：左边的"饣"不能写成"钅"。
Writing tips：The left side "饣" should not be written as "钅".

（九）饿 è

词语：很饿（very hungry）　不饿（not hungry）

析字：形声字。左边的"饣"表示字义，右边的"我"表示读音（由于古今音变，"我"与"饿"的读音稍有不同）。字的本义就是"饥饿"。

Analysis of the character：It is a pictophonetic character. The "饣" on the left side is related to the character's meaning. The "我" on the right side refers to the character's pronunciation(due to the phonetic changes since ancient times，the pronunciation of "我" and "饿" has slight difference). The original meaning of the character was "hungry".

田字格书写 Writing in Tin Word Format：

ノ 夕 亇 亇 忾 忾 忾 饿 饿 饿

书写提示：左边的"亻"不能写成"讠"。

Writing tips：The "亻" on the left side should not be written as "讠".

（十）累 lèi/lěi

词语：很累（very tired）　劳累（tired）

析字：繁体字写作"纍"，上面的"畾（léi）"表示读音，下面的"糸"表示字义。本义是"很粗的绳索"，也表示"堆积"的意思。事情积累多了就成了负担，因此引申出"劳累"的意思。现在简化字写成"累"。

Analysis of the character：In traditional Chinese characters, it was written as "纍". The "畾（léi）" meant pronunciation, and the following "糸" meant meaning. The original meaning was "a very thick rope", also meant "accumulation". When things accumulate more, they become a burden, which means "tired". Now the simplified character is written as "累".

田字格书写　Writing in Tin Word Format：

丿 冂 冂 田 田 甲 罒 罒 罢 累 累 累

累	累	累	累	累	累	累	累	累	累	累	累	累	累

书写提示：下面的"糸"不能写成"纟"

Writing tips：The below part should be written as "糸", not "纟".

（十一）玩 wán

词语：游玩（play）　玩具（toy）

析字：左边的"王"与字义有关，右边的"元（yuán）"与读音有关（由于古今音变，"元"与"玩"的读音稍有差异）。本义是"玩赏玉石"，后来引申出"游戏""进行某种文体活动"等意思。

Analysis of the character：The "王" on the left is related to the meaning of the character and the "元（yuán）" on the right is related to pronunciation（due to the phonetic changes since ancient times, the pronunciation of "元" and "玩" is

273

slightly different). The original meaning was to "play with ornamental jade", and later extended to the meanings of "game" and "carrying out some kind of cultural and sports activities".

田字格书写 Writing in Tin Word Format：

一 二 F 王 王 玡 玩

书写提示：左边的"王"不能写成"王"。
Writing tips：The left part should be written as "王", not "王".

(十二) 球 qiú

词语：足球（football） 打球（play a ball game）

析字：左边的"王"与字义有关，右边的"求（qiú）"表示读音。本义是"美玉"，后来专门用于表示一些圆形立体状的物品，如"地球""篮球""乒乓球"等。

Analysis of the character：The "王" on the left is related to the meaning of the character, the "求（qiú）" on the right is related to the pronunciation. The original meaning was "jade", later specifically used to express some round objects, such as "the earth" "basketball" "table tennis" and so on.

田字格书写 Writing in Tin Word Format：

一 二 F 王 王 玗 玡 玡 球 球 球

书写提示：左边的"王"不能写成"王"。
Writing tips：The left part should be written as "王", not "王".

(十三) 现 xiàn

词语：现在(now)　发现(find)

析字：左边的"王"与字义有关，右边的"见(jiàn)"表示读音（由于古今音变，"见"与"现"的读音稍有差异）。本义是"美玉散发的光泽"，后来由"光泽"引申出"出现"的意思，由"出现"引申出"现在"的意思。

Analysis of the character: The "王" on the left is related to the meaning of the character, and the "见(jiàn)" on the right indicates the pronunciation(due to the phonetic changes since ancient times, the pronunciation of "见" and "现" is slightly different). The original meaning was "the luster of beautiful jade". Later, the meaning of "luster" was extended to mean "appearance", and then the meaning of "present" was extended from "appearance".

田字格书写 Writing in Tin Word Format：

一 二 F 王 丑 玑 现 现

书写提示："见"不能写成"贝"。

Writing tips: The "见" should not be written as "贝".

 汉字锦囊 Idea Box of Chinese Characters

常用偏旁——斜玉旁(王)

Commonly-used Component — Xieyupang(王) Component

"王"是常用的汉字表义偏旁，常表示"玉石""美玉"之类的意思。出现在字的左边时，最下的横要写成提。

The "王" is a commonly-used Chinese character meaning component, often means "jade" "beautiful jade" and so on. When it appears on the left side of the character, the bottom 横(héng) should be written as 提(tí).

（十四）贵 guì

词语：宝贵（valuable）　贵姓（surename）

析字：小篆写作"貴"，上面的"臾"表示读音，下面的"貝"表示字义，楷书写作"貴"，简化字写成"贵"。本义是"价值高"，由此引申出"重要""地位高"等意思。

Analysis of the character：It had been written as "貴" in Seal Script (Xiaozhuan)，the part "臾" above represents pronunciation，and "貝" below represents meaning. Then it had been written as "貴" and "贵" in Regular Script(Kaishu) and simplified character. Its original meaning was "high value"，which extended to "important" "high status" and so on.

田字格书写　Writing in Tin Word Format：

丨　口　口　中　虫　串　贵　贵　贵

贵	贵	贵	贵	贵	贵	贵	贵	贵	贵	贵	贵	贵	贵

书写提示：上面的"串"不能写成"虫"。

Writing tips：The upper part should be written as "串"，not "虫".

（十五）南 nán

词语：南门（south gate）　南方（south）

析字：古代汉字写作"南"（像古代一种乐器的形状）。古代借用这个字来表示"南方"，至今没有改变。秦代隶书写成"南"，后来楷书写成"南"。

Analysis of the character：It had been written as "南"（it looks like an ancient musical instrument）in ancient Chinese character. At ancient times this character had been borrowed to show the "south"，which stays the same till now. It also had been written as "南" in Clerical Script（Lishu）from Qin Dynasty，and "南" in Regular Script(Kaishu).

田字格书写 Writing in Tin Word Format：

一 十 十 冇 冇 冇 肉 南 南

书写提示：里面的"羊"不能写成"羊"。

Writing tips：The inner "羊" should not be written as "羊".

（十六）回 huí

词语：回家（home）　回去（go back）

析字：金文写作"☉"，楷书写作"回"，表示"旋转"的意思。后来，由"旋转"的意思引申出"返回""回答"等意思。

Analysis of the character：It had been written as "☉" and "回" in Bronze Script(Jinwen) and Regular Script(Kaishu) respectively to refer to "rotate". Later，it was extended to the meanings of "return" "answer" and so on.

田字格书写 Writing in Tin Word Format：

丨 冂 冂 冋 回 回

书写提示：最下面的横笔应最后写。

Writing tips：The lower 横(héng) should be written last.

（十七）放 fàng

词语：放学（after school）　放心（be at ease）

析字：形声字。左边的"方"表示字音，右边的"攵(pū)"表示字义。"攵"是汉字中常见的偏旁，古代写作"攴"，像手上拿着打击的工具，表示"行为动作"的意思。"放"的本义是"驱赶""抛弃"，后来引申出"放置""释放"的意思。

Analysis of the character: It is a pictophonetic character. The "方" on the left side refers to the character's pronunciation, the "攵(pū)" on the right side refers to the character's meaning. "攵" is a commonly-used character component. It had been written as "⺙" in ancient Chinese, like holding a tool in the hand, with the meaning of "actions". The original meanings of "放" were "expel" and "abandon", later the meanings were extended to "place" and "release".

田字格书写 Writing in Tin Word Format：

丶 亠 方 方 方 放 放

书写提示：右边的"攵"不能写成"文"。

Writing tips: The "攵" on the right side should not be written as "文".

(十八) 听 tīng

词语：听音乐(listen to the music)　听写(dictation)

析字："口"与字义有关，"斤(jīn)"与读音有关(由于古今音变，"斤"与"听"的读音有差异)。

Analysis of the character："口" is related to the meaning of the word, "斤(jīn)" is related to pronunciation(due to the phonetic changes since ancient times, the pronunciation of "斤" is different from that of "听").

田字格书写 Writing in Tin Word Format：

丨 丨 口 口 听 听 听

书写提示：右边的"斤"不能写成"厅"。

Writing tips: The right part "斤" should not be written as "厅".

第十四课 假借字

(十九) 新 xīn

词语：新闻(news)　新同学(new student)

析字：甲骨文写作"𣂺"，像用斧子(斤)砍木柴，左上的"辛"表示读音，楷书写作"新"。本义是"木柴"，后来被借用作为"旧"的反义词。

Analysis of the character: It had been written as "𣂺" in Oracle Bone Script (Jiaguwen). It's like chopping firewood with an axe, "辛" on the top left indicates pronunciation. It had been written as "新" in Regular Script (Kaishu). The original meaning was "firewood", which was later used as the antonym of "old".

田字格书写 Writing in Tin Word Format：

丶　亠　立　立　辛　辛　辛　亲　新　新　新

新 新 新 新 新 新 新 新 新 新 新 新 新

书写提示：左边的"亲"不能写作"亲"。

Writing tips: The left part should be written as "亲", not "亲".

(二十) 写 xiě

词语：写作业(do homework)　写字(write)

析字：繁体字写作"寫"，上面的"宀(房屋)"表示字义，下面的"舄(xì)"表示读音，简化字写成"写"。本义是"从别处把东西搬到房屋里"。"书写"是后来引申出的意思(用笔把别处的文字抄录过来)。

Analysis of the character: Its traditional Chinese character form was "寫". The upper part "宀(house)" indicated the meaning, and the lower part "舄(xì)" indicated the pronunciation. Its simplified character form was "写". Its original meaning was "to move things to the house from other places", and the meaning of "writing" was the later extended meaning (transcribe words from other places with a pen).

田字格书写 Writing in Tin Word Format：

丶㇖冖写写

写	写	写	写	写	写	写	写	写	写	写	写	写	写

书写提示：上面的"⼀"不能写成"⼍"。

Writing tips：The top part should be written as "⼀", not "⼍".

三、词语练习 Phrase Practice

1. 找出方框 B 中由方框 A 中的每个汉字构成的词语，同学们互相检查正确与否。

Find out the phrase in Table B formed by each Chinese character in Table A and check with your classmates.

A
前　别　班　经　给　纸　红　累　玩　球　贵　员　回　听　新

B
红色　不给　经过　班级　别人　前面　累了　玩具　篮球　贵重　队员
回家　听说　足球　新旧　上班　白纸　前进　很累　贪玩　球员　太贵了
重新　返回　听见

2. 看拼音写汉字。

Read the following pinyin to write Chinese characters.

① 踢 zú qiú（　　　　）　② huí（　　　　）学校　③ 很 lèi（　　　　）

④ tīng 说（　　　　）　⑤ 昂 guì（　　　　）　⑥ jīng（　　　　）历

3. 读出下面的句子。

Read out the following sentences.

① 你别去了,已经来不及了。

② 事情的经过,请你再说一遍吧。

③ 听说他回国了,不能来参加后天的足球赛了。

④ 他就是太贪玩了,所以周末忘了写作业。

⑤ 你给丽丽的礼物准备好了吗?

⑥ 上周末我一直在上班,真的很累。

四、综合练习 Comprehensive Practice

1. 写出下列汉字的两个组成部件。

Write out the two components of the following characters.

① 给:_____ + _____　　② 特:_____ + _____

③ 骗:_____ + _____　　④ 听:_____ + _____

⑤ 杂:_____ + _____　　⑥ 蛇:_____ + _____

⑦ 灯:_____ + _____　　⑧ 球:_____ + _____

2. 选字组词。

Choose characters to make out words.

① 高(A. 山　B. 臣　C. 田)

② (A. 斤　B. 听　C. 沂)见

③ 足(A. 求　B. 球　C. 现)

④ (A. 近　B. 折　C. 听)写

⑤ 冰(A. 水　B. 土　C. 木)

⑥ 放(A. 字　B. 学　C. 宇)

3. 选字填空。

Choose a character to fill in the blank.

跑　泡　炮　袍　饱　抱

① 有饭能吃（　　　），有水把茶（　　　）。
② 有足快快（　　　），有手轻轻（　　　）。
③ 有衣穿长（　　　），有火放鞭（　　　）。

五、课外任务 After-class Task

1. 用拼音在电脑或手机上打出下面的词语。

Typy out the following phrases on your computer or mobile phone with pinyin.

分别　班级　剪纸　现在　所以　新衣　到达　书写

2. 请在卡片上写出与天气有关的词语。请你的同学们随机抽取卡片读出来，并造句。

Please write down the weather-related words on the card. Please let your classmates reads the words randomly, and makes sentences using the words.

第十五课　字和词的网络关系
Lesson Fifteen　Network of Characters and Words

一、汉字知识 Knowledge of Chinese Characters

这一课,我们来介绍建立字和词语的网络。
In this lesson, let's introduce building a network of characters and words.

学习汉字,不仅要注意学习掌握汉字的读音、字形、字义,了解字的结构、字形结构中哪个是与字义有关的部分、哪个是与读音有关的部分、如何正确书写汉字等,还要注意把汉字放到"字-词"的网络中进行学习。例如,"学"字,在了解这个字的结构的基础上,尽量联系由这个字构成的词语,如"学校""学生""学习""上学""放学""大学""小学""中学"等。学习"生"字时,在了解这个字的本义"小草长出来"的基础上,联系"生长""生命""生活""学生"等词语,这样可以帮助我们更好地掌握由"生"构成的一系列词语。

Learning Chinese characters, we should pay attention to learning and mastering the pronunciation, form, meaning, the structure of Chinese characters, and also should know which part is related to the meaning of Chinese characters, which part is related to the pronunciation, how to write Chinese characters correctly and so on. What's more, we should also pay attention to putting Chinese characters in the "character-word" network for learning. For example, the character "学", on the basis of understanding the structure of the character, trying to connect the words formed by the character, such as "学校""学生""学习""上学""放学""大学""小学""中学" and so on. Learning the character "生", on the basis of understanding the original meaning "grass grows out", try to connect the words "生长""生命""生活""学生" and so on, which can help us better learn a series of words formed by "生".

二、汉字形音义 The Form, Pronunciation and Meaning of Chinese Characters

 目标汉字 Learning Objective

国 些 要 左 马 真 着 网 用 风 就 零 朋 师 医 帮 兴 京 饭 的

（一）国 guó

词语：国家(country)　中国(China)　出国(go abroad)

析字：繁体字写作"國"，"囗"表示字义，"或"表示读音，本义是"邦国——古代以一座城市为中心的周围地区"。宋代以后，常常简写成"国"（意思是"城中有国王"），现在简化字加上"丶"，写成"国"。

Analysis of the character: Its traditional Chinese character form was written as "國". "囗" denoted the meaning, "或" denoted the pronunciation. The original meaning was "a city-state — the surrounding area centered around a city in ancient times". Since the Song Dynasty, it has abbreviated as "国"(the meaning of this form is "there is a king in the city"). Now the simplified character form adds "丶", so the writing form turns into "国".

田字格书写 Writing in Tin Word Format：

丨 冂 冂 月 用 国 国 国

国 国 国 国 国 国 国 国 国 国 国 国 国

书写提示：注意按照"丨、冂、王、丶、一"的顺序书写。

Writing tips: Please write as the order of "丨、丂、王、丶、一".

(二) 些 xiē

词语：这些(these) 那些(those) 一些(some)

析字：上面的"此(cǐ)"表示读音（由于古今音变，"此"与"些"的读音有差异），下面的"二"是起区别作用的记号。本来表示"略微"，后来表示不确定的数量，如"这些书""某些人"。

Analysis of the character: The upper part "此(cǐ)" of the character denotes pronunciation(due to the phonetic changes since ancient times, the pronunciation of "此" and "些" has differences). The part below the character "二" is a distinguishing mark. The original meaning was "a little", but now it means indeterminate amount, such as "these books" "some people".

田字格书写 Writing in Tin Word Format：

书写提示：下面的"二"不能写成"一"。

Writing tips: The lower part "二" should not be written as "一".

(三) 要 yào

词语：重要(important) 要求(request)

析字：古代汉字写作"𦥑"，像人两只手叉腰的形状，表示人的身体部位"腰"。楷书写作"要"。后来主要借用这个字来表示"需要""要求"等意思。

Analysis of the character: Its ancient Chinese character form was "𦥑". It looked like those two hands were put on the man's waist, and the original meaning was one's "waist". It had been written as "要" in Regular Script (Kaishu). Later, it was mainly borrowed to indicate the meanings of "need" "request" and so on.

田字格书写 Writing in Tin Word Format：

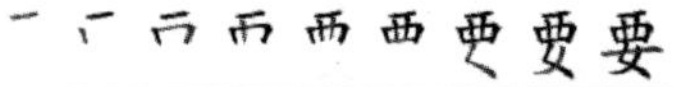

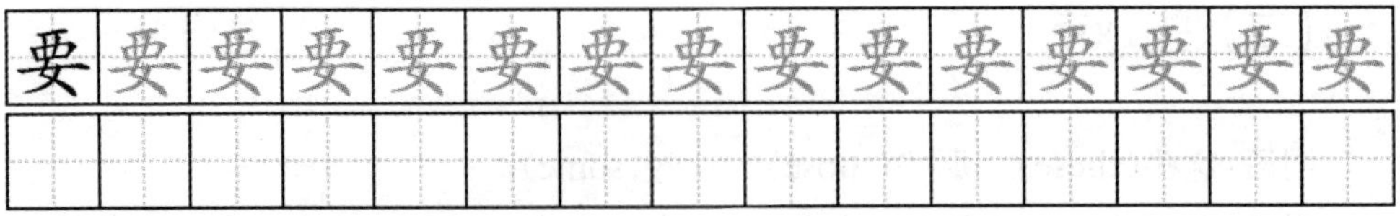

书写提示：上面的“覀”不能写成“西”。

Writing tips：Please do not write the upper part “覀” as “西”.

(四) 左 zuǒ

词语：左手(left hand)　左边(left side)

析字：古代汉字写作“𠂇”，像左手的形状，后来加上起区别的记号“工”，小篆写成“[illegible]”，楷书写作“左”。

Analysis of the character：The ancient Chinese character form was written as “𠂇”, it was like the shape of left hand, and then added the distinguishing mark “工”, and had been written as “[illegible]” and “左” in Seal Script(Xiaozhuan) and Regular Script(Kaishu).

田字格书写 Writing in Tin Word Format：

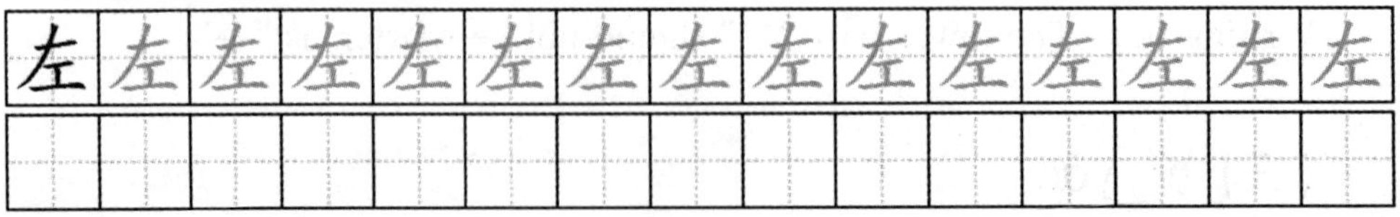

书写提示：下面的“工”不能写成“土”。

Writing tips：The lower part “工” should not be written as “土”.

(五) 马 mǎ

词语：马上(right now)　骑马(ride a horse)

析字：甲骨文写作“[illegible]”，像马这种动物的外形。金文写作“[illegible]”，秦代小篆写作“[illegible]”，楷书写作“馬”，简化字简写作“马”。

Analysis of the character：It had been written as “[illegible]” in Oracle Bone Script

(Jiaguwen), like the shape of a horse. It also had been written as "𢒰" in Bronze Script(Jinwen), "𢒔" in Seal Script(Xiaozhuan) from Qin Dynasty, "馬" in Regular Script(Kaishu), and the simplified character form was "马".

田字格书写 Writing in Tin Word Format：

乛 乜 马

马	马	马	马	马	马	马	马	马	马	马	马	马	马	马

书写提示：注意按照"㇆、㇄、一"的顺序书写。

Writing tips：Please write as the order of "㇆、㇄、一".

（六）真 zhēn

词语：真实（reality） 认真（earnest）

析字：金文写作"𧴪"，像用食具从鼎中取食。后来字形发生变化，小篆写作"𧵆"，楷书写作"真"。本义是"美食美味"，后来引申为"本质""本性"，再引申为"符合客观事实"的意思。

Analysis of the character：It had been written as "𧴪" in Bronze Script (Jinwen), it was like taking food from the tripod with utensils. With the shape of the character changes, in Seal Script(Xiaozhuan) it was written as "𧵆", and in Regular Script(Kaishu) it was written as "真". The original meaning was "delicious food", and later meaning was extended to "essence", furtherly, it was extended as "accord with objective facts".

田字格书写 Writing in Tin Word Format：

一 十 广 疒 疒 肯 肯 直 真 真

真	真	真	真	真	真	真	真	真	真	真	真	真

书写提示："真"中间是三个短横，不能写成两个短横。

Writing tips：The form of "真" has three short 横（héng）in the middle, not has two short 横(héng).

(七) 着 zhāo/zháo/zhe/zhuó

词语:听着音乐(listen to the music)　睡不着(sleepless)

析字:古代汉字写作"箸","箸"的意思是"筷子"。上面的"⺮"表示字义,下面的"者"表示读音。后来上面的"⺮"换成了"艹",另外造出"著"。宋代以后,上面的"艹"简写成"⺍",下面的"者"变成"看",产生了"着"字。"着"字主要用来表示"接触""贴近"的意思,其他用法是由此引申出来的。

Analysis of the character: In ancient Chinese character, the form was written as "箸". The meaning of "箸" was chopsticks. The upper part "⺮" was used to express meaning, the lower part "者" was used to express pronunciation. Then the upper part "⺮" turned into "艹", and then the character form turned into "著". After the Song Dynasty, the upper part "艹" was replaced by "⺍", the part below the character "者" became "看". So the character "着" came into being. The "着" mainly indicated "touch" "adhere", and the other meanings were extended from the original meanings.

田字格书写 Writing in Tin Word Format:

丶 丷 ⺍ 丷 兰 羊 养 着 着 着

着	着	着	着	着	着	着	着	着	着	着	着	着

书写提示:下面"目"不能写成"日"。

Writing tips: The lower part "目" should not be written as "日".

(八) 网 wǎng

词语:渔网(fishing net)　上网(surfing online)

析字:象形字。甲骨文写作"⺁",像用来捕鱼或捕捉鸟兽的网状工具。小篆写作"⺁",楷书写作"网"。本义是"捕捉动物的网",后来引申出"像网络一样的东西"的意思,如"互联网""电网""路网"。

Analysis of the character: It is a pictographic character. It had been written as "༙" in Oracle Bone Script(Jiaguwen) to refer to those reticular tools for hunting fishes, birds or other animals. It had been written as "网" in Seal Script(Xiaozhuan), and "网" in Regular Script(Kaishu). The original meaning of this character was "the net for hunting", and then it was extended to the meaning of "something like the network", such as "internet" "electric network" "road network".

田字格书写 Writing in Tin Word Format:

丨 冂 冈 冈 网 网

书写提示:正确的书写顺序是"丨、冂、乂、乂"。

Writing tips: The correct writing order should be "丨、冂、乂、乂".

(九) 用 yòng

词语:有用(useful)　不用谢(no thanks)　用品(daily uses)

析字:古代汉字写作"用",像木桶的形状。由于木桶是日常用具,所以引申出"使用"的意思。小篆写作"用",楷书写作"用"。后来由"使用"这个意思引申出"需要"和"效果"的意思。

Analysis of the character: It had been written as "用" in ancient Chinese character, the shape of it looked like a wooden barrel. As the wooden barrels are used in everyday life, so this character had generated the meaning of "use". It also had been written as "用" in Seal Script(Xiaozhuan), and "用" in Regular Script(Kaishu). Later the meaning extended from "use" to "need" and "effect".

田字格书写 Writing in Tin Word Format：

丿 冂 冂 月 用

书写提示：里面的"丨"不能写成"丰"。

Writing tips：The "丨" inside should not be written as "丰".

(十) 风 fēng

词语：风向（wind direction） 风气（ethos）

析字：甲骨文借用凤凰鸟的字形来表示"风"["风"和"凤(fèng)"的读音近似]。战国时期的"风"字写作"凮"。上面是"凡(fán)"，表示字的读音（由于古今音变，现在"凡"和"风"的读音有差异），下面的"乀"是凤凰鸟的尾部羽毛。楷书字形把凤凰鸟的尾部羽毛变为"虫"，"凮"变成了"風"。现在简化字用"乂"代替里面的"虫"，简写成了"风"。

Analysis of the character：The Oracle Bone Script(Jiaguwen) borrowed the shape of phoenix bird to represent the wind["风" and "凤(fèng)" have similar pronunciation]. "风" had been written as "凮" during the Warring States Period，the upper part "凡(fán)" represented the character's pronunciation，(due to the phonetic changes since ancient times，the pronunciation of "凡" and "风" has slight difference)，the lower part "乀" referred to the tail feathers of phoenix bird. In Regular Script(Kaishu)，the tail feathers was changed into "虫"，and the character "凮" turned into "風". Later the inner part "虫" was replaced by "乂"，the character was simplified into "风".

田字格书写 Writing in Tin Word Format：

丿 几 凡 风

书写提示：里面的"ㄨ"不能写成"又"。

Writing tips：The inner part "ㄨ" should not be written as "又".

（十一）就 jiù

词语：一看就懂（see at a glance）　就业（employment）

析字：左边的"京"（意思是"高处"）表示字义，右边的"尤"表示读音，本义是"登上高处"。后来引申出"靠近""接近"的意思，又引申为时间副词，表示动作和情况很快发生。

Analysis of the character：The left part "京" (meaning "high place") represents the meaning of the character, the right part "尤" represents the pronunciation. The original meaning was "to climb to a high place". Later, it was extended to "close" "near", and then it was extended to be the adverbs of time. The meaning was that action and situation would happen soon.

田字格书写 Writing in Tin Word Format：

书写提示：右边的"尤"不能写成"龙"。

Writing tips：The right part "尤" should not be written as "龙".

（十二）零 líng

词语：零钱（pocket money）　零度（zero degree）

析字：形声字。上面的"雨（yǔ）"表示字义，下面的"令（lìng）"表示字音。本义是"细小的雨丝"，后来产生"细小""零碎""零星""数量少"等意思。

Analysis of the character：It is a pictophonetic character. The upper part "雨（yǔ）" represents the character's meaning and the lower part "令（lìng）" represents its pronunciation. The original meaning of the character was "fine rain", later it was extended to mean "fine" "tiny" "fragmentary" "small quantity" and so on.

田字格书写 Writing in Tin Word Format：

书写提示：下面的"令"不能写成"今"。

Writing tips：The part "令" in the below should not be written as "今".

 汉字锦囊 Idea Box of Chinese Characters

常用偏旁——雨字头（雨）

Commonly-used Component — Yuzitou(雨) Component

"雨字头"是常用的汉字表义偏旁，一般出现在字的上部，表示下雨、下雪之类的意思，如"雷""霜""雪"。

"Yuzitou" is a commonly-used Chinese component that denotes the meaning, it is often used in the upper part of the character, the meanings are to rain or to snow, such as "雷""霜""雪"。

（十三）朋 péng

词语：朋友（friend） 宾朋（guest）

析字：甲骨文写作"拜"，像两串贝（古代货币）连在一起。后来字形发生了一系列变化：拜→角→匆→匆→匆→朋。本义是"古代货币单位（两串贝）"，后来引申出"朋友"的意思。

Analysis of the character：The Oracle Bone Script（Jiaguwen） form was written as "拜", it looked like two strings of shellfish（the ancient currency） connected together. Later, the form of the character changed: 拜→甪→夘→ 𢆶→𢆶→朋. The original meaning was "ancient monetary unit(two strings of shellfish)", then it was extended to the meaning of "friend".

田字格书写 Writing in Tin Word Format：

丿 几 月 月 朋 朋 朋 朋

书写提示：注意与"明"字的区别。

Writing tips: Mind the difference between "明" and "朋".

（十四）师 shī

词语：老师（teacher） 工程师（engineer）

析字：繁体字写作"師"，简化字写作"师"。本义是"军队"，后来指"精通某种技艺的人"，如"乐师""画师"等，也表示"老师"。

Analysis of the character: The traditional Chinese character form was "師", the simplified character form was "师". The original meaning was "army", later, it referred to "someone who is good at a particular skill" such as "musician" "artist" and so on. It can also refer to "teacher".

田字格书写 Writing in Tin Word Format：

丿 丿 广 庐 师 师

书写提示：右边的"币"不能写成"巾"。

Writing tips: The right part "币" should not be written as "巾".

(十五) 医 yī

词语：医生（doctor）　医院（hospital）

析字：繁体字写作"醫"，上面的"殹（yì）"表示读音，下面的"酉（yǒu）"表示字义。简化字截取了繁体字的左上部分"医"。

Analysis of the character：The traditional Chinese character form was "醫". The upper part "殹（yì）" denoted the pronunciation, the part below the character "酉（yǒu）" denoted the meaning. The simplified character cut off the upper left part "医" of traditional Chinese character.

田字格书写 Writing in Tin Word Format：

一 ㄏ ㄷ ㄹ 亙 夭 医

医	医	医	医	医	医	医	医	医	医	医	医	医	医	医

书写提示：按照"一、矢、乚"的顺序书写。

Writing tips：The writing order is "一、矢、乚".

(十六) 帮 bāng

词语：帮助（help）　帮忙（do a favour）

析字：繁体字写作"幫"，上面的"邦"表示读音，下面的"帛"表示字义。简化字把下面的"帛"简写成"巾"。本义是"鞋子的两个侧面"，由此引申出"帮助"的意思。

Analysis of the character：The traditional Chinese character form was "幫". The upper part "邦" denoted the pronunciation, the part below the character "帛" denoted the meaning. The simplified character wrote the "帛" as "巾". The original meaning was "two sides of shoes", and was extended to the meaning of "help".

田字格书写 Writing in Tin Word Format：

一 二 三 丰 邦 邦 邦 帮 帮

帮	帮	帮	帮	帮	帮	帮	帮	帮	帮	帮	帮	帮	帮

书写提示：下面的"巾"不能写成"冂"。

Writing tips：The lower part "巾" should not be written as "冂".

(十七) 兴 xìng

词语：高兴(joyful)　兴奋(exciting)

析字：古代汉字写作"🈳"，像四只手从四个角上一起用力抬起重物。小篆写作"🈳"，楷书写作"興"，简化字把上面的"𦥑"简写成"⺍"，"興"变成了"兴"。字的本义是"起来""上升"，后来在这个意思的基础上，又产生了一些新的意思，如人的心情好起来就是"高兴""兴奋"；事业发展起来就是"兴旺""兴盛"。

Analysis of the character：It had been written as "🈳" in ancient Chinese character, it looked like there are four hands lifting something heavy from the four corners. It also had been written as "🈳" in Seal Script(Xiaozhuan) and "興" in Regular Script(Kaishu), and in the simplified character, "𦥑" on the top was abbreviated into "⺍", so that "興" now turned into "兴". This character originally meant "get up" "up". Later, it generated some new annotations to this character, for example, when people are in the good mood that is "joyful" "exciting"; when someone's business thrived that is "thriving" "flourishing".

田字格书写 Writing in Tin Word Format：

丶 ⺍ 丷 兯 兴 兴

兴	兴	兴	兴	兴	兴	兴	兴	兴	兴	兴	兴	兴	兴

书写提示：上面的"⺍"不能写成"丷"。

Writing tips: The "⼧" on the top should not be written as "⼧".

(十八) 京 jīng

词语：北京（Beijing） 南京（Nanjing） 京剧（Peking Opera）

析字：象形字。古代汉字写作"𩫕"，像高台上面有建筑。小篆写作"𩫖"，楷书写作"京"。本义是"高的地方"，后来用来表示"都城"的意思。

Analysis of the character: It is a pictographic character. The ancient Chinese character form "𩫕" was like a building on the platform. Then the character had been written as "𩫖" and "京" in Seal Script (Xiaozhuan) and Regular Script (Kaishu) respectively. The original meaning of the character was "high place", later it was extended to mean "capital".

田字格书写 Writing in Tin Word Format：

书写提示：中间的"口"不能写成"日"。

Writing tips: The part "口" in the middle should not be written as "日".

(十九) 饭 fàn

词语：吃饭（have a meal） 米饭（rice）

析字：左边的"饣"与字义有关，表示与饮食有关的意思。右边的"反"表示读音。本义是动词"吃饭"，后来也作为名词使用。

Analysis of the character: The left part "饣" is connected with meaning, and the meaning is about diet. The right part "反" denotes the pronunciation. The original meaning was "eating", later, it can also be used as the noun.

田字格书写 Writing in Tin Word Format：

`丿 𠂉 𠂈 饣 饣 饭 饭`

书写提示：左边的"饣"不能写成"钅"。

Writing tips：The left part "饣" should not be written as "钅".

(二十) 的 de/dí/dì

词语：好的(good)　我的书(my book)

析字：古代汉语中原来写作"旳"，"日"表示字义，"勺"表示读音。本义是"日光明亮"，后来"日"变为"白"，字变为了"的"，引申出"真实"等意思，如"的确""目的"。现代汉语中常作为助词，用在定语和中心语之间，表示修饰和领属关系。

Analysis of the character：In ancient Chinese，the character was written as "旳"，"日" denoted the meaning，"勺" denoted the pronunciation. The original meaning was "the sun is bright". Latter，"日" changed as "白"，the character had been written as "的"，and its meaning was extended to the meaning of "reality" and so on，such as "indeed" "objective". In modern Chinese，it is often used as auxiliary word，and is used between the attributive and the central word to embellish and denote the subordinative relationship.

田字格书写 Writing in Tin Word Format：

`丿 亻 白 白 白 白′ 的 的`

书写提示：右边的"勺"不能写成"匀"。

Writing tips：The right part "勺" should not be written as "匀".

三、词语练习 Phrase Practice

1. 找出方框 B 中由方框 A 中的每个汉字构成的词语，同学们互相检查正确与否。

Find out the phrase in Table B formed by each Chinese character in Table A and check with your classmates.

A
国　要　左　真　着　因　以　色　雪　朋　师　医　帮　为　饭

B
颜色　以为　看着　真实　左边　不要　国家　雪花　朋友　师傅　医生
帮助　为什么　吃饭　国际　因为　花色　老师　帮忙　早饭　左右　认真
必要　可以　睡着

2. 看拼音写汉字。

Read the following pinyin to write Chinese characters.

① 有 xiē(　　　)　② 好 péng(　　　)友　③ tí(　　　)目

④ zhēn(　　　)相　⑤ 下 yǔ(　　　)　⑥ yīn wèi(　　　)

3. 读出下面的句子。

Read out the following sentences.

① 我的理想是长大以后成为一名医生。

② 这道题我不会做，你可以帮帮我吗？

③ 中国是一个幅员辽阔的国家。

④ 你为什么要这么做呢？

⑤ 这些衣服的颜色我都不喜欢，我想再看看其他店的衣服。

⑥ 我想知道这件事的真相，请告诉我吧！

四、综合练习 Comprehensive Practice

1. 选字组词。

Choose characters to make out words.

① (A. 做　B. 左　C. 作)边

② (A. 因　B. 国　C. 困)为

③ 老(A. 归　B. 临　C. 师)

④ (A. 医　B. 知　C. 匡)生

⑤ (A. 期　B. 朋　C. 明)友

⑥ 不可(A. 似　B. 已　C. 以)

2. 用所给汉字组词。

Please make up the words by the given characters.

① 晴_____　_____　　② 特_____　_____

③ 灯_____　_____　　④ 急_____　_____

⑤ 村_____　_____　　⑥ 帮_____　_____

⑦ 国_____　_____　　⑧ 真_____　_____

3. 选词填空。

Please fill in each blank with a word.

① 她是一个爱_____别人的人。

A. 听说　　　　B. 帮助　　　　C. 打扫　　　　D. 吹牛

② _____天气预报说明天有暴雨,所以学校取消了室外体育课。

A. 既然　　　　B. 因为　　　　C. 如果　　　　D. 为什么

③ 我坐在他的_____,小红坐在他的右边。

A. 一边　　　　B. 右边　　　　C. 左边　　　　D. 外面

④ _____了,房子和树木都要变成白色的了。

A. 打雷　　　　B. 下雨　　　　C. 刮大风　　　D. 下雪

⑤ 甲:你好,请问你要去哪里?

乙：你好，_____，我要去天安门广场。

甲：好的，请系好安全带。

A. 医生　　　B. 老师　　　C. 师傅　　　D. 客人

五、课外任务 After-class Task

1. 用拼音在电脑或手机上打出下面的词语。

Type out the following phrases on your computer or mobile phone with pinyin.

需要　彩色　以为　帮忙　题目　就是　左右　晚饭

2. 请在卡片上写出你喜欢的几个职业。请你的同学们随机抽取卡片读出来，并造句。

Please write some professions you like on your cards. Please let your classmates chooses cards and reads it，then makes a sentence with the chosen word.